THE DUBLIN
RAILWAY MURDER

Also by Thomas Morris

The Mystery of the Exploding Teeth

The Matter of the Heart

THE DUBLIN
RAILWAY MURDER

THOMAS MORRIS

Harvill *Secker*

LONDON

1 3 5 7 9 10 8 6 4 2

Harvill Secker is part of the Penguin Random House group of companies
whose addresses can be found at global.penguinrandomhouse.com

Penguin
Random House
UK

First published by Harvill Secker in 2021

A CIP catalogue record for this book is available from the British Library

penguin.co.uk/vintage

ISBN 9781787302396 (Hardback)
ISBN 9781787302402 (Trade paperback)

Map illustration on p. xi © Mike Hall

The photographs which appear in this book were reproduced by the archives of The British Library
via Bridgeman Images, The Irish National Archives, The Royal Collection Trust and by kind
permission of Pat Parsons and Anne Taylor.

Typeset in 12.5/16 pt Sabon MT Std by Jouve (UK), Milton Keynes
Printed and bound in Great Britain by Clays Ltd, Elcograf S.p.A.

The authorised representative in the EEA is Penguin Random House Ireland,
Morrison Chambers, 32 Nassau Street, Dublin D02 YH68

Penguin Random House is committed to a sustainable future
for our business, our readers and our planet. This book is made
from Forest Stewardship Council® certified paper.

MIX
Paper from
responsible sources
FSC
www.fsc.org   FSC® C018179

THE DUBLIN
RAILWAY MURDER

THOMAS MORRIS

CONTENTS

CONTENTS

AUTHOR'S NOTE

In November 1856 the residents of Dublin were shocked by news of a brutal murder at the city's Broadstone railway terminus – a crime without parallel in the Irish capital's recent history. The ensuing police investigation was the most complex and mystifying that Dublin's detectives had ever undertaken, and its many twists and turns seized the public imagination. It was seven months before the prime suspect was arrested, culminating in a sensational trial that was eagerly followed by newspaper readers on both sides of the Irish Sea.

The Broadstone murder, as it became known, was a particularly notorious crime in an age that relished them. Both the victim and his suspected killer became household names, while the outcome of the trial was a national cause célèbre. This level of public interest meant that newspapers competed to uncover any minor development in the investigation, and sent reporters to transcribe every court hearing. These accounts make it possible to reconstruct much of what happened, but more importantly a huge cache of confidential government papers relating to the case has also survived. A 160-year-old file held by the National Archives of Ireland contains more than three hundred pages of police interviews, minutes and memos; correspondence between detectives, government ministers and lawyers; and even letters written by the prime suspect from his prison cell. What emerges is an unusually complete picture of a Victorian murder inquiry, including many details that were deliberately withheld from the public at the time.

This book draws on all these sources, and also includes material from a pamphlet published privately in 1858 by the phrenologist

AUTHOR'S NOTE

Frederick Bridges, who interviewed the main suspect at length over the course of several weeks. Every incident in the pages that follow is based closely on witness statements and other first-hand accounts. All characters identified by name are real people, and biographical details, however minor, are genuine. Even the dialogue is authentic, with two important exceptions. In transcripts of police interviews and court proceedings the questions asked by detectives or barristers were usually omitted, and I have reconstructed these based on the answers given. In one or two places I have taken the liberty of constructing conversations from statements that were originally committed to paper – but in every case using the actual words of the people concerned.

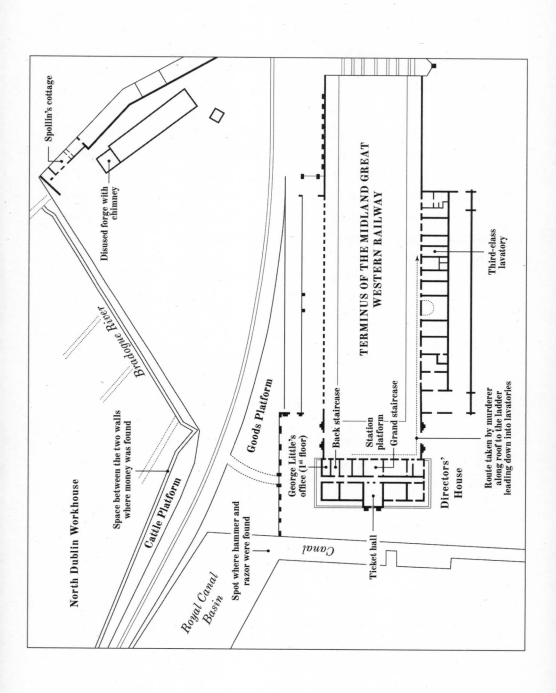

North Dublin Workhouse

Spollin's cottage

Disused forge with chimney

Bradogue River

Space between the two walls where money was found

Cattle Platform

Goods Platform

George Little's office (1st floor)

Back staircase

Station platform

Grand staircase

TERMINUS OF THE MIDLAND GREAT WESTERN RAILWAY

Third-class lavatory

Route taken by murderer along roof to the ladder leading down into lavatories

Directors' House

Ticket hall

Canal

Spot where hammer and razor were found

Royal Canal Basin

LIST OF CHARACTERS

OFFICIALS AND EMPLOYEES OF THE MIDLAND GREAT WESTERN RAILWAY

George Little, cashier
Frances Little, his mother
Kate Morton, his sister

William Chamberlain, clerk to George Little
William McCauley, cash porter
Thomas Moore, messenger boy

Anne Gunning, housekeeper
Bernard Gunning, assistant storekeeper
Catherine Campbell, their servant

Patrick Hanbury, stationmaster
Mrs Hanbury
Mary Mitchell, their servant

John Ennis, chairman
Henry Beausire, company secretary
Thomas Bennett, accountant's clerk

Joseph Cabry, chief engineer
Patrick Moan, chief clerk to engineering department

Walter Kirwan, company solicitor
Joseph Goldsmith, solicitor's clerk

LIST OF CHARACTERS

Henry Thornton, solicitor's clerk
Michael Linskey, solicitor's clerk
Mr Kearney, solicitor's clerk

Richard Russell, audit superintendent
John Jolly, audit clerk
Robert Fair, audit clerk
Isaac Christian, audit clerk and acting cashier
George Burns, audit clerk
John Landy, audit clerk
James Kelly, audit clerk

Archibald Moore, superintendent of transfer office
John Henry Moore, his son, former audit clerk
George Green, transfer clerk
James Magee, transfer clerk

Henry Osborne, storekeeper
William Millar, storekeeper's assistant

James Brophy, foreman of carriage department
Thomas O'Byrne, foreman of painting department
James Spollin, painter
Mary Spollin, his wife
James, Joseph, Lucy and George Spollin, their children

Superintendent Hodgens, railway police
Sergeant Collins, railway police

OFFICERS OF THE DUBLIN METROPOLITAN POLICE

John More O'Ferrall, commissioner
Colonel George Browne, commissioner

LIST OF CHARACTERS

Augustus Guy, superintendent, 'C' division
Joseph Finnamore, superintendent, 'G' division
Detective Inspector Daniel Ryan
Detective Sergeant Craven
Detective Sergeant Murphy
Detective Constable James Meares
Detective Constable James Donnelly

John Ward, sergeant, 'C' division
Abraham Hobson, constable, 'C' division

Joseph O'Donnell, police magistrate
Frank Thorpe Porter, police magistrate

GOVERNMENT AND LEGAL OFFICIALS

Edward Horsman, Chief Secretary for Ireland
Lieutenant Colonel Thomas Askew Larcom, deputy Chief
   Secretary
John FitzGerald, Attorney General for Ireland
Jonathan Christian, Solicitor General for Ireland
Thomas Kemmis, Crown Solicitor for Leinster
William Kemmis, Crown Solicitor for Dublin
John Elliott Hyndman, Coroner for the City of Dublin

Thomas Langlois Lefroy, Lord Chief Justice of Ireland
James Henry Monahan, Chief Justice of the Common Pleas

Gerald Fitzgibbon QC, prosecution barrister
Abraham Brewster QC, prosecution barrister

John Adye Curran, defence barrister
William Sidney, defence barrister

LIST OF CHARACTERS

Charles Fitzgerald, Spollin's solicitor

Dr Barker, physician
Dr Wensley Jennings, physician
George Porter, surgeon
Dr Thomas Grace Geoghegan, professor of forensic medicine

Patrick and Catherine Cullen, the 'Stoneybatter suspects'
John Halligan, servant who reported them to police

Fredrick Bridges, phrenologist
Hannah Bridges, his wife

Mr Thomas, landlord of the Auld Lang Syne

PART ONE

The Murder

1

Thursday 13 November 1856

The mail train was supposed to leave Galway on the stroke of midnight, but once again the GPO delivery was late. The squat Midland Great Western locomotive sat quietly by the 'up' platform, exhaling plumes of steam into the chilly November air, while its driver and fireman chatted in the open cab. Mr Wainwright, the stationmaster, paced the platform impatiently. Dispatching the night train was the last and most important duty of his working day, and he resented being kept from his bed. Sadly this delay was nothing new. The Galway post office was notorious for its inefficiency, and the city authorities had publicly reprimanded the postmaster for his laziness – but without any discernible effect.

Several minutes after the hour the post-cart finally clattered its way into the station. While the sacks were being heaved into a windowless goods wagon, Mr Wainwright double-checked the locks of a sturdy metal cashbox entrusted to him earlier that evening by the station cashier. Satisfied that they were secure, he handed it over to the guard. There were only two keys to this box: one was attached to the chain jangling in his pocket, the other was at the company headquarters in Dublin. It contained the day's takings at the ticket office, well over £100 in gold and silver – five or six times what the average farm labourer would earn in a year. The guard scribbled a receipt and stowed the cashbox in a corner of the break-van at the rear of the train.

Loading was complete; it was time to get going. The guard stepped back on to the platform, made a cursory inspection of the goods wagon and blew his whistle. He gave Mr Wainwright a friendly nod and hopped back on to his van as it passed him. The guard's accommodation for the five-and-a-half-hour journey to Dublin was a small wooden carriage with apertures cut into its walls so that he could keep an eye on the rest of the train. It also contained a charcoal stove, but this was no match for the icy North Atlantic blast that whipped mercilessly through the unglazed windows. Nor did the scenery offer much by way of compensation for his discomfort. At this time of night the distant mountains of County Clare were shrouded in darkness, and all that could be seen of Galway Bay was the steady glow of the Mutton Island lighthouse a mile or so out to sea.

The Galway to Dublin line crossed Ireland due east from coast to coast, from the North Atlantic to the Irish Sea. But for most of its one hundred and twenty-five miles the railway passed through some of the dreariest countryside that this famously beautiful island had to offer. Much of the track had been laid through the vast expanse of bog covering the midlands, a flat and featureless wasteland of peat and standing water. Occasionally the train would emerge from the wilderness into green farmland – but this was no rural idyll. What had once been lush pasture was now a tangle of thistles; last summer's oats and barley had rotted in the fields, choked by bindweed and ragwort. But worst of all, this fertile agricultural land was deserted. It was possible to travel for miles without seeing a single person working in the fields: everywhere cottages lay derelict, their roofs and windows gone, the doors long ago ripped off their hinges and used as fuel.

As the locomotive rolled through the night at a sedate twenty miles an hour, the guard had reason to be glad that the sterile landscape remained out of sight. A decade ago, in the mid-1840s, these fields had been the epicentre of the Great Famine, when a virulent new blight had devastated the potato harvest and left countless numbers in abject poverty. Every empty cottage was an unwelcome reminder of a family displaced or dead. Many, unable to pay the rent, had been evicted by the local landowner and were now living in squalid mud huts in the bog, their children running barefoot through the muck and slime. Others had left to take their chances in the slums of Dublin, or joined the mass exodus to America. A million had emigrated in the space of a few years, and another million had perished from malnutrition or disease. A quarter of Ireland's population, killed or driven from her shores, in the greatest catastrophe the island had ever known.

Few places bore the scars of this calamity as obviously as Athenry, second of the fifteen stops on the line. One tourist guidebook even described the town, reputed to be the oldest in County Galway, as 'the very acme of human misery'. Wretched shacks had sprung up around the ruins of grand aristocratic houses and ancient monasteries, the terrible deprivation of modern Ireland cohabiting with the excesses of its past.

Ballinasloe, Athlone, Moate: large or small, in the early hours these places were almost indistinguishable – a solidly built station-house and a small patch of platform illuminated by oil lamps. As the mail train continued its stately progress eastwards, the baggage wagon became heavier and the pile of cashboxes in the guard's van grew ever larger. At Mullingar, three hours into the journey, there was quite a heap of boxes waiting for him, and he had to make several trips from platform to carriage to stow them all safely.

As the railway left the town behind it joined the course of the Royal Canal, the ninety-mile waterway constructed half a century earlier, at vast expense, between Dublin and Limerick. At the incorporation of the Midland Great Western Railway Company in 1845 its directors had bought the canal, intending to fill it in and lay track over its corpse. But this sentence of execution had been commuted: instead the railway was placed next to it, in the hope that the waterway would provide some welcome extra revenue. This had proved foolishly optimistic. Four-fifths of passenger traffic on the canal had disappeared more or less overnight, and the barges carrying cows and peat were becoming ever more scarce. For the fifty-odd miles between Mullingar and Dublin, canal and railway ran companionably together, the flashy young upstart side by side with its superannuated cousin.

Killucan, Enfield, Kilcock, Maynooth: every twenty minutes another town or village interrupted the train's passage through the 'dreary tracts' – as one visiting writer described it – of the Bog of Allen, a quarter of a million acres of drab peat. As if to ensure that its exhausted occupants were in no danger of falling asleep, the train now began to rattle violently. The Galway to Dublin line remained blandly rectilinear for most of its length, but on its approach to the capital it indulged in a number of extravagant curves. The guard was jolted around uncomfortably in his van, and the contents of the railway company cashboxes – now amounting to several hundred pounds – jangled like a sack of tambourines. At the village of Lucan he had taken custody of the twenty-eighth of these receptacles; and the last, for they were already in the outskirts of Dublin. Emerging from the long Clonsilla cutting, the train slowed as it passed the Phoenix Park and the Zoological Gardens a mile to the south. The zoo had recently acquired a pair of lions, and on a clear night one could sometimes hear a distant roar from one or other of these lucrative star attractions.

It was almost 5.30 in the morning when the mail train finally pulled under the impressive glass roof of Broadstone terminus. The guard's long night was nearly over. All that remained was to supervise the porters unloading the mailbags, sign over the cashboxes to the stationmaster Mr Hanbury, and then he could begin his weary walk home. Outside the gaslight of the station building, most of Dublin still slumbered. A few bleary-eyed apprentices were taking down the shutters from the fronts of their shops, and here and there a policeman walked his beat, looking out for the petty criminals who had plagued the capital since the famine years.

*

It was just after 8 a.m. when George Little, cashier of the Midland Great Western Railway Company, emerged from number 58 Waterloo Road and set off for his office at the Broadstone terminus. George lived in an elegant villa on a broad street of recently built town houses in south Dublin. With two storeys and a basement it was not much bigger than some of the workers' cottages to be found in the less salubrious parts of town, but the high-ceilinged rooms and intricate fanlight over the front door were indications that this was a residence intended for a superior class of person. Each house was set back from the road by a sizeable front garden, with an even larger one to the rear. Although some distance from the city centre, it was a desirable place to live. Mr Little's neighbours included judges and bankers, surgeons and government officials – some of the most successful professionals in the city.

Despite these affluent surroundings, George Little was far from wealthy. He shared his home with his sister Kate, their elderly mother, and an aunt who was in poor health. George's father, a prosperous solicitor, had died suddenly when George was fifteen. His mother Frances then found herself widowed at the age of thirty-two, with four children to look after and no source of income. Selflessly she decided that their modest savings should go towards her eldest son's education. George attended Trinity College for a couple of years, but when their funds ran out he had to leave without taking a degree. With no hope of entering one of the professions he became a clerk, supporting the family on his meagre salary until his younger brother James was old enough to make a contribution of his own.

That, at least, had been the plan. Kate married a doctor and moved forty miles away to the country, but within a few weeks the newly-wed returned to Dublin a widow, her husband having died suddenly from a fever. The younger sister, Fanny, met an Englishman and settled down with him in Cheshire. And then George's brother James, an engineer, announced that he was emigrating to Canada. The decision was understandable, since his employment prospects were poor in an Ireland still reeling from the effects of the Great Famine. But it was a major blow for the rest of the family, who had counted on him to help ease their precarious financial situation. George Little was now forty-two and unmarried, the sole breadwinner for a household of four: himself, and three impecunious widows.

His responsibilities weighed heavily on him, and he found solace in religion. Brought up a Church of Ireland Protestant, in his thirties he joined an evangelical sect known as the Exclusive Brethren, a Nonconformist group recently founded in the city. The Brethren's rather severe approach to personal morality had left its mark: he was devout, abstemious, and had a powerful sense of personal duty. One colleague described him as being 'of a gloomy cast of mind', but this was putting it too strongly; he was not a pessimist, but approached life with an intense seriousness that left little room for levity. Though George had few close friends he was well liked, a quiet and amiable soul who avoided conflict and treated everybody with courtesy.

In the 1850s the Littles' house in Waterloo Road was at the very edge of the city, where the modern housing of southern Dublin petered out and gave way to woods and fields. George's office was in the north, three miles away, a walk of about forty-five minutes through the city centre. His route took him over the Grand Canal and through the Georgian splendour of St Stephen's Green – sixty years earlier the scene of public executions, but now Europe's largest and most elegant garden square. From there he turned northwards and passed Dublin Castle, then and for the last seven centuries the seat and symbol of British power in Ireland. While he walked he thought about the day ahead. His work often detained him late in the office, but the week's accounts had been submitted the previous day, so he saw no reason why he should not be home for supper. In his bag was a paper package containing a few pieces of bread and butter for his lunch; his sister had offered to make him a chicken sandwich, but he had told her he needed nothing so substantial.

'I'll be back early,' he had said as he left the house.

As he crossed the Liffey, George grimaced and clamped a handkerchief to his nose. The stench of raw sewage was overwhelming: beneath him, standing knee deep in the river, a group of labourers was shovelling a foul mixture of mud and human ordure on to a barge. The unlucky residents of Temple Bar had to put up with this appalling smell for eight hours in every twenty-four, but after months of debate the members of the city corporation still could not agree what to do about it.

George hurried away from this foul miasma and into the commercial hubbub of Capel Street, with its glorious muddle of umbrella makers and pawnbrokers and haberdashers and seed merchants. These businesses and the nearby food markets attracted the most prolific of Dublin's 'strokers', the professional thieves whose ability to make a watch or a wallet disappear would not have disgraced a stage conjuror.

But as George Little continued northwards and away from the city centre, the character of the streets began to change. The shops gave way to large institutional buildings full of lawyers, doctors and prisoners. This was a densely populated part of the metropolis, but few of the residents would call it home; indeed, barely any lived here by choice. People might come here because they were sick, and needed treatment at one of the three hospitals on Brunswick Street; or because they were destitute, and had been placed in the workhouse on Constitution Hill; or even because they had been declared insane, and committed to the Richmond Lunatic Asylum. Many of those George walked past every morning were only passing through, travellers en route to Galway or Belfast or London, perhaps staying at one of the hotels that had sprung up to cater for the large transient population.

This area, Broadstone, was Dublin's gateway to western Ireland. The Royal Canal ended here in a wide harbour where barges had been disgorging their loads of goods, livestock and people for almost half a century. There was still the odd boat on the canal, but for most people the name Broadstone now signified the railway. After all, it made little sense to spend four shillings for an uncomfortable eight-hour journey in the laughably named fly boat to Mullingar, when the train covered the fifty-two miles in a quarter of the time, and for only sixpence more.

The directors of the Midland Great Western Railway Company had wanted their new headquarters to make a bold statement, and the architect had certainly met his brief. Broadstone station was built on the highest spot in the vicinity, so that as one climbed Constitution Hill the station's weighty granite facade loomed impressively, dominating its surroundings completely. It was a two-storey building whose proportions and chimneystacks were reminiscent of a grand Regency town house, but the first thing most visitors noticed was the colossal doorway in the centre of the building, and above it a blank face of stone. It was an entrance worthy of some ancient monument, and after dark it was easy to imagine the hefty double doors slowly swinging open to admit a torchlit procession of robe-clad priests. To the traveller nervous about the novel dangers of rail travel, the high speeds and fatal accidents that appeared in the newspapers with worrying frequency, the solidity and permanence of the Broadstone terminus offered some reassurance.

It was a bitterly cold day, but George had stopped noticing by the time he crossed the pontoon bridge over the canal on to the station forecourt. The last passengers from the morning 'up' train were just leaving the building as he walked through the entrance. Inside was the ticket hall, an echoing stone atrium which with its Doric columns and massive lintels looked like a cross between a Greek temple and an Egyptian burial chamber. Above his head a wrought-iron gallery encircled the room at first-floor height, and above that the wintry daylight filtered through a glass cupola set in the roof. George crossed the hall and walked through a second doorway which led to the platforms – but instead of turning right into the train shed he climbed an elaborate iron staircase to the first floor. This part of the building was known as Directors' House, and it contained the offices and administrative staff of the Midland Great Western Railway Company.

George Little had joined the railway as a clerk in the Transfer Office in 1853, three years after the station opened. The company was rigidly hierarchical, and an employee's progress through its ranks was typically slow and difficult. But his superiors soon recognised his quiet diligence and valued his fastidious, even pedantic, approach to his work. Six months earlier, in May 1856, he had been promoted to cashier, beating sixty other candidates to the job. It was not a position of any great status, but one carrying grave responsibility. Thousands of pounds in cash passed through his office every week, the majority of the company's revenues. George's appointment was a sign that his bosses trusted him implicitly.

At the top of the staircase George turned right, walked to the end of the corridor and opened the last door on the right. The cashier's office occupied a corner of the building, and although small it was light and well ventilated, with windows on two sides. A few feet inside the door was a stout wooden counter topped by railings, like that of a high-street bank, dividing the room into two. In the middle of the counter was a small aperture at shoulder height, through which money or documents might be passed. Underneath this opening was a door which opened like a wicket gate, giving access to the cashier's private sanctum within. This arrangement was a recent innovation: when George had assumed his new role six months earlier security had been so lax that a stranger might easily have walked in and helped themselves to the piles of cash that were routinely on his desk. It had taken some effort to persuade the company directors that this situation was not acceptable, but eventually they had relented, and arranged for a carpenter from the workshops downstairs to build the barrier that now prevented unwelcome incursions from members of the public.

George went to the end of the room and sat down at his desk, a large plain table facing the door. It was empty, since it was his unvarying habit to clear it of every atom of clutter when he left the office in the evening. Behind him was a safe set into the wall, and a window which opened on to a sloping expanse of glass and iron, the massive pitched roof that covered the station platforms. Its proximity to the train shed meant that the room was seldom quiet, even when there was no locomotive at either platform. Voices swirled and echoed underneath the glass canopy, as did the never-ending cacophony of bells. A bell was rung ten minutes before a train was due to depart, and again when it actually left. Another bell indicated when an incoming train was ten minutes away, and when it had reached the platform. The incessant noise had been disconcerting at first, but George soon learned to shut it out.

To his right was a wooden dresser containing his ledgers and stationery, and a large sash window which offered the best view in the building, a tableau worthy of a Bruegel. In the foreground the goods yard teemed with men and cattle, their forms dwarfed by the dark edifice of the North Dublin Workhouse. Beyond that could be seen the open green space of the Phoenix Park, the wilder tracts of the plains of Kildare, and a shapely line of undulating hills. A fire had been laid in a small grate opposite this window, and next to it were the high stool and lectern used by his clerk William Chamberlain. There was no other furniture, apart from rough matting covering the floor; the walls were bare, giving the office an air of monastic austerity.

William arrived at 10.00, an hour after his boss. He was a lad of eighteen who had joined the company the previous July. Although the clerk's duties consisted mainly of mundane administrative tasks, such as copying figures into the official ledgers, a great deal of trust was placed in him, given that he was often asked to handle large amounts of cash. George had kept a watchful eye on his new subordinate at first, looking for any sign that he might succumb to temptation, but soon concluded that he was reliable and honest.

As cashier, George Little was responsible for counting and recording every penny taken at all the ticket offices on the line between Dublin and Galway – as well as every fare taken on the boats of the Royal Canal. Each week he was required to present his accounts to the company directors for scrutiny, and on Thursdays he also had to prepare the weekly wage packets for distribution to the hundred or more employees who worked at the Broadstone terminus. Twice a week he visited the bank to deposit the takings, check the balance of the company accounts and report what he had learned to the accountants. His workload varied considerably, since the amount of cash coming into the office was entirely dependent on the volume of traffic being carried by the railway. Not all the passengers were human: the greater part of the company's revenues throughout the year came from transporting livestock, and the sound of lowing cattle often drifted in through the window as the beasts were being unloaded on to the platform beneath the office.

The cashier's hopes for a quiet Thursday were confounded by the arrival of William McCauley, one of the station porters. Every day McCauley was in and out of the office at regular intervals, bringing the heavy cashboxes from the platform in batches, and collecting them once they had been emptied. Today as he set down the wicker basket containing the first load of boxes he grunted apologetically that there were rather a lot of them. It was Mullingar Fair, he explained: the entire line had been unusually busy for the last two days. The annual livestock fair at Mullingar, fifty-odd miles west of Dublin, was the biggest in Ireland, attracting sheep and cattle farmers from all over the country. In recent years it had also become an important marketplace for the sale of horses, and the leading dealers from England now travelled hundreds of miles to be there, paying as much as £200 for the finest specimens.

When George Little had helped McCauley stack the cashboxes against the wall he acknowledged with a sigh that he was likely to be stuck in the office until unusually late. George was not obliged to work any later than 5 p.m., but he also loathed the idea of leaving a task unfinished. His predecessor as cashier, a man called Nugent, had not been quite so particular about his duties, and his bookkeeping had often been chaotic. Mr Little was determined never to let his accounts get into such a state, even though it meant that he often had to stay at work long after everybody else had gone home.

George placed the first of the day's boxes on his desk, and opened it with a key from his chain. It was an object about the size of a doctor's bag, made from sheet iron. Inside was a mass of notes and coins, and an official docket detailing how much money the box contained, what tickets had been purchased and at which station it originated. His task now was to check that the cash amounts all tallied with the dockets, make a note of the receipts in his ledger, and then transfer the dockets to the accountant's office downstairs to ensure that there was a duplicate record of the day's takings.

That was the theory, but the reality was nowhere near as simple. Although most of the cash that came out of each box belonged to the railway company, a significant proportion did not. Passengers using the stations on the Midland Great Western line often continued their journeys beyond Dublin: they might buy a through ticket to Belfast or Wicklow or even to London. In that case, part of the fare was passed on to another railway, or to the firm that operated the regular ferries across the Irish Sea. This portion of the ticket-office revenues, known as 'surplus money', had to be placed in a different pile and accounted separately, before being bundled up and labelled with the name of the company that was to receive it – a laborious and complicated task. The packets of surplus money were sent periodically to a bank in London, but they sometimes accumulated in the office – amounting to considerable sums – for weeks at a time.

After an hour of industrious activity, George Little's desk was covered in piles of money, cheques and papers. To the casual observer the scene might have appeared chaotic; but, if asked, the cashier could have explained precisely what was in each pile, where it had come from and its final destination. He processed each cashbox with methodical care. When he had sorted the money and dockets, and made a record of each in his ledger, the notes were arranged into bundles and the coins wrapped in paper cartridges, each according to their denomination. The empty box and cash were then placed on a mahogany shelf underneath the large window to his right. Occasionally he asked William to take some document downstairs to the accounting office, but such interruptions were rare, and for several hours the pair continued their labours in silence.

It was mid-afternoon that Thursday when the peace was abruptly shattered by the noisy arrival of an uninvited guest, a scruffily dressed man of indeterminate age carrying a leather satchel. Mr Little stood up and went to the other side of the counter to investigate. The man produced a box of spectacles from his satchel and launched into an enthusiastic but rambling sales patter which he managed to keep up, almost without interruption, for the next quarter of an hour. George asked the pedlar to leave, but this did nothing to stem the verbiage. In desperation he agreed to try on a couple of pairs of glasses. Squinting theatrically through them, he declared that they were not as good as his own, and said firmly that he would not be making a purchase. At length the disappointed salesman was reluctantly evicted into the corridor. George and William, who were equally glad to see the back of him, laughed about their limpet-like visitor, and William asked if the fellow was perhaps Jewish.

'Yes, I think you are right, William,' said Mr Little.

Another hour passed before McCauley returned to the office to pick up the final load of empty cashboxes, which needed to be returned to their various stations by the five o'clock train. William had left them out for him, piled neatly on the counter. Seeing the cashier hunched over his work, McCauley decided not to disturb him, closing the door quietly on his way out. Twenty minutes later another visitor entered the room. It was a while before George Little, glancing up from his ledgers, noticed him at the counter and hurried over to see what he wanted. It turned out to be William Tough, a local builder who sometimes dropped into the office in the hope of cashing a cheque. George was happy to oblige: with several hundred pounds sitting on his desk in notes and coins it was no great inconvenience. He handed over £104 5s 3d in cash, countersigned the builder's cheque and wrote him a receipt.

Mr Tough had just left, his transaction complete, when William Chamberlain looked up at the clock and saw that it was already after 5.00. He put away his work, gathered up his coat and retrieved his hat from the shelf beneath the window. He wished his boss a good evening, ducked through the opening in the counter and departed. All over the building, clerks and managers were doing the same – but the cashier still had work to do. He followed his clerk to the door of the office and locked it behind him. It was the last time that anyone who knew George Little would see him alive.

George was often the last to leave, and disliked being left alone surrounded by so much money. Ten days earlier he had been startled by the sudden intrusion of a rough-looking stranger wearing a dirty jacket and carrying a length of rope. It transpired that the man was only looking for Mr Cabry, the chief engineer, and had taken a wrong turn in the labyrinthine corridors. It was an honest mistake, but the incident had shaken the cashier considerably. He decided that in future he would lock himself in when working on his own, but was alarmed to discover that his door would not lock from the inside. Since the office was readily accessible from the ticket hall, this made him an easy target for a would-be robber. At George's insistence, the door had been modified so that he could shut himself in with relative security.

Night was falling, and there was still a significant amount of work to be done. George reckoned that it would take three or four hours to get through it all. He returned to his desk and sat down amid the piles of coins and sheaves of notes – a fortune to most Dubliners, more than £1500 in cash. From elsewhere in the building he could hear movement and voices; evidently he was not the only employee working late. The trains would be running for a little while longer, and underneath the great glass roof behind him the cavernous space still echoed with the shouts of porters and the vaporous sighs of locomotives. George adjusted the sputtering mantle of the gas lamp on the table in front of him and picked up his pen. He had told his sister Kate that he would not be late tonight, but she appreciated that his work was often unpredictable. She would not be worried.

The railway offices were looked after by a housekeeper, Anne Gunning, who lived in a basement flat with her husband and children. Every evening she walked through the building, turning down the gaslights and checking that Catherine Campbell, the housemaid, had cleaned the floors and raked out the fires to her satisfaction. At a quarter past seven she began her tour of inspection on the ground floor. In the downstairs passage she met a clerk from the solicitor's department, Mr Thornton, who was unexpectedly – and rather unwillingly – returning to work. He had been at home eating supper with his wife when he was summoned back to the office to copy an important document which needed to be sent to Parliament the following morning.

Mrs Gunning climbed a back staircase to the first floor. The building was in darkness, but as she turned into the long corridor she noticed a patch of light on the wall opposite the cashier's office. Approaching closer, she realised that it was caused by the gaslight shining through the keyhole. Mrs Gunning was on friendly terms with Mr Little, and was used to seeing him at work long after everybody else had departed. She turned the handle of his door, but found that it was locked. The noise would usually prompt a shout of 'Not gone yet!' from the cashier, but this time there was no reaction from within. Supposing that Mr Little did not wish to be disturbed, she left him to it. She lit a candle and continued with her evening rounds.

A distant clanging, followed shortly by the thunderous music of steam pistons, told her that the 7.30 p.m. train to Galway – the last departure of the day – was under way. The ticket office was now closed, and the porters and other staff were hurrying home to their families. The train shed fell gradually into darkness as the lamps were extinguished one by one. Just three were left burning, illuminating a small portion of the arrivals platform next to Directors' House. Inside, the housekeeper walked past the open door of an office where Catherine, who also lived in the building, was laying a fire for the following morning. Remembering that the coal scuttle in her own bedroom was empty, Mrs Gunning went to refill it. Her chores completed, she returned to the basement to spend the evening with her children.

At 9.00 there was a knock on the door of the Gunnings' parlour. It was another of the legal clerks, Mr Linskey, who asked apologetically if he might have a light, as he needed to fetch something from the solicitor's office on the top floor. Such interruptions were to be expected when one lived in a busy railway station, and Mrs Gunning did not mind them. As it happened, the worst disturbance of the day was yet to come.

The railway company was obliged by law to provide one train per day to cater for those who could not ordinarily afford rail travel, with tickets priced at a penny a mile. The fare from Galway to Dublin worked out at a mere 10s 6d, but the journey was likely to be as uncomfortable as it was inexpensive. The parliamentary train, as it was known, consisted entirely of third-class carriages with hard wooden seats, and was often unpleasantly overcrowded. Its arrival at Broadstone at 9.30 p.m. could be a raucous affair, as bad-tempered passengers, cooped up in the airless and unheated compartments for hours, spilled out noisily on to the platform. There followed an undignified scramble to secure one of the few cabs still waiting at the side of the station, while suitcases and trunks were unloaded and – in the absence of anything so convenient as a porter – dragged unceremoniously along the dark platform.

This Thursday evening the parliamentary train was half an hour late. The delay was particularly unwelcome to Patrick Hanbury, the stationmaster, who had personally supervised every arrival and departure on these platforms – be it people, goods or livestock – since 5.30 in the morning. If he was lucky he might get six hours' sleep before tomorrow morning's mail train, but he could not even think about going to bed until the last passenger had left the station. At length the great terminus fell silent, and the exhausted stationmaster could perform his final task of the day. Brandishing a large bunch of keys, he walked the length of both platforms, locking up the waiting rooms, the separate lavatories set aside for first-, second- and third-class passengers, and the porters' room. As he headed for the alluring warmth of Directors' House, Mr Hanbury passed the nightwatchman, John King. A few gaslights still glimmered in the offices upstairs; but soon they too would go dark, leaving the custodian to his solitary vigil in Broadstone station.

Henry Beausire, company secretary to the Midland Great Western Railway, sat in his spacious office on the ground floor of Directors' House. It was midday on Friday, and he was just beginning to contemplate the possibility of lunch when Bennett, his clerk, put his head around the door to tell him that something was amiss. Every Friday morning Mr Beausire signed a number of cheques which were then sent up to the cashier's office and added to the pile of moneys to be taken to the bank later that afternoon. On this occasion Bennett had taken the cheques upstairs but found to his surprise that the office was locked and Mr Little nowhere to be found. The secretary agreed that this was strange, and sent one of the office juniors, a youth called Magee, to enquire for the cashier at his home in south Dublin, three miles away.

But it was not long before the mystery deepened. Half an hour later his clerk knocked on the door to say that a lady wished to see him. The woman he then admitted, Mrs Morton, was in her mid-thirties, smartly dressed and spoke with an educated formality that suggested a privileged upbringing. She seemed unsettled, and fidgeted nervously as she explained that she was the sister of George Little, the cashier. Beausire knew him well: George had entered the company as his personal clerk three years earlier, and the secretary had quickly warmed to his quiet dedication and his guileless, unassuming manner. Kate Morton told him that her brother had not returned home the previous night. She was very worried, and feared that he had been taken seriously ill, or perhaps attacked while walking home in the dark.

Mr Beausire's response was not at all what she had expected. He became agitated and spoke of calling the police, as if he assumed that George had absconded with the week's takings. Kate was offended by the implied slur on her brother's character, and begged Mr Beausire not to take this course of action. She left shortly afterwards, telling him that she intended to check that George had not spent the night with a relative who lived nearby. Kate asked him not to do anything until her return, but the secretary decided that he had better begin making enquiries straight away. It was not unheard of for a railway employee to turn up late for work after a night of drinking or gambling, but he knew George Little well enough to be quite sure that such nocturnal vices were not his style. And it seemed inconceivable that a man so conscientious would deliberately stay away from home overnight without letting his family know.

Mr Beausire strode up the grand staircase to the first floor and found William Chamberlain loitering in the passage outside the cashier's office. When asked why he was not working, the clerk replied that the office was locked; he had asked the housekeeper to let him in, but she had told him that Mr Little had the only key. Beausire gave the door a quick rattle to confirm the truth of this statement, and then bent down to look through the keyhole. But there was nothing to see: the metal keyhole cover on the other side of the door entirely obscured his view.

Awful thoughts coursed through Mr Beausire's mind. Perhaps George had suffered a stroke or heart attack, and was now sitting slumped at his desk just a few yards away, dead or dying. But if he was still alive they must do everything in their power to help him; there was not a minute to lose. Mr Beausire had just decided that they would have to break down the door when a messenger boy, Thomas Moore, emerged from the office opposite. The secretary instructed him to run downstairs to the carriage workshop and ask for Mr Brophy, the foreman. Brophy must send a carpenter to the first floor, urgently, and help them gain access to the cashier's office. The boy listened attentively and then told Mr Beausire that he knew how to get into Mr Little's room. There was a window on the back staircase that gave access to the station roof. From there it would be easy to get into the office through one of the side windows. The secretary agreed to this plan, on condition that he summon the carpenter first.

A few minutes later Mr Beausire and William heard noises from the other side of the locked door. Thomas had succeeded in getting on to the roof, but was struggling to open the window from outside. He shouted to them that he was not strong enough to lift the heavy sash. Assistance soon arrived in the muscular form of James Brophy, carrying a basket of tools. A builder and joiner by trade, Brophy was quite at home clambering about on the roof, and in a moment he was outside the window of Mr Little's office. The blinds were down, and the only news he could pass on to the small crowd now waiting anxiously in the corridor was that the gas was still lit.

Just then a clerk from the engineering department, Patrick Moan, returned from lunch. He was surprised to find so many people standing around in the corridor outside the cashier's office. Before he could ask what was going on, Mr Beausire barked an instruction at him.

'Moan, run for a doctor. There is something wrong.'

As Moan scurried off on his errand, the company secretary shouted to Brophy that he should get inside the room as quickly as he could, by whatever means were necessary. Brophy tried the window and found that it would not open. Looking more closely, he noticed that it had been roughly secured by a single nail driven through the bottom sash. One firm yank proved enough to dislodge it, and on the other side of the door Mr Beausire soon heard the protesting squeal of a warped window frame being forced open. Brophy swung his legs round and jumped lightly to the floor, then gave an involuntary cry of horror.

'He is here, lying dead,' he yelled, 'and there is no key in the door.'

'Quick!' said Mr Beausire. 'Prise that door open!'

With a rising sense of panic, those in the corridor – who now numbered five or six – tried to force the door, while inside the room Brophy attacked the lock with a chisel. When it finally gave way, Beausire led the charge into the cashier's office. Brophy looked at him blankly and, without saying a word, turned his head towards the window through which he had entered. Beausire followed his gaze, taking in the gas lamp still burning in broad daylight, the desk with its neat piles of papers and coins, and, on the floor behind it, a motionless human form. George Little was lying on his front, his right cheek resting on the floorboards and his eyes fixed open in a glassy stare. His neck was disfigured by a gaping wound; and all around him was blood, endless blood, more blood than Henry Beausire had ever seen.

2

Friday 14 November

To those who made the ghastly discovery it seemed that George Little must have taken his own life. The door to his office had been locked, apparently from the inside; the windows were fastened and the blinds down. There was nothing to suggest the presence of an intruder, no indication of forced entry or a struggle. The cashier's table was conspicuously tidy, as if he had just arranged everything for the day's work. The only sign that anything might be amiss was a small spot of blood on his blotter. The position of George's body suggested that he had been sitting in his chair when he had cut his own throat. On the desk was an office knife, and on the floor next to his hand a towel matted with blood, as though in his last moments he had made a desperate attempt to undo what could not be undone.

As Henry Beausire took in this dreadful tableau he was suddenly conscious of the press of bodies behind him. Looking round, he noticed that George Little's assistant William had entered the room. Instinctively Mr Beausire moved sideways to block the boy's view, took his elbow and gently steered him into the corridor, anxious that William should not see anything that might distress him. Then he strode back into the throng to take charge of the situation.

He had already sent for a doctor, at least. It was obvious that the cashier had been dead for hours, but they would need to obtain a death certificate and an expert opinion of his injuries. The next priority was securing the money, which lay in piles on almost every surface. Mr Beausire asked Archibald Moore, who worked in the office opposite, to gather and count the cash before storing it in the safe behind George Little's desk. The safe had been left open, with the key inside. Moore got on with this task without complaint, but his demeanour betrayed his true state of mind. His hands shook as he moved around the room picking up the piles of notes and cheques, and he studiously avoided looking in the corner, where the mutilated body of his friend and colleague lay.

Mr Beausire helped James Brophy look for the missing door key. There was no sign of it on the desk, and a rummage through the drawers yielded only a small penknife and a pair of scissors. Brophy had also looked in the large wooden dresser, without success. The disappearance of the key seemed inexplicable, until it occurred to one of them that it must be in Mr Little's pocket. This put an end to the search, since Mr Beausire had decreed that nobody was to touch the body until the doctor had examined it.

But finding a doctor was proving difficult. Patrick Moan had tried to get hold of Dr Kelly, whose surgery was a short walk away on the Phibsborough Road, but the boy he sent to fetch him returned a few minutes later saying that the doctor was out. One of the porters recommended a Dr Holmes in Dorset Street, but he too was unavailable. Moan then tried Dr O'Reilly in Dominick Street, where his knock went unanswered, and the apothecary's shop in Capel Street, where the lad who was minding the counter told him that the doctor was out on his rounds. Since he could not think of any other options nearby, Moan decided to run back to Broadstone and get further advice. He had not gone far when he bumped into Michael Linskey from the solicitor's office.

'Moan, have you heard?' Linskey said. 'Poor Little is dead, his throat was cut.'

'Oh my God!' exclaimed the clerk. Assuming that the time for medical assistance had passed, Moan stopped running and walked the rest of the way back to the terminus. His return aroused little enthusiasm. Joseph Cabry, the chief engineer, asked him when the doctor would be arriving, and swore at Moan when he learned that the clerk had not found one. So the clerk went out again, this time accompanied by Bennett from the secretary's office. The two men jumped in a cab and took a frustrating drive around north Dublin, trying another four medical practices before they eventually succeeded in finding a physician who was at home: a general practitioner named Barker, who immediately agreed to accompany them.

It was a little before 2 p.m. when they reached Broadstone, and the station was in uproar. News of a death on the premises had rapidly penetrated every department of the company, and dozens of railway workers – impelled more by morbid curiosity than sympathy for their late colleague – had taken advantage of the lunch hour to come and gawp. Moan and Dr Barker fought their way through the melee at the top of the stairs and looked for Mr Beausire. They eventually located the company secretary at the end of the corridor on the other side of the landing, where he had evidently retreated in search of privacy. He was deep in conversation with two men in their forties dressed, like him, in frock coats. They appeared to be professionals of some description, lawyers or bankers perhaps, and although Dr Barker could not hear what was being said, the shock and distress in their faces told its own story. Mr Beausire bade them each farewell with a sympathetic handshake, and came over to greet the doctor.

The pair were friends of George Little, he explained. After learning of his disappearance from Kate they had come straight to Broadstone, pausing only to pick up a doctor of their acquaintance in case the cashier had been taken ill. Mr Beausire had managed to intercept them on the threshold of the blood-soaked office, and narrowly prevented them from seeing a sight they would have found impossible to forget. He had told them about the cashier's apparent suicide, supplying as few of the unpleasant details as he thought consistent with perfect honesty. The doctor was still in the office examining the body, but the other two were now on their way to the Littles' house in Waterloo Road, having volunteered to break the news to George's mother and sister.

Mr Beausire led Dr Barker to the cashier's office. Many of the bystanders suddenly remembered pressing obligations elsewhere, recognising signs in the glowering countenance of the company secretary that their presence was not desired. Moore had collected all the cash and locked it in the safe, and was now bundling up the cheques and dockets. Dr Barker ducked through the wicket gate in the wooden counter and surveyed the scene dispassionately. At first glance the room looked in good order, with the desk now cleared and the clutter tidied away. But a cold wind whipped in through the open window, and the matting underneath the table was marred by a huge and ugly stain. Around its edges the blood had dried to a dirty brown, but in places it was brighter and still slightly wet, like a puddle of recently spilt wine. At the centre of this drying lake the dead man lay on his front, his right arm underneath the stomach and his left extended in front of him, as if reaching out for something.

Another person was stooping over the body, inspecting it closely. Dr Barker recognised him as Dr Wensley Jennings, one of the younger physicians who practised in the area. Dr Jennings gently lifted one of the dead man's shoulders to get a better look at the face.

'Throat cut,' he said, choking on the words.

All the colour had drained from Dr Jennings's face. He looked profoundly shocked. After taking a moment to recover his composure he explained to his colleague that he was related to George Little, and had come to the station on the understanding that the cashier had been taken ill. He had never expected to find his relative dead, and particularly not in such dreadful circumstances. Muttering his apologies, Dr Jennings withdrew, leaving Dr Barker to conduct his own examination.

The doctor realised that his presence was a formality. He

could only sign a death certificate if the cashier had died from natural causes, and there was self-evidently nothing natural about this death. He could see at once that the wound to George Little's neck was catastrophic, enough to kill anybody within a matter of minutes. But there were proprieties to be observed, so dutifully he produced a stethoscope and listened to the dead man's chest in sombre silence for a minute, before confirming that life was indeed extinct. With the reluctant assistance of Archibald Moore he heaved the body back into its original position. His examination complete, he returned to the corridor where Mr Beausire was waiting for him. The doctor delivered his assessment.

'I fear there is little I can tell you that you did not already know. His throat has been cut, and I suspect that it was he who cut it. There will have to be an inquest, of course. You had better communicate with the police in Frederick Street, and send somebody for the coroner.'

Mr Beausire summoned Moan, who had been waiting nearby, and told him to take Dr Barker home in a cab, and then to continue to the police station and report what had happened.

An inquest! This was unwelcome news, but Mr Beausire had been expecting it. An inquest meant a public hearing on railway premises, journalists, and a lot of undesirable publicity. Still, it was Friday afternoon. If he could persuade the coroner to assemble a jury straight away, they could hear the case before the weekend. The verdict was surely straightforward: the cashier had killed himself while temporarily insane. Suicide still carried the taint of illegality, but in practice juries usually chose to exonerate the deceased, and thus spare the family further distress, by casting doubt on their mental state. With a bit of luck, Mr Beausire reasoned, they could get the whole affair out of the way before the newspapers got wind of it.

But he was out of luck. A few hours later a Dublin newspaper, the *Evening Freeman*, published a short but sensational story:

SUICIDE OF A RAILWAY CASHIER THIS DAY

We regret to have to state that Mr. Little, the cashier of the Midland Great Western Railway (Ireland) committed suicide this day in his office at the Broadstone Terminus, by cutting his throat with a razor. At the usual hour for taking up the cash to deposit it in the bank, the officer deputed for that purpose found the cashier's door locked; and on the door being broken open, the unfortunate gentleman was found dead, his throat being literally severed from side to side. The cause of this frightful suicide is, of course, not yet known, though various surmises have been suggested by the lamentable frequency, of late, of railway defalcations.

The newspaper must have had an informant at Broadstone, given that this report appeared before the coroner or police had even visited the station. And, as the *Evening Freeman* hinted, it was not just the immediate circumstances of George's death that suggested suicide.

What was meant by that phrase 'the lamentable frequency . . . of railway defalcations'? Defalcation is embezzlement, the dishonest appropriation of funds. The previous decade had seen an epidemic of corporate fraud, and 1856 proved to be the golden age of the embezzler. In February that year a prominent Irish financier, John Sadleir, was found dead on Hampstead Heath in London. He had taken cyanide, and it soon emerged that he had debts totalling well over £1 million. In order to finance a series of rash speculations he had pillaged the funds of numerous companies with which he was involved. As chairman of the Royal Swedish Railway Company he had forged thousands of share certificates; he had also run up a colossal overdraft at the Tipperary Joint Stock Bank, a family firm established by his grandfather. The inevitable collapse of the Tipperary Bank caused a national scandal in Ireland, since many of its victims were labourers and peasant farmers, members of the rural working class who had survived the Great Famine only to lose everything for a second time.

But it was not just the bosses who were fiddling the books. A mere two weeks before the death of George Little, a clerk with the Crystal Palace Company in London had been convicted of forgery and sentenced to transportation to Australia. In little over two years, William Robson swindled more than £30,000 out of his employers, using the cash to fund an extravagant lifestyle of racehorses, fine clothes and wine – and accommodating two mistresses, separately, in apartments of considerable opulence. Before he embarked on this criminal spree Robson had worked for the Great Northern Railway Company, where by a strange coincidence his colleagues included another fraudster even more shameless than himself.

Leopold Redpath was the registrar of the Great Northern Railway, responsible for keeping track of the company's share-holders and how much stock they each owned. Soon after his appointment he began falsifying documents, creating non-existent shares and selling them for his own profit. He bought a substantial house next to Regent's Park and a country estate in Surrey, complete with its own fishing lake and more than a dozen servants. Unlike the dissipated Robson, Redpath appeared to be a pillar of the community, a generous patron of the arts and trustee for several charities. There were some who wondered, rea-sonably enough, how a middle-ranking official at a railway company could afford to live in such style, but the urbane Red-path let it be known that he had made a fortune speculating in the City. The truth of the matter was that he had siphoned off more than £250,000 of other people's money – the equivalent of around £27 million today.

Crucially, news of Leopold Redpath's gigantic scam broke on the very day that George Little's body was discovered. After learning of the cashier's apparent suicide, readers of that Friday's *Evening Freeman* would have seen a report under the headline 'Serious Defalcations on the Great Northern Railway' on the fol-lowing page. Three of the most significant frauds in corporate history had taken place in quick succession, all perpetrated by individuals intimately connected with the railways. Now George Little, a railway company official routinely entrusted with thousands of pounds in cash, had been found dead. It was easy to assume, as many did, that he had been caught with his fingers in the till and had chosen to put an end to his life rather than face the consequences.

But there were also reasons for doubting the theory that Mr Little had killed himself. Where, for example, was the key to his office? If he had locked himself in – as was generally assumed – it must be somewhere in the room, but a careful search had so far failed to locate it. And the wound to his throat had evidently been inflicted by some fearsomely sharp blade, yet the only implements found near his body were a blunt pair of scissors, a small office knife and an even smaller penknife. Could any of these really have been the instrument of his destruction? These were points that a jury would have to consider before delivering a verdict.

It was late afternoon when John Elliott Hyndman, coroner for the City of Dublin, finally arrived at Broadstone station, accompanied by his clerk. Like most coroners of the day he was an elected official, and had no particular expertise in medicine or the law; the only essential qualifications for the job, in fact, were that he should be a man, own property, and have an income of more than £50 a year. Mr Hyndman was the archetypal establishment figure, a former High Sheriff of Dublin and head of the local Masonic lodge. He was also, infamously, one of Ireland's last and biggest slave-owners, the heir to a family fortune built on the unpaid toil of generations of black Africans. A white-haired man of sixty, Mr Hyndman was known for his polished manners and brisk efficiency – although he was not without self-regard.

Mr Beausire met the coroner downstairs in the grand hall. The pair had often encountered each other, but never before in such sombre circumstances. Mr Beausire gave a brief account of events earlier that day, then took Mr Hyndman to inspect the cashier's office. Gossip, travelling through the city like some air-borne contagion, had taken news of the death to both sides of the Liffey, and curious members of the public had started to arrive in some numbers, hoping to catch a glimpse of the corpse. The object of their ghoulish fascination was, however, inaccessible, since a large and unfriendly policeman now blocked the entrance to the corridor. The constable stepped aside when he spotted the coroner, touching the brim of his top hat in salute as the official passed him.

Three more officers were at work inside the room, making a minute examination of the body, the furniture, the floors and windows. Much of this industrious activity was quite pointless, since the chances of learning anything new or useful were now remote. In the five hours since the discovery of the body a small army of visitors had turned the office upside down. Every move-able object had been picked up, tidied or taken away, every cupboard and drawer emptied by at least three pairs of hands. The matting on the floor was a palimpsest of street dirt, soot and sawdust tramped in from the workshops downstairs, an inde-cipherable muddle of footprints old and new. If the scene of George Little's death ever had any forensic secrets to give up, they were long gone. A search of the cashier's clothing had yielded a few personal effects, but nothing surprising. The constables were now solemnly contemplating an elderly and rather crooked poker which one of them had found propped next to the fireplace. They broke off their discussion when they saw the coroner enter, and the senior officer conducted him on a guided tour of the room. The coroner's clerk took notes while his superior listened atten-tively to the policeman's narration. There was not much to say, or to see.

Mr Hyndman lingered longest next to George Little's body, taking a sharp intake of breath when he saw the obscene incision that had cut his throat open from one side to the other. At his request the constables rolled the corpse over, and with a crisp

'Thank you' he returned to the corridor and an expectant Henry Beausire. The secretary had already made plain his desire for a quick inquest, and began to reiterate this plea, but the coroner cut him off. It was quite out of the question, he said. Assembling an inquest jury would mean sending police officers out to find twelve local men of good character and demanding that they drop everything to come to Broadstone. This hardly seemed reasonable at such a late hour; in any case, it was almost dark, and daylight was essential for the jurors to make a proper inspection of the body.

Mr Hyndman appreciated that speed was of the essence, not least because George Little's remains could not be moved or prepared for burial until after the inquest. Tomorrow was a Saturday, of course. But the coroner was expected to hold his inquiry within forty-eight hours of being notified of a sudden death, and it was illegal to conduct any judicial business on a Sunday. This made the decision straightforward: the inquest would take place the following day, at noon. Mr Hyndman had already compiled a mental list of tasks, which he now communicated with some urgency to his clerk. He needed the names of everyone who had visited the cashier's office on the last day he was seen alive; anybody who lived in the building, or had visited it overnight; and those who had been present when the door was forced and the body discovered. If they had any useful information they would be summoned to give evidence, on pain of prosecution. The coroner also wanted two surgeons to perform a thorough post-mortem and determine the cause of death. Then there was the jury to be found, of course, and a room big enough to accommodate everybody. The clerk made a note of these requirements, then hurried off to start work. It was going to be a long night.

3

Saturday 15 November

In stipulating that the inquest would take place at noon on Saturday, the coroner had overlooked one important fact. In a railway station there is an authority higher even than an official of Her Majesty the Queen, an authority more sacrosanct than holy writ, and more capricious than the weather. This higher power is the railway timetable, a document which is simultaneously prediction and promise, best-guess estimate and downright lie. The timetable ruled the Broadstone terminus with the arbitrary whim of a tyrant, dictating the actions of its subjects while regularly confounding their plans.

It now delayed the pursuit of justice, because at a few minutes before midday the first express train of the day, the 08.50 from Athlone, arrived with deplorable punctuality. Carriage doors were being flung open even before it had squealed to a halt, and passengers piled on to the platform, impatient to get on with their Saturday business in the capital. As the hordes thundered into the ticket hall they ran into a miscellany of policemen, office workers, labourers, and, standing slightly apart, a group in black mourning. This was, or soon would be, the inquest, awaiting admission to the ground-floor room where the hearing was to take place. The noise and confusion continued for some minutes after the doors were finally opened, and to preserve the dignity of the occasion Mr Hyndman waited until the last echo had faded away before opening proceedings.

The makeshift court over which he was presiding had been set up in the large meeting room – the grandest that the Broadstone station had to offer. Unlike the public areas of the building, it was expensively carpeted, with high ceilings and wood panelling. This was where the company directors met in conference every week, and where they entertained major investors and government officials.

Mr Hyndman was not accustomed to such splendid surroundings. Dublin did not yet have a purpose-built coroner's court; when a sudden death was reported it was usual for the body to be taken to a nearby pub and laid out in the bar, there to await an inquest later the same day. Thanks to a recent change in the law, publicans had no say in the matter: they were required to close their establishment until the inquest had taken place, or accept a hefty forty-shilling fine. They received no compensation for the loss of revenue, even though the temporary presence of a corpse on the premises could harm their custom for days or weeks.

Pub inquests were by necessity often rather informal affairs, and given the degree of interest in this case it was fortunate that the station contained a room so well suited to the purpose. The coroner sat in front of the windows at its far end, behind a heavy oak table that usually occupied the middle of the room. Chairs had been arranged along one of the side walls to accommodate the jury of twelve men. At the front of the room, nearest the coroner and facing him, sat Mr John Ennis, chairman of the Midland Great Western Railway, accompanied by six of the company directors and a number of other officials including Mr Beausire. Behind them were several male relatives of George Little, but not his mother or sister, who were at home. There were only a few dozen chairs, so most of the spectators were standing. In the little remaining space, next to the door, was a contingent of uniformed police constables and detectives – the constables in their regulation top hats and brass-buttoned blue tunics, the detectives in plain clothes.

After the jurors had been sworn in one by one, Mr Hyndman gave a sombre little speech to explain the purpose of the afternoon's hearing, underlining the gravity of the decision the jury would be asked to reach. Their first and most important task would also be the least pleasant. It was fundamental to the very nature of inquests that they were held *super visum corporis* – a legal phrase, the coroner explained, meaning 'upon a viewing of the body'. Before any evidence could be heard, they must see Mr Little for themselves; now all twelve of them would accompany him upstairs to discharge this responsibility.

There was a shifting of chairs, and the policemen nearest the doors stood aside to let the jurors pass. The impromptu procession, with Mr Hyndman and his clerk bringing up the rear, filed through the ticket hall and up the grand staircase to the cashier's office. Their visit was brief: although this viewing of the body was required by law, the procedure was rapidly becoming an empty ritual, a vestigial remnant of medieval practice. The jurors would learn little from their sight of the bloodied corpse, except that a man was dead. It was no longer their role to determine the cause of death, anyway. That job fell to the expert medical witnesses, a surgeon and physician who were already lurking outside in the corridor, waiting to be left alone so that they could get on with the post-mortem. One of them was Wensley Jennings, who had recovered from his shock of the previous day, and who to general surprise had volunteered to assist at his own cousin's autopsy.

In the meeting room downstairs an uneasy hum of muttered conversation had broken out, the sound of a bored congregation at a funeral delayed by the late arrival of the priest. All fell silent as the doors were flung open to admit the coroner, and those lucky enough to have a seat rose to their feet as he and the jury returned to their places. Mr Hyndman asked for the first witness to be called.

Henry Beausire made his way to the small table which was serving as the witness stand, and the clerk administered the oath. Inquests in Victorian Ireland entailed little of the official rigmarole seen today: though the family of the deceased (and the suspect, if there was one) were permitted legal representation, on this occasion there were no barristers in the room, or indeed lawyers of any kind. The witnesses would be questioned by the coroner, but jurors and even members of the public were encouraged to interject at any time. It was also in the jury's power to call a witness back to the stand if they wanted clarification, or to revisit a subject if fresh evidence had come to light.

Mr Beausire was asked to confirm first of all that he knew George Little. He explained how the cashier had started work at the station three years earlier, and that he had been in that role since the previous March. The coroner then plunged into what seemed the obvious line of questioning.

'Mr Beausire, how often did Mr Little submit his accounts for inspection?'

'His cash account was laid before the directors every Wednesday. It was laid before them in the usual manner last Wednesday.'

'And were you or your colleagues in the habit of making some test that the figures he gave you were in agreement with the moneys he had received?'

'Yes. A few weeks earlier the cash in his hands was checked by the directors, who went to his room for the purpose, and they found it perfectly correct. In fact, the cash in hand was further checked up to the previous Sunday night or Monday morning.'

'Five days have passed since then, of course. As far as you know, are the accounts in order for this week?'

'A large amount of money found in his office last night was counted, and found, as well as I can now state, to be substantially correct.'

The coroner paused before asking the question he had been building up to.

'Mr Beausire, you will be aware that in recent months a number of companies have fallen prey to the avarice of their employees.

Is there any suggestion that there has been any defalcation in this case?'

'I know of no defalcation.'

This answer was far from the end of the matter, as Mr Hyndman knew all too well. When a company had been swindled, the bosses were often the last to know. Indeed, a mere two months before Leopold Redpath's gigantic frauds came to light, the chairman and directors of the Great Northern Railway had received a complacent little note from the company auditors expressing their 'entire approval' of the annual accounts, 'with our usual certificate of their correctness'. A quarter of a million pounds was missing, but they had no idea; Redpath had been far too canny to let his dishonesty show up on the balance sheet.

There were numerous ways of concealing wrongdoing in the accounting, but one of the simplest was to document the settling of debts that had not yet been paid. The coroner decided to probe further.

'Now, it would be perfectly ordinary for an official in Mr Little's position sometimes to accept a promissory note, a written guarantee of future payment, in lieu of cash, would it not?'

'Yes, certainly.'

'Did he include such promissory notes in his weekly accounts, or would he wait until the debt had been settled?'

'No, sir. He constantly advanced money on IOUs, and he would not enter them till there was a final settlement with the parties.'

Mr Hyndman was about to pursue this line of inquiry further, but the next question died on his lips. There was a commotion at the end of the room as the door was opened violently, and Dr Jennings emerged from the scrum of policemen blocking the coroner's view. The doctor stammered an apology, and, without waiting for a response, turned the entire inquest on its head.

'There is no doubt that he was murdered, sir. His head is covered with wounds.'

A subsequent newspaper report inserted the single word 'sensation' at this point, an economical way of describing the gasps and cries of surprise and anguish that followed the doctor's stunning intervention. The coroner waited a moment for the shock to subside before responding.

'Thank you, Dr Jennings. This justifies the course I took yesterday evening, when I declined to proceed then with the inquest. I was far from being satisfied, at the time, that this was a case of suicide. I did regret exceedingly that I felt unable to comply with the request for an immediate inquest.'

Sir Percy Nugent, a former MP and one of the company directors, stood up and observed ingratiatingly that Mr Hyndman had acted with great prudence, and had been perfectly vindicated in the course he chose to pursue.

Since this new information seemed likely to alter the outcome of the hearing, the coroner offered the jurors a chance to view the body for a second time. Again they climbed the stairs to the fateful office, where a terrible sight awaited them. Looking at the corpse had not been easy the first time; but now, barely twenty minutes later, it presented an even more frightful appearance. It had been lifted off the floor and placed on the table, and the clothes removed. The medics had washed the blood off Mr Little's head and shaved his hair, and it was as if they had stripped off the last remnants of his personality.

It was now apparent that the head had been all but severed from the body, and the pallid face in front of the jurors seemed more animal than human, a freakish anatomical specimen rather than the remains of a friend, a beloved brother and son. Now the scalp was bare, it was quite clear that the gash to his throat was not the only injury. Both the front and back of George Little's head were livid with bruising, and there was a deep indentation in what should have been the smooth dome of his skull. He had been savagely beaten, his cranium shattered by numerous blows of devastating force.

On the other side of the wooden counter, a young surgeon named George Porter opened a bag of instruments and waited for the jurors to leave. As soon as the last of them had reached the stairs he closed the door, picked up a knife and a surgical probe and stepped towards the body with grim intent.

In the meeting room downstairs the atmosphere had changed. The mood was sombre, but there was now also an air of expectation, a sense that further revelations would soon be made. The company secretary had not left the witness stand, and with the coroner once again in his place he resumed his questioning. Circumstances now dictated that he take a different tack.

'Mr Beausire, how much money was there in the cashier's office?'

'There was over eleven hundred pounds yesterday in the office after the body was discovered.'

'And when did you last see Mr Little?'

'I don't think I have seen him for some eight or ten days.'

'And why was there so much cash on Mr Little's desk?'

'Mullingar Fair was held on Tuesday and Wednesday, and there was an increase in the receipts: on one day there was over eight hundred pounds, and over six hundred the next.'

At the coroner's request he explained the niceties of Mr Little's job: how the money was delivered to him, what he did with it and where it went afterwards.

'Mr Beausire, you are talking about very large sums of money. How many people in this station would know that Mr Little regularly handled such sums?'

'It would be known amongst the majority of the clerks that he received daily the receipts of the line from all the stations. It would also be known to a certain extent, but I don't know to what extent, by the porters.'

'And how would you describe Mr Little's character?'

'The deceased was a quiet, amiable, unpresuming and as unoffending a creature as ever breathed.'

'Had he quarrelled with anybody here at the station?'

'As far as I know, he had no dispute of any kind with any clerk or porter in the establishment, or with any other person.'

'Had he any enemies, anybody who might wish him harm?'

'I am not aware that anyone bore any ill will towards him.'

Mr Beausire then narrated the events of the previous day, from the impromptu visit of George's sister up to the arrival of the coroner himself. The jury asked for more detail about the security arrangements. The company secretary told them about the unexpected visitor whose arrival late one evening, while George had been counting the gold, had given the cashier such a fright; and about the modifications he had had made to the lock on his office door as a result. He spoke of Mr Little's thoroughness, and his habit of staying at work after all the clerks had gone home.

A final thought occurred to the coroner.

'Mr Beausire, had the deceased finished his work when he was attacked?'

'It appears to me that he had finished counting the money. There was no loose cash, and a slip with the receipts for November the twelfth, the previous day, was on the table in front of him.'

Mr Hyndman thanked the company secretary and asked him to resume his seat. During the latter part of his evidence two figures had slipped into the room virtually unnoticed. The medics had completed their post-mortem examination, and were now ready to present their conclusions.

First to take the stand was the surgeon George Porter, who delivered his evidence in the drily factual manner of a chief executive reading out a quarterly report. His tone was at odds with the litany of horrors he had to relate. Mr Little had been the victim of a sustained attack of staggering ferocity. The doctors had found wounds over both eyebrows; five more on the forehead; three on the left cheek; a deep wound above the left ear, and another in front of it. There were seven wounds on the back of the head and one on top. The tip of the right ear had been nearly severed.

The most obvious injury was a five-inch wound to the front of the throat, which ran from underneath the left ear to an inch or so beyond the Adam's apple. Both the jugular veins on the left-hand side had been entirely cut through, as had the oesophagus and all the muscles in front of the spine, all the way to the bone. When the surgeon peeled back the scalp he had found a massive haemorrhage underneath it. The skull was fractured in several places, with one fissure running from over the right eyebrow to the left temple. The entire left side of the skull had been shattered into small pieces, causing catastrophic injury to the underlying portion of the brain.

Even the coroner was taken aback by the extent of the dead man's injuries, and the savagery they implied. After a moment to collect his thoughts, he asked the surgeon what weapon the attacker might have used.

'I am of opinion that the fracture over the left ear was inflicted by some heavy instrument, while the deceased was in a stooping posture, by someone standing in front of him. The other lacerated wounds of the head and the incised ones of the face and throat being inflicted while he was lying insensible on the ground. And, in addition to the blunt weapon, some exceedingly sharp instrument was employed to cut the throat and face.'

'Is it possible that the deceased inflicted these injuries on himself?'

'No, sir. I am satisfied the case is not one of suicide, but that the deceased was injured by another person.'

'And, independently of the cutting of the throat, would the wounds on the head have caused death?'

'The fracture of the skull would, certainly.'

'And you say that the skull where it is fractured is broken into innumerable small pieces?'

'We could not count them.'

Dr Jennings now took the surgeon's place, and spoke briefly to endorse his colleague's assessment. Mr Little, he said, had been 'barbarously murdered'.

Since both medical witnesses agreed that the skull fractures had been caused by a blunt instrument, a boy was dispatched upstairs to fetch the bent poker which the police had noticed in the office. This object was handed around and examined closely, but both Mr Porter and Dr Jennings agreed that it could not be the murder weapon, since there were no marks on it.

That being the end of the medical evidence, both doctors were excused. Mr Little's assistant William Chamberlain was now examined, and gave a detailed account of his movements on Thursday, the last day that George Little had been seen alive. Like Mr Beausire, he had never heard anybody in the station say a word against the cashier, who appeared to have been a man without enemies.

Mr Hyndman turned to the possibility of robbery. William acknowledged that most people at Broadstone knew that the office generally contained large sums of money. He told the story of the rough-looking stranger whose unexpected visit one evening had frightened Mr Little. William had bumped into him on his way out of the building, and had asked him where he was going. The man gave him a crumpled piece of paper with a name written on it, that of Mr Cabry, the chief engineer. William was just telling him that Mr Cabry had gone home when another railway employee had interrupted to suggest that he go upstairs and leave a message with the office boy. Although he had not thought much of it at the time, William noticed that he was carrying a length of heavy rope – a plausible weapon, and one sometimes used by muggers.

The coroner asked whether he knew the man, or had seen him since that occasion a few weeks ago.

'I would know him again, both from his appearance and his voice; but I never saw him before.'

One of the jurors asked William about the lock on the door of the office he shared with the cashier. The young man described how Mr Little had discovered that the door would not lock from inside, and how the carpenter had altered it just the previous week.

'And what happened to the key of this lock when Mr Little went home at night? Did he take it with him?'

'No, sir, he never took the key home. On the day the lock was altered he told me to put the key inside the room when we left. During the day the key was left in the lock on the outside of the door.'

This was an important point: the only real purpose of the lock on Mr Little's door was to prevent intruders from entering the office if he happened to be there alone. George had not thought it necessary to lock up the office when he went home every evening, since any money left in the room overnight was secured in a stout iron safe.

Despite the earlier doubts of the medical witnesses, the coroner asked for William to be shown the office poker.

'Chamberlain, you no doubt recognise that poker. It is rather bent, you see. Was it like that when you left the office on Thursday evening?'

'I think the bend has been in it for some time, though it may be a little more bent now than it was. It is difficult to be sure.'

Suddenly recalling what might have been a significant incident on that fateful day, William described the visit of the spectacle salesman, and his stubborn refusal to leave the office. Mr Hyndman's interest was piqued.

'Was there cash lying about the office when this man, this pedlar, came into the room?'

'Yes, sir, there was a large sum of money on the desk.'

'And how would you describe him?'

'I never saw the man before. I think he was a foreigner, from the way he spoke. He had one of those leather cases.'

'A satchel?'

'Yes, sir. I think he was a Jew. Mr Little said he thought so too.'

There was an interruption from the floor which Mr Hyndman tolerated, since it appeared to put an end to this line of questioning. One of the station employees, backed up by several of his colleagues, said that he knew the Jewish pedlar well: he was often around the building, and it was generally agreed that he was harmless.

With this potential suspect apparently absolved of suspicion, William was excused. But that still left the unidentified stranger with the length of rope, who had claimed to be looking for Mr Cabry. The obvious thing was to ask the chief engineer himself, but Mr Cabry could not be found. A boy sent to his office to fetch him returned with the news that he was laid up in bed, having sprained his ankle the previous morning while attempting to break down Mr Little's door.

There was, in truth, no need for further evidence, since the function of the inquest was simply to decide whether a crime had been committed. It was already clear what the jury's verdict would be, and today a coroner might not think it necessary to call any more witnesses; but Mr Hyndman was keen to speak to the permanent residents of Directors' House to see if any important facts about the likely killer would emerge.

First to speak was Anne Gunning, the housekeeper, who lived on the premises. The coroner asked her about the key to Mr Little's door.

'He sometimes remained as late as ten o'clock, and always left the key in the door when he left. The servant cleans the offices at night, and she leaves the keys in the office doors all night.'

Mrs Gunning described her visit to the cashier's office at 7.30 p.m. the previous Thursday: how the door had been locked, and the office gaslight shining through the keyhole. She also recalled that her servant Catherine had asked for the keys the following morning because the door was still locked; this was an unusual occurrence, but Mrs Gunning had assumed at the time that the cashier had taken his key home with him, perhaps because he had left important papers on his table.

A juror asked how easy it would be for an outsider to gain entry to the cashier's office in the evening, once the clerks had gone home.

'The door leading to the platform is not locked before half-past eleven, and through this door access can be had to the entire building by a back staircase. Before the door is locked at night, a search is made to ensure that there are no strangers on the premises.'

'Say a stranger were to enter through that door. Would it be easy for them to find Mr Little's office?'

'No, a person would need to know the house well to get to the office from the platform door.'

Before Mrs Gunning was allowed to step down, she too was asked to inspect the poker. She declared firmly that the bend had been in it 'for some time', a statement which put an end to this exhibit's evidential, if not its practical, utility.

Catherine Campbell was next to speak. She also lived in the house, working as servant to the Gunnings and assisting with general housekeeping duties. She explained that she usually went round the offices at about 5.00 every evening to rake out the fires and clean the grates. That Thursday she had arrived at Mr Little's office at around 5.30 and found the door locked. She rattled the handle but got no answer.

A juror interrupted to ask whether the key was in the door.

'The key was not outside, and I could not tell whether it was on the inside of the door or not.'

She had then gone downstairs to the office of the canal administrators, and cleaned all the fireplaces on the ground floor.

'And did you meet any stranger in the building?'

'No. But while I was in the canal office, which is underneath Mr Little's, I heard footsteps, as if somebody was walking across the room upstairs.'

'At what time was that?'

'That was just as the first bell rang for the departure of the mail train, so it would be at ten minutes past seven.'

'And do you think that it was Mr Little's footsteps that you heard?'

'Yes, sir. I am sure it was Mr Little's step, as his boots creak very much. I would know it at any time.'

The coroner asked if Catherine had returned to the cashier's office later that evening.

'Yes, sir: when I was shutting the boardroom door, about eleven o'clock, I went to his door. I turned the handle and gave it a shake, but it was locked. I suspected that Mrs Gunning had locked the door and taken away the key, so decided to leave his fire till the morning.'

Sir Percy Nugent, who was not a member of the jury, interrupted with a question of his own, having apparently decided that his eminence as a director of the company permitted this minor departure from normal protocol.

'Miss Campbell, did it surprise you that Mr Little did not answer when you rattled the door?'

'Well, sir, in general if he was inside he would say, "Not gone yet." On Monday night I found the door locked and him inside, about six o'clock. I heard his papers rustling, and he answered me.'

One of the jurors asked Catherine whether it would be possible for somebody to leave the station building after 11.30 p.m., when the outer door was locked.

'That door has no lock, but two bolts, and anybody inside can get out at any time. I locked the doors to the upstairs corridors at eleven o'clock, and if there was anyone in Mr Little's office after that he could not get out except by the back stairs. But I found the doors locked the next morning.'

As coroner and jury were now discovering, the internal layout of Directors' House could be baffling to the uninitiated. For most of the day, the main route to and from the company offices was through the ticket hall and the main entrance at the front of the building. But after 5.00, when the ticket hall closed, anybody leaving the offices would have to use another exit at the bottom of the grand staircase. This door, which opened directly on to the station platform, was the 'outer door' Catherine referred to in her evidence. Complicating matters still further, there were two ways of getting there from the upper floors of the building. The simplest was down the grand staircase, but this route was not always accessible, because in the early evening a series of internal doors separating the office corridors from the stairwell were locked. The only option then was to take a smaller back staircase which went straight from the first floor to the basement, and thence up a single flight of stairs back to ground level.

Given these complexities, the question of how the killer had reached Mr Little's office and left the building afterwards now appeared an important one. Patrick Hanbury, the stationmaster, was next to speak.

'I live on the premises, and the outer door leading to the platform is opened every morning either by Mr Gunning or myself. I went out at half-past six yesterday morning and found the door open.'

Bernard Gunning, Anne's husband, was the Broadstone assistant storekeeper, responsible for ordering and issuing supplies for the workshops. He and his wife lived in a basement apartment next to that of Mr Hanbury. The coroner asked him to step up.

'Mr Gunning, we have just heard the stationmaster say that in the mornings the outer door leading to the platform remains locked until either you or he opens it. Did you open it yesterday morning?'

'No, sir. It is usually my duty to open it but I did not do so yesterday morning. It was open before I went out. Mr Hanbury went out before me.'

Since both men denied having unlocked the door, one of the jurors suggested that perhaps it had been left open all night.

Catherine Campbell was called back to the witness box and asked if she might have forgotten to lock it, but was adamant that she had bolted it some time after 11.00 on Thursday night.

James Brophy then gave a detailed account of how he had broken into the cashier's office and found the body, subjecting George's family to one last description of their relative's mutilated corpse.

The final witness to speak was William Hughes, one of the police constables who had searched the office. He had little to offer, confirming that they had been unable to find either the key to the door, or anything that might have been the murder weapon. He told the jury that he had emptied the dead man's pockets and found his spectacles, some small change, a watch key and a pocket-watch. The watch had stopped at twenty past seven. Was this a clue, an indication of the time of the murder? It seemed plausible that the heavy impact of the cashier's body against the floor might have caused the watch to stop. Yet, strangely, nobody involved in the subsequent investigation thought this detail worthy of consideration.

Mr Hyndman decided that it was time for the jury to consider their verdict. He summed up.

'Gentlemen of the jury, after the very great attention you have paid to this inquiry, there is little left for me to say. The medical gentlemen who gave their sworn testimony were of opinion that the unfortunate deceased met his death by violence, that he had been brutally and foully murdered, by his skull having been fractured with some blunt and heavy instrument, and his throat afterwards cut. According to the evidence of Catherine Campbell, he was alive after seven o'clock on Thursday evening, and between that hour and half-past eleven the same night he must have been assassinated, as the doors were locked soon after the latter hour, which prevented ingress or egress to that part of the building where Mr Little's office is situated. It remains for the present a perfect mystery as to the object the murderer had in view in committing the deed: whether it was for plunder or otherwise. If it was the former, it seems strange that he did not take some or all of the money, for fifteen hundred pounds was found untouched on Mr Little's desk. But perhaps something prevented the murderer from executing his purpose; maybe he intended to return in the middle of the night; and, finding the doors locked, was compelled to go away by the door downstairs, which was not locked but bolted. However, that is only surmise.'

The coroner offered the jury the option of retiring to a quiet room to discuss the evidence, but after conferring briefly with his colleagues the foreman declared that this would be unnecessary.

'Very well. Do you mean to say that you have reached your verdict?'

'Yes, sir. We find that George Samuel Little was wilfully murdered by some person or persons unknown, between five o'clock on Thursday evening, and eleven o'clock on Friday morning.'

PART TWO

The Investigation

4

While rumours of a suicide at the Broadstone terminus had set tongues wagging all over Dublin, the verdict of wilful murder electrified the city. One local newspaper even suggested that 'it is not too much to say that nothing which has ever occurred in Dublin has created so great an amount of painful excitement'. The idea that an official of one of the major railway companies could be viciously murdered in his own office, and the perpetrator escape without trace, was chilling for a populace unaccustomed to such savagery. There was a killer on the loose; would he stop at one victim?

Moreover, the circumstances of George Little's death were both sensational and mysterious. He had been found in a locked room, his body horribly mutilated. The money lying all over his office appeared to have been left untouched, so what was the motive behind such a brutal murder? And, most importantly, who was the killer? The relatively inaccessible location of the crime scene suggested that a railway employee was responsible, though it had also been established beyond doubt that at least two members of the public had gained entrance to Mr Little's office on the fateful day.

But it was not just the unusual features of the murder that caused such horror; it was the fact that it had happened at all. For murders were exceptional events in Dublin, whatever the London newspapers might suggest. Among outsiders – and especially the English – there was a perception that mid-nineteenth-century

53

Ireland was a uniquely dangerous place, and that its working classes had some inborn propensity for mindless violence. Even those who had grown up there often believed it. In 1849 the Anglo-Irish historian George Lewis Smyth wrote:

> The magnitude of crime in Ireland is enormous, and its character most hideous. Murders the most savage are so frequently perpetrated in that country that the worst possible opinion of the social qualities of the Irish peasant are entertained by a numerous and not always an ill-meaning class of the community of the empire at large.

Smyth counted himself an Irishman, but it was no accident that he made this uncomplimentary assessment from the comfort of his luxurious home in central London, a stone's throw from the Palace of Westminster. Many of his neighbours, members of the patrician ruling class, regarded the Irish as a backward and morally primitive people, and violent conflict their natural state.

Violent crime was a genuine problem in rural Ireland, although arguably one of Westminster's own making. The epidemic was at its worst in the areas hit hardest by the Great Famine – and caused so much concern in London that the police were obliged by Parliament to submit an annual 'Return of Outrages', a statistical summary of all serious offences reported in agricultural communities. In 1849 there were 203 murders recorded by the police; by 1855 this number had halved, thanks largely to the greater prosperity of the post-famine years. Ireland as a whole was becoming much safer, but there was also one surprising anomaly in the figures: even during the darkest days of famine and rebellion, Dublin was a city in which homicide was almost unknown. In the aftermath of George Little's death the *Freeman's Journal* even claimed that 'there has not been a conviction for murder in the city of Dublin for more than thirty years'. The writer seems to have overlooked the case of Thomas Delahunt, a British government spy who was hanged in 1842 after confessing to the murder of a nine-year-old boy* – but there is no doubt that such crimes were exceptionally rare in the Irish capital.

By contrast, England was in the grip of what one newspaper called a 'murder mania'. Barely a week went by without news of some fresh outrage: poisonings, stranglings, drownings. On a typical day in November 1856 a single column of the Irish *Daily Express* carried the stories of a young woman murdered in Worcester, a man from Wokingham who had killed his five-year-old son, a murder-suicide in Hackney and a fatal stabbing in Erith. The crime reporters of Dublin could not compete with this orgy of violence, rarely encountering anything more serious than a mugging or a stolen joint of meat.

Murders might have been more frequent in the large towns and cities of England, but the acres of newsprint devoted to them were not necessarily evidence of a homicidal crime wave. Ever since the birth of the modern newspaper in the eighteenth century the British had always enjoyed a good murder, and editors were quick to realise the commercial benefits of satisfying that craving. Salacious accounts of ghastly atrocities, and of the public executions that often followed, soon became staples of the broadsheets. For many readers there was more to their enjoyment of such stories than simple bloodlust. While the majority of murders were mundane offences committed by brawling drunkards, violent robbers or jealous lovers, a few were altogether more complex. An unfathomable motive, a hint of conspiracy, an exotic method of dispatching the victim – these were ingredients that could elevate a quotidian crime into an extraordinary one.

Thomas De Quincey, the author of *Confessions of an English Opium-Eater*, was among the first to recognise that the public were turning into connoisseurs of crime. In 1827 he mocked this morbid

---

* Coincidentally, the scene of this vicious crime was just round the corner from the Littles' house in south Dublin.

fascination in an essay entitled 'On Murder Considered as One of the Fine Arts', which imagines a dining club for those who are 'curious in homicide; amateurs and dilettanti in the various modes of bloodshed; and, in short, Murder-Fanciers'. De Quincey was himself a murder-fancier: he became obsessed with the Ratcliffe Highway Murders of 1811, the savage and apparently random killing of seven residents of London's East End. In 1854 he published a detailed reconstruction of this notorious event – an early example of what would now be called literary true crime.

For aficionados of homicide the 1850s was a golden age – the beginning of 'our great period of murder', as George Orwell describes it in his famous essay 'Decline of the English Murder'. A significant precursor to the case at the Broadstone terminus was a sensational trial that had taken place in London six months earlier. In May 1856 William Palmer was tried at the Old Bailey and found guilty of killing his friend John Cook by poisoning him. Palmer, who was deeply in debt, had spiked Cook's drinks with strychnine, intending to steal the young man's inheritance. This was the only crime of which he was convicted, but he may also have poisoned several other people, including his own brother, wife and children.

Palmer became an object of fascination almost as soon as his crimes had been discovered. He did not seem to fit people's preconceptions of a cold-blooded killer: he was a doctor, a figure of some standing in his home town of Rugeley in Staffordshire. In his public appearances he was composed, dignified, and protested his innocence in a calm and reasonable manner. His self-possession in court prompted many to aver that he could not possibly be guilty. One newspaper even declared that 'there is no denying that Mr William Palmer is the hero of the day'. A frustrated Charles Dickens was moved to write an article in his journal *Household Words* urging his readers to see through this act, describing Palmer as 'the greatest villain that ever stood in the Old Bailey dock'.

Dickens's plea went unheeded. William Palmer was hanged at Stafford Prison on 14 June 1856, but the notoriety of a criminal the press had dubbed the Rugeley Poisoner lived on. While many were horrified by what he had done, the audacity and ingenuity of his deeds also imbued them with a degree of glamour. Despite Dickens's misgivings, Palmer – a man seen as both healer and killer, hero and villain – created a new legend of murder and the often complex individuals who committed it.

In that context, it is not difficult to understand why news of events at the Broadstone terminus was greeted with as much fascination as horror. If an unscrupulous Victorian newspaper editor had been minded to cook up a fictional murder in a desperate attempt to increase sales, he could hardly have written a more intriguing story than that of George Little. The crime was gory, the details lurid. There was pathos in the desperate plight of the victim's family. There was the enigma of how, and why, the deed had been committed. To top it all, there was the elegant fact that the perpetrator had vanished without a trace, his (or her) identity unknown. The case the Dublin Metropolitan Police were being asked to solve was not merely unusual for the Irish capital; it would have been exceptional anywhere.

It was late afternoon on Saturday when the inquest jury delivered its shocking verdict. Mr Hyndman, the coroner, thanked the jurors for their time and dismissed them. That brought an end to proceedings; the doors were opened, and as members of the public left the building the grand ticket hall of the Broadstone terminus echoed with animated conversations about what they had heard. But many stayed inside the meeting room, where a scrum soon formed around Mr Ennis, the railway company chairman. Some of those wanting to talk to him were small investors, anxious about any effect that this dreadful event might have on their modest shareholding; others were journalists, hoping to get the inside track on what would happen next. Mr Ennis dismissed these inquiries as politely as he could, since he wanted to speak to George Little's relatives before they left. Finally he managed to extricate himself from the clutches of the press, and ushered the family members into his private office on the other side of the ticket hall. As well as expressing his condolences, he wanted to discuss the possibility of offering a reward to hasten the capture of George's killer.

As the crowds finally melted away, Mr Beausire could be seen deep in conversation with three young men. Their presence at the inquest had gone virtually unnoticed, since all three wore street clothes, but they were police officers. More precisely, they were detectives, members of the Dublin Metropolitan Police's elite 'G' division. The city was divided into six wards, each with its own dedicated police station. The Broadstone terminus fell into the territory of the 'C' division, whose officers usually dealt with the manifold petty crimes that routinely occurred at a busy railway station. But whenever a really serious offence was committed, the plain-clothes officers of 'G' division would be summoned to begin an investigation, wherever in the city they were needed. The detective department had been set up in 1842, shortly after the formation of a similar unit in London. It was small, consisting of just seventeen officers – and in contrast to the London Metropolitan Police, which had plain-clothes officers attached to every local force as well as those based at Scotland Yard, the members of Dublin's 'G' division were the only detectives in the city.

The advent of the police detective was not a popular development. In both cities they were initially regarded with suspicion, seen as undercover government agents who in their ordinary clothes could spy on the public with impunity. In London their stock soon rose, however, as they proved effective at clearing up major crimes including robberies, murders and forgery. They found a persuasive advocate in Charles Dickens, whose articles about the Met's detective officers represented them as resourceful public servants doing work that was daring, valuable, and above all glamorous.

The situation was very different in Ireland. Dubliners resented the cost of their Metropolitan Police, which was funded by a tax levied only on residents of the capital; since they also helped pay for policing the rest of Ireland through general taxation this seemed more than a little unfair. Theirs was also an exceptionally large force, given the size of Dublin's population. When Friedrich Engels visited the city in May 1856 he was appalled by this exhibition of state authority, observing in a letter to Karl Marx that he had never seen so many policemen before. While the DMP was grudgingly respected by the locals for its discipline and efficiency, there was no getting past the fact that it was a tool of the British state, imposed on the city by politicians in Westminster. Most of the officers were Irish, but their orders came, ultimately, from London. That did not matter so much when it came to the constables walking their beat, ordinary Catholic lads from nearby villages like Leixlip or Tallaght, but the detectives were another matter entirely.

The headquarters of 'G' division were in Dublin Castle, the seat of the British administration in Ireland, and Dubliners joked that the 'G' stood for 'government'. This was not mere paranoia. Almost as soon as it was founded the detective force was being used as a covert political intelligence network. In the 1840s, and particularly after the outbreak of famine, there were signs that Irish nationalism was reinventing itself, with new radical groups and newspapers springing up in Dublin and elsewhere. The London government, wary of any threat to the status quo, relied on the plain-clothes officers to gather information about nationalist activities. The fact that a police department supposedly created to catch murderers and gangsters was actually being used to snoop on private citizens caused outrage. A newspaper editorial published in 1845 gives some idea of the repugnance many Dubliners felt for their detective force: 'We never will be contented till the huge army of spying scoundrels . . . shall have been banished from our city.'

The three 'spying scoundrels' now talking to the railway company secretary were Acting Inspector Daniel Ryan and his colleagues Sergeants Craven and Murphy. An investigation of this significance would normally have been led by the division superintendent, Joseph Finnamore, but he was off sick. His stand-in Ryan was a sergeant who had recently been given a temporary promotion because the force was short of senior officers. The DMP tended to recruit its constables from outside Dublin, and Ryan hailed from Philipstown, a small country town in the Irish midlands. After working as a carpenter for a few years he had joined the police in 1840, and transferred to the detective division three years later. Those who worked with the thirty-eight-year-old knew that he was a talented and ambitious officer. A few months before the Broadstone murder he had made his name by solving the perplexing 'Jack in the box' case, a series of mysterious thefts from the locked and guarded stores of a Dublin steamship company. Ryan worked out that the perpetrator had been hiding inside a specially constructed wooden chest, arranging for it to be delivered to the warehouse, and then emerging from a secret compartment under cover of darkness to fill it with valuables – before employing the steamship company's unwitting porters to convey his plunder to his own front door.

Inspector Ryan explained that he and his colleagues were likely to spend a great deal of time in the terminus over the next few days. Mr Beausire assured him that the company would do everything possible to help: the detectives would have the run of the station buildings, and members of staff would be instructed to cooperate fully with their investigation. He even promised that one of the directors would be present at every interview to ensure that the railway workers – many of whom had a hearty dislike of plain-clothes policemen – were as forthcoming as possible.

Trains were running all weekend, but Inspector Ryan decided that it would be better to wait until Monday before interviewing any witnesses. None of the administrative employees would be in the building until then, and the few staff who remained on duty were stretched enough as it was. He decided that his first priority must be a close examination of the crime scene. He told Craven and Murphy that he was going upstairs to Mr Little's office; in the meantime they should inspect the ground floor for any possible clues.

When Ryan reached the cashier's office, two men were crouched over Mr Little's body, which had now lain in the same spot by the desk for almost forty-eight hours. One he recognised as the surgeon, George Porter; the other was a stranger. When he saw the detective enter, Mr Porter stood up and introduced his companion as a local undertaker. With the post-mortem now complete, they were preparing the body for removal, stitching up the most obvious wounds and removing any trace of blood. When they had finished they would transfer it to a coffin and load it on to a hearse now waiting downstairs. The undertaker would then drive to the Littles' house in Waterloo Road, where the family planned an overnight vigil over the body before its burial on Sunday.

Inspector Ryan had already examined the room for clues and now repeated the exercise, though without much hope of further enlightenment. So many people had passed through the office in the twenty-four hours since the discovery of the body that it seemed impossible to distinguish the marks made by these visitors from any traces that might have been left by the murderer. How had he gained access to the locked office? Clearly not through the window, since the sash had been nailed shut. Through the door, then; this implied that the killer was somebody known to the cashier, for surely Mr Little would not have opened the door to a stranger out of business hours. But there was another possibility. The assailant might have concealed himself behind the counter while the door was unlocked, perhaps when Mr Little was visiting the lavatory or talking to a visitor. This was not difficult to imagine: after dark the room was only dimly lit, even with the gas turned up high, and an intruder might easily slip in unobserved.

That was only the beginning of the puzzle, since it was equally unclear by what route the killer had left. The door was locked, but the key was missing – evidently the murderer had taken it with him. Maybe he had left via the corridor and locked the door behind him, in which case he would have had to walk through Directors' House in order to leave the building. This was no simple matter, as several internal doors were locked at the end of the working day, rendering the grand staircase and ticket hall inaccessible. It was then only possible to reach the ground floor via a complex route involving the back staircase. The alternative explanation was that the killer had left through the window of the back staircase, carefully securing it behind him. Then he had a choice: either he could traverse the side of the building and re-enter via another window on the same floor, or walk along the duckboards that crossed the roof of the train shed, before descending a ladder that would take him down to the third-class passenger lavatory on the station platform. None of these options was straightforward, and it seemed to Inspector Ryan that whoever the murderer was, he must have a reasonable knowledge of the building.

But was it even a he? Everybody had so far assumed that the killer was a man, but even taking into account the severity of Mr Little's injuries there was nothing that ruled out the possibility of a female assassin. The inspector was interrupted in these ruminations by the sudden appearance of one of the sergeants, who announced that he had found bloodstains on the woodwork downstairs. Ryan followed him to the foot of the grand staircase, where the other officer was looking closely at the frame of the door into the ticket hall. He pointed out some red marks at about waist height, on the right side of the door. The inspector squinted at them uncertainly. They looked like finger marks, all right, but it was not clear how recently they had been made, or what had made them. Was that blood, or paint? He could not tell.

That was not all. Behind them, opposite the door into the

ticket hall, was a high window overlooking the station platforms. In front of the window was a stool which the housekeeper
had placed there to make it easier to reach the sash in case anybody needed to open it. It was several months since it had been
used for this purpose, and the top of the stool was thick with
dust. Clearly visible, however, was the fresh impression of a
workman's boot, complete with hobnails. One side of this foot-
print was more distinct than the other, as if something had
disturbed the dust after the foot had been removed. The three
detectives discussed this finding for a little while before they
agreed on a likely explanation. The stool was three feet off the
ground, so whoever had climbed on to it must have been using it
to get through the window. Once he had opened it he had waited
until the coast was clear before jumping through the window and
down on to the platform. The skirts of his coat had brushed over
the dust as he leapt from the stool, causing the slight distortion
they had observed.

If the murderer had gone via the platform he might have left
other clues. There was the possibility that he had escaped by
train, but the mail train had been the only departure after the
likely time of George Little's death, and the stationmaster
would surely remember every passenger at that time of night.
No, it seemed more probable that the killer had used one of the
platform exits. Daniel Ryan and his colleagues went out on to
the platform and considered the routes an escaping criminal
might use to leave the building. It did not take them long to find
something else of interest. On one of the gates leading from the
arrivals platform to the street was another red smear. This and
the other red mark might yet prove to be significant, but they
would need to get samples to an expert for analysis. That could
not happen until Monday at the earliest, but the traces might
easily be destroyed if left in situ before then. Ryan told the sergeants to find a carpenter, and ask him to remove the sections
of timber from both door frame and gate as carefully as

possible, so as to preserve any evidence for scientific examination. When that was done, they could both go home. They would reconvene at the station the following day; in the meantime, Inspector Ryan was off to the Castle to make a preliminary report to his superiors.

The detective office at Exchange Court was open at all times of day and night, with an inspector on duty round the clock. Whenever a serious offence was committed anywhere in the city the local constabulary would notify this official, and if he thought it necessary, plain-clothes officers would be ordered to attend the incident. Detectives were required to make a report of their activities, and the status of any investigation, at the end of the working day. When Daniel Ryan arrived back at base on Saturday evening he gave the duty inspector a brief summary of all that had transpired at the Broadstone terminus that afternoon. Even before he had finished his statement, he assumed that the government would have to be informed. It was a serious business, and not just because a man had lost his life. This was not some drunken brawl or tawdry domestic squabble; the victim was a respectable, educated clerk, a religious and utterly harmless individual. He had been brutally killed in a railway station, a building that was a symbol of Ireland's new-found optimism, its long journey from poverty to prosperity. And, most seriously, the murderer remained at large. The inspector concurred. He instructed Inspector Ryan to write a report and submit it to the Chief Secretary's office the following day.

The Chief Secretary for Ireland was the British government's representative in Dublin. The incumbent, Edward Horsman, was MP for Stroud in Gloucestershire, but gained some local credibility from the fact that he had been born in the Irish capital. As a cabinet minister he spent much of his time in Westminster, so most of the day-to-day administration was undertaken by his deputy, Lieutenant Colonel Thomas Askew Larcom. Colonel Larcom's bald, bullet-headed features were unmistakable, his efficiency legendary. He was decisive but never impetuous. He had a remarkable ability to assimilate information at great speed, devouring the briefings he was given before scrawling his instructions in terse and almost indecipherable memoranda that were the despair of his clerks.

Colonel Larcom was just the man for a crisis, but alas he did not work on Sundays. The Chief Secretary's office, the nerve centre for the government of Ireland, was normally well staffed, with a profusion of private secretaries, assistant under-secretaries and no fewer than fourteen clerks. When Daniel Ryan arrived on Sunday afternoon, however, the place was almost deserted, staffed by a single and rather bored-looking clerk. This functionary accepted the detective's report and promised to pass it on to the Under-Secretary as soon as possible.

Thomas Kemmis, Crown Solicitor for the Leinster Circuit, lived at number 45 Kildare Street, a short distance from Trinity College Dublin. Born and brought up in this imposing Georgian town house, Kemmis had never lived anywhere else, except for four years spent studying at Oxford; his grandfather, also Thomas, had bought the house almost eighty years earlier. Bricks and mortar were not the only things that the younger Thomas had inherited from his forebears. Both his grandfather and father had served as Crown Solicitor to Dublin or the surrounding province of Leinster, a dynasty that stretched back unbroken to 1784. Thomas's own appointment to the post four years earlier had prompted accusations of nepotism, and even calls for an inquiry in the House of Commons.

As Crown Solicitor for Leinster, Thomas Kemmis was the government's chief prosecutor in the province, responsible for putting together an effective case and ensuring that there was sufficient evidence to secure a conviction. His work brought him into frequent contact with the police, since he was often required to supervise their inquiries. The role was much like that of a

District Attorney in the American legal system, but had no equivalent in English law.

It was lunchtime on Monday 17 November when one of the servants knocked on the door of Mr Kemmis's study and told him that a message had arrived from the Attorney General, the most senior legal officer in Ireland. The note he handed over was brief and to the point: it asked Mr Kemmis to go to the Broadstone terminus immediately, to learn everything he could about the murder that had taken place there the previous Thursday, and then to return for a meeting with the Attorney General and his deputy, the Solicitor General, at 5 p.m. There was no mistaking the urgency of the request, or the fact that that sense of urgency emanated from the highest echelons of Dublin Castle. But the message also gave no hint that this was any more than a brief errand, or that it would turn into one of the most significant and lengthy cases of Mr Kemmis's career.

When Colonel Larcom had finally seen Inspector Ryan's report earlier that morning he had been horrified. Four days had elapsed since the murder, and yet he was only just learning about it. Even to his inexpert eye, failure was writ large on every page. There had been inexcusable delays in breaking down Mr Little's door, in summoning the police, and ordering the post-mortem and inquest. And the police had apparently achieved nothing. The colonel scribbled one of his impenetrable missives and summoned a clerk to dispatch it to the Attorney General, setting in train the sequence of events that resulted in Thomas Kemmis sitting in the back of a carriage on its way to the Broadstone terminus.

On his arrival at the station the Crown Solicitor went straight to the chairman's office, where he was granted an immediate audience. Several directors of the company were already there, discussing the possibility of offering a reward for information about the murder. Mr Kemmis believed that such a financial incentive might cause the police to be inundated with irrelevant or even false information. He decided to speak up.

'Mr Chairman, experience has shown that an injudicious offer of an award sometimes tends to defeat justice. At this juncture it might be better to wait and see what course the government will pursue with respect to a reward.'

His concerns were well founded, but Mr Kemmis was over-ruled. The meeting came to an end, and he was escorted upstairs to inspect the murder scene, where a clerk was working method-ically through a forest of paperwork. The clerk explained that there was now some uncertainty about the amount of money found in the office, and whether any had been taken. Despite Mr Beausire's evidence at the inquest, the auditors had been unable to make their accounts tally with the paperwork. It appeared that something was missing, and it was the clerk's task to work out what and how much.

Once again there was a crush of bodies in the cashier's office. Several members of the press who had been hanging around the station all day had quietly added themselves to Mr Kemmis's pri-vate tour, and a couple of George Little's male cousins had also arrived to find out what was going on. Then there were Inspector Ryan and several of his detective officers. Kemmis had worked on a number of investigations with Ryan, and rated him highly. The inspector answered the government lawyer's questions crisply, but his manner betrayed embarrassment. It was clear that the police had gleaned almost nothing from their inquiries to date: pressed by one of the journalists, Inspector Ryan admitted that they had not even identified a suspect.

This was not a surprise to Mr Kemmis, who had already guessed the true state of affairs. But George Little's relatives and one or two of the directors seemed staggered by the revelation, and the journalists responded by peppering the railway company executives with questions. Inspector Ryan took advantage of this distraction to exchange a quiet word with Mr Kemmis. The detective was more forthcoming when the directors were not lis-tening. He told the Crown Solicitor that he had asked for a section of the canal immediately outside the station to be drained, in the hope of discovering a weapon, but he was finding it impossible to achieve anything. Several directors had taken it upon themselves to be helpful, but their assistance consisted largely in asking unnecessary questions, and Inspector Ryan was growing irritated by their interference. What with regular complaints from the victim's family that nothing was being done, and hourly requests for information from newspaper reporters, he was finding it nearly impossible to organise a systematic inquiry.

As if to illustrate these problems, one of George Little's cousins then cornered Mr Kemmis to make his views plain. He had lost all faith in the police, he said: so much time had been wasted that he now doubted their ability to catch the killer. He announced his intention to telegraph London and engage a private investigator called Field.

Mr Kemmis had never heard of him, but Charles Frederick Field was arguably the best-known detective in the English-speaking world. He rose to prominence as the officer in charge of the London Metropolitan Police detective department in the late 1840s, and when Charles Dickens started to write about their work it was Field who became his most important contact. In 1851 Dickens published an article entitled 'On Duty with Inspector Field', based on an evening he had spent with the detective on the streets of London. After his retirement from the Met the following year Field was able to capitalise on his new-found fame, and set up his own private detective agency.

Mr Kemmis was not keen on the idea of an outsider being brought in so early in the investigation, and assured Mr Little's cousin that the government would do everything to ensure that the case was solved. He promised that if the local police failed to make progress, they would ask Scotland Yard to send their most experienced detectives to assist. This undertaking seemed to satisfy Mr Little's cousin, who added that – despite police misgivings – the family was also intending to offer a reward for any information.

All things considered, Mr Kemmis felt that his visit to the Broadstone terminus had been most unsatisfactory. He had learned little, except that the police were making slow progress under trying circumstances. He returned to town for his 5.00 meeting with the Attorney General and the Solicitor General, to whom he made a downbeat report of the situation. They told him that they had been unable to get hold of either Mr O'Ferrall or Colonel Browne, the commissioners of the Dublin Metropolitan Police, so had decided to appoint the Crown Solicitor to supervise the police investigation. John FitzGerald, the Attorney General, issued his instructions.

'Mr Kemmis, please inform Superintendent Finnamore and Inspector Ryan that you have been asked to give every assistance in your power, whether by consultation or the examination of witnesses. We will ensure that as many police as are needed will devote their best energies to the case. The government has decided against offering a reward, but otherwise no necessary expense will be spared. If Mr Finnamore feels unequal to the task through ill health, you should let him know that we will apply to the commissioners for the most experienced available officer to be appointed in his place. You are to let us know of any significant developments, and of course you must feel free to ask us for advice or direction, as circumstances require.'

Mr Kemmis was delighted. The work of the Crown Solicitor rarely entailed anything as lively as supervising a murder investigation, and he set about the task with enthusiasm. It was now late, too late to achieve anything at the railway station, so he decided to walk home via the detective office in Exchange Court. He learned from the duty inspector that Superintendent Finnamore was quite unwell and unlikely to return to duty for some time. This was inconvenient: they would have to find another senior officer to work on the inquiry. But he already had a candidate in mind. He wrote a brief note and asked for it to be sent immediately to Mr O'Ferrall, the police commissioner who looked after such matters. He would expect a reply in the morning.

A thick pall hung over Dublin as dawn broke on Tuesday 18 November. This was not uncommon in a city where residents still lived cheek by jowl with factories that belched out smoke night and day. The fumes of metal casting often drifted over Capel Street from the great iron and brass foundry of Joshua Edmundson & Co., while just over the river in Fishamble Street the furnaces of the railway works of Kennan & Son were always lit. The Guinness brewery, Jacob's biscuit factory and a sulphuric acid plant were all near the city centre, polluting the air in every season; in winter, the coal soot of thousands of domestic chimneys constantly poisoned the atmosphere, while in the poorer areas of town the pungent, but not entirely unpleasant, aroma of peat smoke was added to this toxic cocktail.

It was even worse than usual this morning. In the early hours a serious fire had broken out at Richmond Prison, in the south of the city. There were no casualties, but the prison chapel had been burnt to the ground. Some of the better-behaved convicts had been let out of their cells to help extinguish the blaze, but at 6 a.m. the chapel roof collapsed and the destruction was complete.

A distant black plume of smoke was still visible from the high ground of Broadstone several hours later, when Thomas Kemmis's carriage arrived at the front of the station. Workmen had begun the long and tedious business of draining the canal, and a crowd was gathering in the hope of seeing some new development. Again Mr Kemmis headed straight for the chairman's office, where there was a delicate conversation to be had. He had practised as a barrister before becoming a public servant, and years of sweet-talking judges had taught him that tact and a little flattery were often more effective than making demands. He thanked Mr Ennis profusely for the assistance he and the directors had given to the investigation, though refrained from observing that their interventions had been largely unhelpful. Instead he emphasised the excellence of the police officers now working on the case, and added that the government was treating the investigation as an urgent priority. An experienced detective had been drafted in to oversee matters, said Mr Kemmis, and he thought it might be best if the new man were allowed to pursue matters undisturbed. To that end, he wondered if one of the directors might be nominated as the single point of contact between the police and railway management.

The chairman saw the logic behind this request, and was happy to comply. Having succeeded in neutralising this source of interference without causing offence, Mr Kemmis went into the ticket hall, where Inspector Ryan was waiting for him with reinforcements. Commissioner O'Ferrall had responded promptly to the Crown Solicitor's request, and several constables would be coming from the local division later that morning to assist. But an advance party had already arrived, the senior officer seconded to run the investigation: Superintendent Guy.

At the age of forty-six, Augustus Guy was one of the most experienced officers in the Dublin Metropolitan Police. He joined the force as a beat constable the year after its formation in 1836, and was among the first recruits to the new detective department six years later. He had risen quickly through the ranks, and while still in his thirties was made superintendent of the 'G' division, at around the same time that Charles Frederick Field was appointed to the equivalent role in London. But while Field's reputation – and that of his department – soon grew, the Dublin detectives became only more unpopular.

Superintendent Guy's promotion coincided with an upsurge in nationalist sentiment, and for much of his tenure the detective force was preoccupied with the battle against Irish separatism. He was in the thick of things in 1848, a year that saw a short-lived armed rebellion and the forcible suppression of several nationalist newspapers. Guy was heavily involved in the prosecutions that followed, and personally arrested one of the most influential and outspoken voices of republican activism, John Mitchel, who was subsequently convicted of treason* and transported to Tasmania. As the public face of the British state's *de facto* secret police, Guy was therefore not universally popular. It did not help matters that he was an English immigrant who had been born in Pimlico and spoke with a London accent.

Perhaps it was his growing notoriety that led Augustus Guy to accept a transfer in 1849 to one of the uniformed divisions. At the time of George Little's murder he was superintendent of 'C' division, responsible for the crime-ridden docklands in the east of the city. With years of experience of detective work and intimate knowledge of the Dublin underworld, he seemed the obvious choice to take over from the indisposed Finnamore.

Mr Kemmis and the two police officers shut themselves in the ground-floor meeting room for a council of war. After giving the superintendent a detailed account of all that was known so far, the Crown Solicitor asked how he intended to proceed. Mr Guy's plan of action was simple but exhaustive. He wanted witness statements from anybody known to have been in Directors' House on the day of the murder or the following morning. The police had already spoken to many of the railway employees, but a cursory chat was not enough. Everybody must be questioned in minute detail, and their answers written down so that there was a permanent record of any discrepancies. It was agreed that Mr Kemmis would take part in these interviews: a lawyer's perspective would be invaluable, and he might easily pick up on details that the detectives overlooked.

The superintendent also ordered a fingertip search of the entire building. He wanted every inch of the station, from the cellars to

---

* More accurately, the newly defined crime of 'treason felony'. Before 1848 Mitchel would have faced a charge of high treason, which carried the death sentence.

the roof, examined for clues. And if they had grounds for suspecting any of the witnesses they examined, they would obtain a warrant and turn their homes inside out. The immediate object was finding the murder weapon, but they also needed to locate the missing key. Mr Guy stressed the importance of establishing a motive for the killing. Did George Little have an unknown enemy? Did anybody owe him money? Or had he died at the hands of a robber? They did not even know whether any cash was missing, an elementary but vital piece of information which the superintendent wanted his officers to establish without delay.

His final point concerned publicity. Naturally there would be a great deal of interest from reporters, he said, particularly since the London newspapers had now got wind of the story. Most detectives were accustomed to sharing details of their inquiries with journalists, believing that the resulting coverage was a useful way of getting potential witnesses to come forward. But the latest thinking in Scotland Yard was that this practice was counterproductive. With a murderer at large, it was crucial that they did not make public any information that might be useful to him. A suspect might destroy crucial evidence, or change his hiding place, if he could easily find out what the detectives knew and what they didn't. Superintendent Guy had decided to make this what he called a 'confidential' investigation. He and Mr Kemmis were the only officials authorised to talk to the press, and they would limit their revelations to the most basic developments.

Their conference was just coming to an end when there was an urgent rap at the door. One of the detective sergeants entered. He had news.

'Sir, there *was* a robbery. A considerable sum of money is missing from the cashier's office, Mr Beausire says two hundred pounds or more. And an informant has come forward. He believes he knows who did it.'

5

One of that morning's newspapers had declared despondently that 'this horrible tragedy still remains shrouded in the deepest mystery'. Was the gloom now starting to lift? It was not yet 10 a.m., and already it felt as if the police had learned more than they had in the preceding four days. The sergeant told Superintendent Guy and the Crown Solicitor what he knew.

'A servant man in the employment of a Captain Hartley, who lives in Clonsilla, tells us that he came into town on business on Friday last, and while passing through Stoneybatter he went into a public house for some refreshment. He saw two men and a woman sitting in the taproom drinking. One of the men was short and wore a cap without a peak, the other was strong and burly. The short man asked the woman for some money, which she refused. He swore a terrible oath and said, "You had better give it to me, you know what I can tell." The woman got frightened and pulled out of the bosom of her gown a pocket-book, which burst open on the table. Our man believes that there could not be less than three hundred pounds in notes in the pocket-book. The three parties subsequently agreed with a carman to drive them twenty miles, but the informant was not close enough to hear their destination.'

The superintendent weighed this information carefully. The tip-off could be significant, or it might be no more than hearsay. That morning's papers had announced that a substantial sum was now being offered as a reward for information: the railway company, despite police advice to the contrary, was putting forward £200, and the victim's family another £150. With this financial incentive in place it was inevitable that much of the intelligence they received would be irrelevant trivia. Nevertheless, it was a lead, and Stoneybatter was only twenty minutes' walk away. Mr Guy decided to send two officers to find out who these people were and where they lived. The detectives were to track them down, in the countryside if necessary, and bring them in for questioning.

As for the missing money, the superintendent hoped to find out more from Henry Beausire, who had supervised the audit of George Little's books. They went to the secretary's office, where Mr Kemmis introduced his detective colleague, explaining that he would be taking a note of the conversation as consultant to the inquiry. His instructions were to examine these unfortunate circumstances minutely, he said, adding apologetically that it might prove necessary to go into rather tedious detail.

After a few gentle preliminaries, Superintendent Guy asked about Mr Little. When had Mr Beausire first met him?

'He entered the company's service in 1853, as Secretary's Special Clerk. Then in about May 1856 he was promoted to the office of cashier. After that period I saw very little of him.'

'And why did the vacancy arise?'

'Mr Little succeeded Mr Nugent as cashier. Mr Nugent had been a defaulter for over two thousand pounds to the company.'

So Mr Little's predecessor had been an embezzler! This was an unexpected piece of news, and one that suggested a motive for the crime.

'And what happened to Nugent?'

'He was dismissed, but a brother of his is still in the goods department, and a relative named Christian in the audit office.'

'And how was the fraud discovered? Did Mr Little have anything to do with it?'

'Well, the attention of the directors had been drawn to the fact of Mr Nugent's account being unsettled on one or two occasions, which resulted in an inquiry, and the defalcation was discovered. But Mr Little had nothing to do with the investigation.'

The secretary then gave a detailed account of the cashier's responsibilities, the cashboxes and dockets, and the late hours that Mr Little was accustomed to keeping.

'Mr Beausire, you were one of the first into the room when the body was discovered. Did it appear to you that any money had been taken?'

'From the appearance of the paper found after his death he must nearly have completed the balancing of his cash when he was so fatally interrupted. On the table was a pile of notes and drafts, and all seemed very orderly. In the window there was silver in open piles. I think the gold had already been made up into paper cartridges. There is one curious fact, which is that all the money on the table and window appears to tally with the money sent up that day, allowing for the cash advance made to Mr Tough, who had come to ask for change. I supposed at first that the murderer had not taken any money, but when the contents of the safe were examined, there appeared to be a deficiency.'

'And how much do you believe is missing?'

'It seems to be over one hundred pounds in gold, and about one hundred and forty in silver, but I cannot say whether any notes are deficient. I think not.'

This was a greater sum than either man had expected – although, as they would soon learn, even this estimate was a conservative one.

'Mr Beausire, at the inquest you expressed your confidence in Mr Little, but of course that was before this theft had been discovered. This company has already been defrauded by one of its cashiers. Do you think it possible that Mr Little did the same?'

'I do not. I had the highest possible opinion of his integrity.'

The secretary appeared to have forgotten that on the morning of George Little's disappearance he had been the first to suggest that the cashier had absconded. Mr Kemmis then asked him to recount once more the events of Friday, when the body had been discovered. Both investigators made frequent interruptions to check a detail, without eliciting any new information. But one thing intrigued Mr Guy.

'At the inquest Mrs Gunning, the housekeeper, said that the previous night she had seen a light on the wall opposite the door, as if the gaslight were shining through the keyhole. But you say that you tried to look through the keyhole but could see nothing. Are you sure of that?'

'Yes. When we opened the door we found that there was a metal cover hanging on the inside of the keyhole, so that no light could shine through. Yesterday I tested it in the presence of the police. Both lamps were fully lit inside and placed in the most favourable position, but even then no light appeared through the keyhole in the passage. Mrs Gunning was present and pointed out the spot where she thought it had been, but no light appeared on the wall.'

Mr Kemmis and Mr Guy exchanged a glance. It appeared a minor point, but both realised that it was one that merited further investigation.

The detective was curious to know why there had been so little urgency in investigating the cashier's death. Mr Beausire explained that he had not felt able to look closely at the body, but several people had told him that Mr Little had cut his own throat. This rumour of a suicide had become general, and was not disproved until the day of the inquest.

'The station has a nightwatchman, and there is always a police constable here. They were both on duty on the day of the murder. Why did they not give evidence at the inquest?'

'They were not examined because they were not at the terminus on Saturday. They are both here today if you wish to speak to them.'

The superintendent asked about the other people who were in

the offices on the day of the murder. Mr Beausire mentioned the solicitor's clerks, who had stayed at work until at least 11.00 that night.

'And what of Chamberlain, Mr Little's clerk? Do you think him trustworthy?'

'He is a newcomer. I have known him only four months, but I have been told that he has a bad character. His predecessor was Mr Fair, who is now in the audit office. I heard a little time ago that Mr Fair had been in bad company in town, but there was no charge proved against him.'

'And is there any indication that he was untrustworthy?'

'Well, I understand that Mr Little lost some money from his office shortly after he was appointed cashier, when Fair was working there. It was never known how Mr Little made up the deficit in his accounts.'

'There are two families that live on the premises, are there not? What is your opinion of them?'

'Yes, there is the storekeeper Mr Gunning and his wife, who is the housekeeper. I think highly of them, and of Mr Hanbury, the stationmaster. There is also the housekeeper's servant, Catherine Campbell, but I do not know her.'

'Finally, Mr Beausire, would you tell us your movements on the evening of Thursday the thirteenth? Please do not assume that you are suspected, but of course we must look at every possibility.'

'Of course. I left my office at half-past four, and went directly home. I remained there till five to eight, and then went to the Ancient Concert Rooms in Great Brunswick Street, and was there till about ten, and returned home at half-past.'

The detective and the lawyer took their leave of Mr Beausire and ascended the grand staircase to the first floor. They found the corridor outside the cashier's office thick with people, and it was only with difficulty that they managed to push their way into the room. The scene of the crime had, it seemed, become a tourist attraction, and numerous Dubliners had made the macabre pilgrimage to Broadstone to see the place of George Little's death at first hand. Mr Kemmis saw, to his disgust, that there was plenty to interest these ghoulish visitors. The matting underneath the desk with its grotesque dark stain had been left in place, and George Little's black necktie lay discarded beside his chair, soiled with his blood. Worst of all, locks of the dead man's hair, which had been shaved off during the post-mortem and were strewn about the floor, were being pocketed as souvenirs.

The Crown Solicitor was furious, and wasted no time in clearing the room of these interlopers. Once they had been ejected he showed Superintendent Guy where the body had been found, and talked him through the other features of interest. A few minutes later one of the messenger boys arrived from downstairs, bearing a message from Mr Beausire. He wished them to know that Mr Bennett, one of the clerks in the accountants' office, had finished checking Mr Little's books, and would now be able to tell them exactly how much cash had been taken from the office.

The accountants occupied a cramped room on the ground floor. Rather than going back to the grand staircase, Mr Kemmis and the superintendent pushed open a door next to that of the cashier's office. This concealed the back staircase by which the housekeeper and her servant reached the offices from their apartments in the basement, and which was often used by the railway employees as a shortcut. Mr Guy paused on the landing. At the top of the stairs was a window which opened on to the parapet. He undid the catch, and found himself looking at the roof of the locomotive shed. The detective realised it would be quite simple for anybody to climb out, walk gingerly along the side of the building and then enter Mr Little's office via the window. As it happened, this was exactly the route taken by Thomas Moore, the boy who had been the first to try to gain entry when the alarm was raised on Friday morning.

Thomas Bennett was waiting for them downstairs. Although

barely into middle age, he was one of the company's longest-serving employees. He had joined the Midland Great Western Railway in 1845, before it owned a single locomotive or had laid a yard of track. This did not mean that he was above suspicion. A decade of unblemished service was a useful character reference, but it would hardly do as an alibi: during the recent spate of corporate fraud, it was the journeymen rather than the high-flyers who had proved the biggest villains.

Superintendent Guy asked first about the movement of cash around the building. Bennett told him that in addition to the sums he lodged at the bank, the cashier was responsible for making up the weekly wage packets, and for passing on regular sums to the canal and locomotive departments. The clerk doubted very much that there was any opportunity for embezzlement: everything Mr Little had done was checked by the audit and canal offices, even before the accountants scrutinised the books.

'So you are confident that Mr Little's affairs were in order at the time of his death?'

'There is no reason to suppose otherwise. On the Wednesday morning – that is, the day before he died – these accounts were balanced up to the Sunday night previous.'

Mr Kemmis asked about shares and dividends and other financial instruments, but they lay outside the cashier's purview. It appeared that there was little scope for the sort of complex fraud that had brought other companies to their knees.

'You say that the accounts were balanced up to the previous Sunday. But the receipts for the three days between then and his death must have been considerable. What do you know of that period?'

'The accounts have been examined with great care. We have ascertained from the audit and canal offices how much money was received on the line on those three days, and compared these sums with the dockets which were lying on Mr Little's table. We also found two handwritten documents which recorded all the money in the office, both on the table and in the safe, and showing how much was in gold, how much in silver, and so on. The result of our inquiry was that there was found wanting one hundred and three pounds in gold, and one hundred and forty-eight in silver. There was also eighty pounds which was owed to the bank in London, which in all probability would have been in gold. That left a total debit against Mr Little's account of about three hundred and thirty pounds.'

Three hundred and thirty pounds. This was almost three times as much as Thomas Bennett would earn in a year. Yet it represented only a small fraction of the riches laid out on George Little's table when he had been left, alone and unguarded, to his death. The clerk continued.

'The actual receipts from the line which came in on Thursday morning amounted to six hundred and sixty-three pounds. Mr Little ought to have lodged money with the bank on Thursday but had not, so he had more money on his hands than was usual. It seems that he had taken everything out of the safe and was about to tot it all up, and balance his cash, when he was murdered. The last known act of his life was cashing a cheque for one hundred and four pounds, for Mr Tough . . .'

'Wait a minute,' said Superintendent Guy. 'Why do you say that was the last act of his life?'

'Mr Little was a very particular man. If he had had time, he would have altered his own private calculations to indicate that the cash balance had been reduced by one hundred and four pounds and the cheques increased by a corresponding amount. Yet he had not done so. This suggests strongly to me that he was murdered within a few minutes of Chamberlain leaving the room.'

This was a plausible theory, but it also contradicted the evidence of the gaslight supposedly seen by Mrs Gunning more than two hours later. The key must have been removed from the lock after that time; otherwise the light would not have been visible. The detective asked Bennett about the discovery of the body, but the clerk could add nothing that they did not already know.

When Mr Guy and Mr Kemmis emerged from the accountants' office they sought out Inspector Ryan. The superintendent
told him the news: they were now looking for a great deal of
money as well as the murder weapon. In addition, they needed
to find out whether any strangers had been seen near the cashier's office on the evening of the murder, particularly around
5 p.m. when most of the staff were leaving for the day. Mr Guy
wanted to know more about the pedlar who had tried to interest Mr Little in buying spectacles: at the inquest this man had
been dismissed as harmless, but they could not eliminate him
from their inquiries without first identifying him. Finally, the
superintendent announced that the detectives were to take statements from everybody who lived or worked in the Broadstone
terminus – every messenger boy, ticket inspector, engineer,
accountant and lawyer, whether or not they were in the building
on the day of the murder. Once this major undertaking had
been completed, Mr Guy and Mr Kemmis would personally re-
interview any they believed to have important information. It
would be a time-consuming process, but Mr Kemmis felt
strongly that the approach was necessary. Until he had proof to
the contrary, everybody was a potential witness, and everybody
a suspect.

It would be fair to say that Mr Kemmis was not terribly
impressed by Mr Little's assistant William Chamberlain. In his
notebook the Crown Solicitor wrote that 'he seems very stupid;
a washy, weak-looking lad; seems fretted'. But William was an
important witness – and possibly the last person to see George
Little alive, which was why he had been summoned to the meeting room to talk to the two investigators. The young man lived
with his family in Jervis Street, about ten minutes' walk from
the Broadstone terminus. Their house was advertised in the
local press as the 'Chamberlain Academy', an establishment
where William's father Robert offered instruction in 'dancing,

deportment and calisthenic exercises' to the socially ambitious youth of Dublin.

The interview was something of an ordeal, since William was distressed and at times unable or unwilling to answer the questions put to him. He was very sorry that Mr Little was dead, he said, because the cashier had been kind to him. Mr Guy asked about his daily routine.

'I am usually in the office between ten and five, sir, give or take five minutes. I do whatever the cashier needs me to: I run errands, take messages between the various departments, count banknotes or weigh gold.'

'What time did you leave the office on Thursday last, William?'

'It was about ten minutes after five.'

'Do you remember anybody coming in to the office around that time, just before you left?'

'Yes, sir, Mr Tough came in asking for change of a draft. I was sitting at the table with my back to the door.'

'Was there anybody with him?'

'I don't remember, sir.'

'Did you hear any of the conversation between Mr Little and Mr Tough?'

'I heard someone say "tomorrow". I think Mr Little replied, "I would rather this evening." But that is all I remember.'

'And were there any other visitors about that time? Do you recall Mr Little going behind you to speak to a strange man, somebody he hadn't met before?'

'I think there was a stranger, sir, but I don't recall whether Mr Little went out to speak to him.'

'And when you left at ten past five, what was he doing?'

'He was sitting at the table in his ordinary place, but I cannot say exactly what he was doing. I remember him sitting down about seven or eight minutes before I left.'

'When you came out of the room, did you notice whether the key was in the lock?'

'Well, sir, when I spoke to one of the policemen before, I thought I had seen the key. But now I am not at all certain. I would be inclined to say not.'

'Hmm. And what did you do next?'

'I went to the police office on the platform to get my pay. But Mr Hodgens, who looks after it, was not there, so Sergeant Collins told me to come back the next day. Then I went back into the hall and met three of the clerks . . .'

'Hold on,' said the superintendent. 'Which ones?'

'Mr Jolly, Mr Green and Mr Magee.'

'Did you see the porter, Mr McCauley?'

'No, he was not there. I have been raising money for the orphans' refuge, and was trying to get the other three to give me subscriptions. We talked for a while in the ticket hall, then we went out through the parcel office.'

'And where did you go next?'

'Down Dominick Street towards Dunbar's Hotel. Then Mr Green and Mr Magee went off down Dorset Street, and Mr Jolly and I continued down Dominick Street. Oh, and when we got to the Duke of Leinster's house I saw Fair, who went into Keegan's public house to meet somebody. I was pressing Jolly for a donation, but he would not give it. When we reached Simpson's Hospital we parted, but as I crossed the street Mr Jolly whistled to me, and when I turned back he gave me sixpence for the orphans. I went home, where I saw my sister who works at the Theatre Royal, and she gave me a pass for the theatre.'

'For that night's performance?'

'Yes. It was for two people. When I had taken my tea I went to call at Jolly's place. Since he had given me sixpence I thought I would treat him to the play. But he wasn't in.'

'What time was it now?'

'I think about half-past six. Then I went on to see another friend and took him to the theatre instead.'

'When you left Jolly, did he say where he was going?'

'No, he had his railway rug on his arm, but he did not tell me what he was going to do.'

A 'railway rug' was a fashionable accessory in the 1850s, originally marketed as the solution to chilly legs in unheated railway carriages. It seemed an odd detail, but Jolly might simply have been planning to catch an omnibus. The superintendent decided that they were rather getting away from the point.

'William, to return to the office for a moment. Since the wooden counter was installed, most visitors stay on the other side of the railings, is that correct?'

'Yes, sir.'

'But were there some people, members of the railway staff, perhaps, who were allowed to come through into your part of the office?'

'Yes, Mr Little would admit Mr Russell on business. Mr Browne from the canal office used to come in to sign the book. I have seen Mr Cabry there a couple of times. Mr Forbes the traffic manager has been there maybe three times.'

'And of course Mrs Gunning and Catherine Campbell were also allowed in to clean, and so on. Did Mr Gunning ever visit the office?'

'No, I never saw him there at all.'

This was as much as they could get out of William Chamberlain. The young man's grief seemed genuine enough, but Mr Kemmis was not ready to exonerate him just yet. As he and the superintendent left the building and crossed the pontoon bridge over the canal, the Crown Solicitor recalled something that the company secretary had said to them earlier.

'Mr Beausire seems greatly impressed against young Chamberlain, although I cannot see myself that the lad is dishonest.'

'We heard a rumour that he had a kept mistress, an actress called Mrs Bedford. This is not the case, as far as has been found out . . .'

'Indeed!' said Mr Kemmis with a smile. 'To look at the boy is to answer for it.'

'In fact one of our officers, Sergeant Bergan, lives opposite him in Jervis Street and gave him a good character. But he has since said that he once saw Chamberlain with his arm round Mrs Bedford's neck.'

'I am told the boy also admits that he had an uncle, a man of bad character, who was landlord of some slum houses in Dublin; he went to Malta and died there. But Mr Little seems to have trusted Chamberlain. Several people have said that he liked his new clerk very much.'

They had now reached their destination, Temple View, a group of buildings recently erected at the top of Constitution Hill, just over the road from the station. Behind one of these houses was a builder's yard, a jumble of bricks and timber, ropes and pulleys, chimneys, lead pipes and scaffolding poles. There was an out-house containing a forge and anvil, two large carts, and at the far end of the yard a stable, from which two draught horses looked out on the visitors without much interest.

Such were the premises of William Tough, builder. Like his horses, he was currently idle: business was slow, and he found himself with a yard full of materials and nothing to do with them. Creditors now outnumbered the customers in his order books, and the situation was rapidly becoming desperate. So desperate that Mr Tough was teetering on the edge of bankruptcy, although – for the time being, at least – he was the only person who knew that.

Summoned by a smart rap on the door, the builder led Mr Kemmis and the detective into his ground-floor parlour where they explained the purpose of their visit. He had not been asked to give evidence at the inquest, but of course he had heard about it.

'Mr Tough, I believe you saw Mr Little the day he died?'

'Yes, I was in his office on business.'

'At what time did you go there?'

'It was twenty minutes to five until about a quarter to, or thereabouts.'

'Were you on your own?'

'No, a boatman named White came with me on that occasion.'

'Was there anybody else in the office when you visited?'

'There was somebody, as I recollect, yes. He was at my right hand on the counter, when I stood at the door of the hatch, but who he was I cannot say. He had a piece of paper in his hand, said something about income tax.'

'Was he still there when you left?'

'I think so, yes.'

'What were you doing in Mr Little's office?'

'I wanted change from a banker's draft, to pay the boatman four pounds. The draft was for one hundred and four, and I told Mr Little I could wait till tomorrow for the rest, but he gave me all of it straight away.'

'Did you know Mr Little?'

'Yes, he was a friend of mine. He was an amiable, accurate man. He often obliged me with change.'

'One more thing, Mr Tough: where can we find White, the boatman you mentioned?'

'That's easy, sir: unless he's up the canal this afternoon, his barge will be moored at the harbour next the terminus.'

Sure enough, the two investigators had little difficulty in finding White. Close to the Broadstone terminus the canal ended in a wide basin known as the harbour, where goods and passengers were loaded and unloaded. Night was falling, but in the dusk the labourers were still hard at work draining the last section of the canal, between the first lock and the harbour. Stakes and boards had been driven into the bed to form a makeshift dam, and over the next day or so water would be pumped out to expose whatever lay beneath. A crowd of spectators was still watching this minor feat of civil engineering, and among them was Nicholas White, whose lumber barge was one of several vessels being slowly beached on the muddy bottom of the Royal Canal. He soon confirmed the builder's story.

'Yes, sir, I went up there with Mr Tough, so that he could pay me four pounds.'

'Did you see anybody on the way upstairs to the office?'

'No, we met nobody.'

'Who else was in the office when you got there?'

'Well, besides Mr Tough there was Mr Little, Mr Chamberlain, and a gentlemanly man who I did not know.'

'Where was this person standing?'

'Between the door and the screen, with his face against the hatch.'

'Would you know him again if you saw him?'

'No, I would think not.'

'Did you and Mr Tough go behind the counter?'

'No, we stood outside.'

'So what happened when you went into the room?'

'Mr Tough got his money and paid me four pounds. Mr Little asked me what I wanted, and I said I was there with Mr Tough. Then I left, leaving the others in the office.'

'Did you meet anybody else on your way out?'

'No, nobody.'

The boatman had nothing more to offer, so Mr Kemmis and Mr Guy strolled back towards the station. The 'gentlemanly man' mentioned by White and who, according to Tough, had said something about income tax, seemed a credible lead – but this would turn out to be the last they heard of him. Despite the best efforts of Mr Guy's men he was never identified.

Mr Kemmis needed to get back to town to speak to the Attorney General, who he had promised to keep updated with daily progress reports, but first he wanted to perform an experiment. He intended to establish whether Mrs Gunning really could have seen a light shining through the keyhole. Once again he and the superintendent climbed the stairs to the cashier's office, where they lit both the gas lamps and lowered the blinds. The key to the door was still missing, so Mr Kemmis found a pen and inserted it into the keyhole so as to dislodge the scutcheon, the metal cover that normally blocked the aperture. Then he went outside, closing the door behind him. Although it was now quite dark in the corridor, there was no glimmer of light through the keyhole.

This was in line with what Mr Beausire had found the previous evening, but the superintendent was not yet satisfied. He pointed out that the desk lamp was mounted on a flexible stand which allowed it to be placed at different angles. He tried moving it into various positions, but without managing to recreate the effect they were looking for. They were still engaged in this frustrating pursuit when Bernard Gunning, the storekeeper, arrived in the corridor on his way to the engineers' office. Mr Kemmis explained what they were doing, and Gunning offered to help. After several failed attempts he spotted something that the other two men had missed. The counter between the desk and the door contained a hatch which could be opened to allow parcels and other small objects to be passed to the occupants within. When the hatch was lowered, and with the lamp placed in a particular spot on the desk, light did indeed penetrate through the keyhole.

The superintendent and the Crown Solicitor both stood at the far end of the corridor, near the top of the staircase, and agreed that a patch of the wall was distinctly illuminated. Mrs Gunning's claim was at least plausible; and if she was telling the truth this was important, for it gave a clue to the time of death. She had been in the corridor at 7.30 on the night of the murder. If there was light visible then, that meant that the key was still in the door; yet by the following morning the key was gone, and the keyhole was blocked by its metal cover. The implication was that George Little had been murdered later in the evening – but there was an alternative scenario: maybe he was already dead by then, but his killer had returned to the scene to collect more cash, removing the key as he left.

Wednesday morning dawned, dank and grey, on a scene of extraordinary industry. Passengers arriving at Broadstone for the

7.30 a.m. departure to Enfield were surprised to find the area in front of the station already dense with bodies, as if some person of great celebrity was expected by the morning train. It was, in fact, the promise of cheap thrills that had prompted a crowd of Dubliners to forsake their beds and stand in the cold drizzle by a half-empty canal – though the object of their fascination was not a famous writer or statesman, but a glimpse of whatever gothic horrors the subsiding waters might yield. 'The excitement occasioned by this terrible and mysterious murder still continues unabated,' as one newspaper put it. 'In every direction of the city nothing else is spoken of.' In such strange times, even the dredging of a canal became a major public event.

But not everybody was a spectator. Among the crowds was a battalion of labourers armed with shovels, buckets and other tools. The members of this impromptu workforce, numbering more than a hundred and fifty, had been recruited from railway employees, municipal workmen and unemployed navvies, who had been offered a few shillings for a day's work. An additional inducement had been offered in the form of a cash reward for any man who succeeded in finding an object of evidential value.

The unlikely general of these assorted mercenaries and conscripts was Mervyn P. Crofton, Supervisor of Waterworks for the Dublin Corporation. He had organised his forces into teams of twenty or so, each supervised by a foreman. The original plan had been for the men to start searching the canal bed at first light, but to Mr Crofton's frustration the dam had started to leak. Additional planks were being hammered into place to curtail the flow of water, but it was likely to be a while before enough mud was exposed to make a search worthwhile. Some of the labourers passed the time by trying to catch eels, dozens of which were now trapped in the harbour. Their serpentine forms darted frantically around the legs of their pursuers as the workmen lumbered after them through the shallow water.

It was mid-morning by the time Mr Crofton decided that the

search should begin. The channel was far from dry, with the water still two feet deep in places, but he was under considerable pressure to get the job done quickly. The Midland Great Western Railway Company, which owned the canal, and the boatmen who relied on it for their income, would not tolerate any delay. A ripple of excitement went through the crowds when they realised that something was finally happening, and heads craned over the edge of the basin as the spectators looked eagerly for any object that might have been used by the mysterious assassin. But the workmen shovelled and scraped and gathered mud into smelly piles for hours without finding anything, and as lunchtime came and went the onlookers started to drift away.

By 2 p.m. the searchers had nothing to show for their labours but an old carriage lantern. Mr Crofton, who had spent much of the time pacing the quayside from one end of the harbour to the other, had just passed the pontoon bridge for the umpteenth time when he spotted something. He stopped walking and peered at an object which protruded a few inches from a shallow pool in the canal bed. It appeared to be a stick or piece of wood. Mr Crofton happened to be standing next to Superintendent Hodgens of the railway police, so he pointed it out to him. Though based at Broadstone, where he had a little office on the platform, Samuel Hodgens was barely involved in the murder inquiry. His job was seen as something of a sinecure, and although he arrested a few pickpockets and prostitutes it was arguable that his most important function was supervising the weekly distribution of wage packets. Superintendent Hodgens looked towards the spot Mr Crofton had indicated, then bellowed an order at the labourer standing nearest to it – a man Hodgens did not recognise, since he was not a railway company employee.

'Hey, you! There's something in the water to your left. Pull it out and get it over here. And quickly!'

John Geraghty, a muscular contrarian who after years as a navvy had grown weary of being shouted at by strangers, obeyed the letter of the command, if not its spirit. He ripped the object from the cold and sticky embrace of several inches of mud, and without warning hurled it violently towards the bank. The bystanders scattered, and by some miracle the missile did not hit any of them. That was just as well, because when it was picked up and handed to Hodgens the superintendent found that he was holding a hammer. It was a hefty item, about eighteen inches long, and when he showed it to Mr Crofton the latter identified it as an engineer's hammer. One side of its head was flat and broad, the other more pointed and angular. There was no doubt that it would do considerable damage if brandished in anger. When Mr Crofton looked more closely he noticed that the shaft had split a short distance from the head of the hammer, and something had caught in the crack. It appeared to be a human hair.

There was no hope of concealing the discovery. Dozens of eye-witnesses were already excitedly spreading the news, embellishing it as they went. By the time it reached the ears of the nearest newspaper reporters, it was generally agreed that there had been not a single hair but clumps of the stuff found on both the head and shaft of the hammer, which was also liberally stained with blood. A rumour had also begun to circulate that the workmen had uncovered a body embedded in the mud, which was assumed to be that of the murderer. There was at least a particle of truth to this story, in that a corpse, which turned out to be that of a railway employee called Hill, had been fished out of the canal earlier in the day. But the man had been dead for almost a fortnight, and his body was found a good half-mile away; the discovery was coincidental and could not possibly have anything to do with this case. Amid the hue and cry of the murder inquiry, the tragic death of another railway worker went almost unnoticed.

The hammer was quickly put into the possession of one of the detective sergeants, who hurried to pass it on to Superintendent Guy, conducting inquiries inside the station building. The workmen, who had been standing in the filth and cold of an imperfectly drained canal for several hours, were allowed a break for dinner. After half an hour of bread and cheese and tea and tobacco they returned reluctantly to work, and it was only a little later, at around 4.00, that they made another find. The temporary dam, which had already proved so troublesome, was leaking again, and the men had been told to caulk the cracks with mud. A labourer called Christopher Geraghty was gathering handfuls of sludge from the canal bed for this purpose when he gave a sudden yell. The other men rushed over to see what he had found, and so many spectators surged to that part of the towpath that a few fell over the edge and had to be hauled back up, liberally covered in slime.

Geraghty was suddenly aware that all eyes were on him. His fingers, which were numb with cold, seemed impossibly clumsy as he fumbled with the object he had found, trying to wipe it clean of mud. Finally the grime gave way to the glint of hardened steel, and Geraghty realised what he was holding. It was a razor.

6

Thursday 20 November
Day 6 of murder inquiry

This breakthrough could not have come at a better moment. The authorities in Dublin Castle, and even their masters in Westminster, were beginning to express disquiet. The English newspapers were particularly brutal, with *The Times* thundering that 'the detective police are said to be completely at fault, and so far every attempt to obtain the slightest clue to the assassin has been a total failure'. With the discovery of two possible murder weapons a note of optimism now crept into the news coverage. 'Every hope is entertained,' wrote a correspondent for the *Evening Freeman*, 'that the police will soon be on the right track of the perpetrators of this brutal murder.'

Over the next few days things started to move quickly. The Crown Solicitor Thomas Kemmis and Superintendent Augustus Guy found themselves spending more time in each other's company than with their respective families. Their investigation often kept them in the Broadstone terminus until late into the night, supervising searches and conducting interviews. But while they were making confident noises in public, the detectives were considerably less sure of themselves behind closed doors. Bereft of meaningful evidence for so long, they now found themselves overwhelmed by a confusing mass of it.

The most encouraging development was the finding of the hammer. On examination it was found to be a fitter's hammer of a type not merely used in the locomotive workshops at Broadstone, but actually manufactured there. One of the blacksmiths recognised it as one he had recently made, and he pointed out that the face of the hammerhead had not been ground, indicating that it had never been used for its intended purpose. This left no doubt that it had been stolen from the store.

The police had also been able to rule out one of the possible suspects. After several newspaper reports alluded darkly to the mysterious 'Jew-pedlar' known to have visited Mr Little's office on the day of the murder, the man himself visited a police station to give a statement. His name was Jacob Moses Braun, and he turned out to be a rabbi, a German immigrant who eked out a living teaching German and Hebrew and hawking small goods about Dublin. He appeared entirely benign, and in any case he had a watertight alibi for the evening of the murder.

But there was still a great deal they did not know. Where was the key to the cashier's office, and what had happened to the money? Did the failure of the police to find it mean that it had already been taken out of Dublin? And was this an opportunistic crime, or a carefully planned heist? Almost a week had passed since the murder, and the investigators still had not got round to interviewing everybody with first-hand knowledge of the building and the staff who worked in it.

There was great excitement in the city on Thursday, the day after the discovery of the hammer, when word got round that the police had made an arrest. This time the rumours were true. The two men and a woman seen in a Stoneybatter pub handling a suspiciously large sum of money had been identified, and officers followed their trail to County Meath, where they were apprehended. News that they were being brought to Dublin for questioning caused a vast crowd to assemble around the Capel Street police station. Today it would be usual for a suspect arrested on suspicion of a crime to be interviewed in private, but in nineteenth-century Ireland all such examinations took place before a magistrate. As a result, the police court was inundated with spectators, and constables had to be posted on all the main doors to ensure that lawyers and others who had professional business in the building were able to get in and out.

After a long delay the three prisoners were finally brought in front of the police magistrate, Mr O'Donnell. They gave their names as Patrick and Catherine Cullen (husband and wife), and Hugh Collins. They were then told the grounds for suspicion against them, which consisted of having in their possession a sum of money for which they could not satisfactorily account, and – absurdly – 'being absent from their own place of abode without assigning any proper reason therefor'. The police might as well have accused them of 'having a day out in Dublin'.

First to take the stand was John Halligan, the servant who had reported the trio to the police. He testified that he had seen the couple drinking in a pub, and that Patrick Cullen had threatened his wife, who had produced a pocket-book crammed with bank-notes. At this point an official showed the court a large leather wallet found in Catherine Cullen's possession, which the witness agreed was the one he had seen. Halligan added that while Patrick Cullen was out of the room, Catherine had also produced a large quantity of silver from her pocket, including a number of five-shilling pieces. He finished by observing that Collins was not the third person from the pub; he had never seen him before.

The magistrate asked whether the prisoners had anything to say. Patrick Cullen stepped forward.

'Your worship, everything the gentleman says is correct, save as to the quantity of money. We only had three pounds altogether, and no five-shilling pieces.'

One of the detectives rose from his seat to inform the magistrate that there was another witness the police wished him to examine. This was William Chamberlain, but unfortunately nobody had thought to tell William that he was required, so a messenger was dispatched to Broadstone to fetch him. The young man appeared shortly afterwards, looking flustered and upset. The magistrate asked whether he could see anybody in court who looked like the stranger he had seen near Mr Little's office on the day of the murder, and William gazed anxiously around the room. After an expectant silence, he eventually fixed his gaze on one of the spectators in the public gallery, and said uncertainly that he thought that person might be him. Under gentle coaxing from the magistrate, William conceded that he could not be sure that anybody present was the man he had seen.

Halligan was recalled to the stand. He said that when he encountered the three people in the pub he had asked the woman whether she was married to either of her male companions, and where they were headed. She had replied that one of the men was her husband; he was going to America, but she would not be joining him. There was muttering in court: emigration was a costly business, and robbery was certainly one way to raise the fare.

The next witness was a young man called Williams, who worked in a shop visited by the Cullens shortly after they left the pub. Williams recalled that Patrick Cullen had entered his shop carrying a bundle of banknotes, and asked to change some of them for £25 in gold. Williams had declined and, realising that Cullen was rather drunk, advised him to give his cash to his wife for safekeeping.

The officer who had made the arrest, Head Constable Keating of the Meath police, explained that he had taken the suspects into custody after receiving a description of them by telegraph. He had found on the woman a wallet containing one gold sovereign and 8s 6d in silver; when asked whether they had been in Dublin the previous Friday, the Cullens claimed that they had not visited the city in the last month. Keating also claimed to have seen them in the company of known pickpockets.

One of the detectives, Sergeant Kavanagh, was then permitted to question the prisoners.

'Mr Cullen, where do you live?'

'In Kells.'

'How much money did you have in the pub at Stoneybatter?'

'I had three pounds,' said Cullen, before adding that as he had been very drunk, it was 'probably better to ask the wife'.

When the laughter had subsided, Kavanagh asked the Cullens about their movements the previous Thursday. Catherine was vague and refused to say where she had slept that night, but her husband leapt in to say that they had left Kells together that morning to walk the twenty miles to Drogheda, where they had stayed the night. This was not a terribly satisfactory answer, since it did not come close to explaining how they came to be in a public house almost thirty miles away later the same day. The magistrate agreed to the police request to remand the prisoners in custody, but Collins – against whom no evidence had been presented – was released without charge.

It was a start, but those at the heart of the investigation had a feeling that the Stoneybatter suspects were not the people they were looking for. The circumstances of the crime suggested that the killer was somebody who knew the terminus well, and could find their way through the labyrinth of stairs and corridors at a time when the usual public routes through the building were inaccessible. Both Mr Kemmis and Superintendent Guy were convinced that the perpetrator was a member of the railway staff. The chances were that it was somebody they had already met.

A couple of miles south of central Dublin was the ancient village of Harold's Cross, a community of around a thousand inhabitants, many of whom worked in the nearby cotton mills. But Harold's Cross was a place where the dead outnumbered the living. The village was bounded on two sides by Mount Jerome Cemetery, twenty-five acres of gently rolling parkland adorned with shrubs and venerable trees. Twenty years earlier it had been part of a large country estate, and in the summer months it was a tranquil place to stroll. It was rather less relaxing doing so before dawn on a winter morning, in the face of a sharp north-wester – but this is exactly what Thomas Kemmis found himself doing on Friday 21 November.

The Crown Solicitor was part of a solemn procession which also included Superintendent Guy, Inspector Ryan, the county coroner, two doctors, a priest, the sexton and several gravediggers. They walked the cemetery's avenues in silence, the light from their lamps occasionally picking out a name or a line of scripture engraved into the granite monuments. Somewhere out there in the gloom was the massive stone vault commissioned by Elizabeth Gresham, a woman so terrified of being buried alive that she had insisted on having a bell installed on the pedestal that capped the edifice, with a cord inside the tomb so that she could summon assistance if she woke up after interment. Sixteen years after her burial it now seemed safe to assume that she was not in need of this contrivance, but once in a while a rogue gust of wind would catch the bell with enough force to give the unwary passer-by an unpleasant intimation of the supernatural.

The line of figures halted at a patch of recently turned earth. The grave was unmarked, as the monumental mason had not yet completed the headstone that would soon mark George Samuel Little's final place of rest. Quietly Mr Kemmis indicated that the gravediggers should begin work. Ordering an exhumation was not something he did lightly, but this one was necessary. The most difficult part had been obtaining permission from the Littles: George's sister Kate had agreed to it, but she was concerned about the effect the news would have on her mother, who was said to be in a state of near-total collapse. The operation had been arranged at short notice and strictly in secret, since there was no doubt that members of the press would do almost anything to be present at such an event.

Fortunately George Little's grave was a good half-mile from the nearest road, and the irregular pre-dawn goings-on went unremarked. The damp earth yielded easily to the gravediggers' shovels, and it was not long before a glint of reflected lamplight at the bottom of the grave indicated that they had exposed the polished wood of the coffin. They heaved up the casket and placed it delicately on the turf. The lid was unscrewed and removed, to reveal a sight that even these habitués of death and suffering found difficult to look at. Despite the undertaker's best efforts the ghastly extent of George Little's injuries was all too apparent, their effects now compounded by nine days of decomposition.

The coroner, Henry Davis, made a brief examination of the cadaver. Then the two medics stepped in: Dr Jennings and Dr Barker, who had performed the first post-mortem a week earlier. Inspector Ryan handed them something from a heavy cloth bag. It was the hammer found two days earlier at the bottom of the canal. Dr Jennings held it next to the dead man's skull, comparing the size and shape of the wounds with the head of the hammer. He nodded to his colleague, who repeated the exercise. They seemed satisfied, but the test was not quite complete. Ryan had another three or four hammers in his bag, all of which had been turned up by searches of the Broadstone estate. The doctors tried each in turn. Before the exhumation the two men had disagreed vehemently over whether the canal hammer could be the implement that had killed George Little; but now they were in no doubt that it at least might have been.

There was a final, grisly stage to this second autopsy. Dr Jennings produced a bone saw and a trephine, and with a facility which owed more to brute force than skill removed a large section of the dead man's skull. There was every chance that it would be needed as evidence if the matter should come to trial: an intelligent defence barrister would challenge the doctors' assertion that the hammer was the murder weapon. There was no question of taking a photograph, or even drawing a quick sketch, in these conditions. Nothing about the situation encouraged dawdling, so within a few minutes the lid was replaced and the coffin was lowered back into its hole. The priest said a brief prayer and the party retraced their steps out of the cemetery, leaving the gravediggers to their work.

A few hours later Mr Kemmis was back at Broadstone, in the ground-floor room he had commandeered for his headquarters. According to the morning papers the Dublin murder was big news in London. The city's criminal barristers were on the alert for the possibility of work, and some of the brasher Scotland Yard detectives were boasting that they would be able to solve the case in a few days. Mr Kemmis also read with amusement that the telegram sent to Charles Frederick Field – the 'prince of detectives', as the paper styled him – had been delivered by mistake to an entirely unrelated Mr Field, who was rather surprised to receive a summons to Ireland. The message had eventually found its way to the real inspector, engaged on a case in Jersey, who was said to be preparing to sail for Dublin.

The Crown Solicitor raised his eyes from his newspaper to meet those of Augustus Guy, who had just entered. The detective told him that Dublin Castle was allocating more resources to the case, bringing the Broadstone contingent to well over twenty detectives and uniformed officers. Superintendent Finnamore, the officer in charge of 'G' division, was also back from his sickbed and would be assisting Mr Guy. To allow their inquiries to continue unobserved, Directors' House had been declared off limits to anybody who did not have business in the building, with officers posted at every entrance. It was impractical to close the station entirely – as Mr Kemmis would have preferred – but passengers were now allowed access only to the platforms, which they could reach by a side gate. Mr Guy had more news: the police had sent the razor to an expert for analysis, though the results were frustratingly inconclusive. There was no sign of blood on either blade or handle, but the fact that the metal showed no trace of tarnish suggested that the razor had been in the water for only a few days. The most interesting finding was that it was an item of superior manufacture, the sort of expensive razor that a gentleman might own.

The two men spent some time discussing their next move.

Mr Guy's team of detectives had now spoken to most of the rail-way staff, and several persons of particular interest were starting to emerge. The superintendent's suspicions rested principally on McCauley, the cash porter, for circumstantial reasons. He was one of the few people who was in and out of the cashier's office several times a day, and they had already established that he had been there late on Thursday afternoon. Mr Kemmis was more interested in the assistant storekeeper Bernard Gunning and his wife Anne. Visitors to their basement apartment reported that they appeared to be living beyond their means; moreover, it seemed that the hammer used to kill Mr Little had been taken from Gunning's own store. There were also concerns that one of the clerks from the engineering department, Patrick Moan, had not been entirely honest in his answers. These three, then, were their prime suspects; it was time for the Crown Solicitor to inter-view them in person.

The Midland Great Western Railway Company did not yet have the resources or expertise to manufacture its own locomotives – which were purchased from a company in Manchester – but every engine on the line was maintained at Broadstone. This took place in a cavernous workshop a short distance from the station, on the other side of a scrubby piece of wasteland to the east of the ter-minus. In front of the building was a courtyard known as Locomotive Yard, with a gate which opened on to the Phibsbor-ough Road, where many of the workers lived in houses owned by the railway company.

The building that Mr Kemmis and Superintendent Guy now entered was alive with noise. At one end of the workshop, mechanics were reassembling a boiler which had been disman-tled for cleaning, hammering rivets with a violence which seemed to make the walls shake. The greater part of the space was occu-pied by the carriage builders, a skilled troop of engineers, joiners and fitters who constructed every goods wagon and passenger carriage from scratch. Their domain was less noisy, but there was no let-up in the assault on the senses. The air was thick with sawdust, and permeated with the vapours of paint and varnish, and the sickly aroma of turpentine.

Just off the workshop floor, in a cubbyhole masquerading as an office, they found Bernard Gunning, a portly man in his late forties. On the walls around him an armoury of tools hung from racks: the giant sledgehammers used for laying railway track, saws of all sizes, chisels, drills and paintbrushes. It was Gunning's job to issue these to the craftsmen and to record their safe return at the end of each day, and also to ensure that the workshop never ran out of paint, or grease, or any of the other numerous consumables that were constantly required.

The arrival of the detective and his colleague caused a certain amount of interest, and workmen downed tools to peer at them around the door of the storeroom. Gunning seemed discomfited by the attention, perhaps aware that as a resident of Directors' House he might fall under suspicion. He was keen to emphasise that he rarely spent much time there, except when he went home to sleep or eat.

'Mr Gunning, would you tell us where you were on the evening of the murder?'

'I was here in the stores from three o'clock till half-past five. Then I went home to our sitting room in the basement of Directors' House and asked my wife to give me tea, as I had business in town. I had tea, and then went out.'

Mr Gunning gave an elaborate account of his movements thereafter, which had covered a surprising area of the city. After a business meeting at a central Dublin hotel he had been to see his tailor and then visited friends on both sides of the Liffey, finishing up in a pub near Trinity College. Mr Guy asked what time he had returned to Broadstone.

'About eleven o'clock. I knocked at the gate under the clock, which was opened by the nightwatchman, John King.'

'Did you see anybody else?'

'Not a soul. I went over to the door of Directors' House, where I live.'

'Was it locked?'

'No, only closed.'

'Was it usual for the door to be left unlocked so late at night?'

'Yes. It was locked by half-past eleven that night. I went straight downstairs to our parlour, where my wife was with Catherine Campbell, our servant. I told her to turn off the gaslight and fasten the outer door; that is, the one I had just entered, which leads off the platform.'

'Is the door locked with a key?'

'No, it is fastened by a bolt. Any person inside could open it.'

'So it would be possible for somebody in the cashier's office to get out of the building late at night, even after that door had been secured?'

'Yes. Whenever Mr Little stayed at work until late, his habit was to go down the back stairs to the basement, and then up a flight of stairs by Hanbury's apartments and go out by that door.'

This seemed a strangely circuitous way of getting from the first floor to ground level. Gunning explained that his wife locked the internal door to the grand staircase every evening, making the direct route inaccessible.

'Did she mention that Mr Little had stayed late, or that his door was locked?'

'No, she said nothing of it, except at breakfast the following morning. She remarked then that Mr Little would be cold, as he would have no fire in his room.'

'And why was that?'

'Because it seemed that he had locked the door and taken the key with him, so that Catherine could not get in to clean the grate.'

'And what time did you leave the house on Friday morning?'

'Some time between six and seven o'clock. Hanbury was out

first that morning – I saw him on the platform – so the door was already unbolted by then.'

Gunning claimed to know nothing about the missing hammer, telling them that all tools were issued by his young assistant William Millar. The boy was out running some errand, but Gunning promised that he would send him to them as soon as he returned.

They spoke next to William McCauley, the porter responsible for delivering the cashboxes to Mr Little's office every day. McCauley was a railway company man through and through: he and his wife, who worked as private nurse to a local invalid, lived in a company flat a stone's throw from the locomotive workshop, and two of their seven children were employed at Broadstone as messengers. As well as delivering the cashboxes every day, McCauley was the station factotum – cleaning lavatories, keeping the offices supplied with coal and drinking water, carrying luggage for passengers, and, as he put it, 'making myself generally useful'.

The Crown Solicitor asked him what time he normally started work.

'Usually before six. First I inspect the water closets, and if they're dirty I clean them. Then I light the fires with a match.'

'Do you mean the lavatories in Directors' House?'

'No, the ones on the platform, for the passengers. They have fireplaces to heat them. When I've lit the fires I go with the other porters to look after the seven o'clock train. It's my duty to bring in the money boxes to the cashier and take out the empty ones.'

'Would you tell us what happened on Thursday the thirteenth?'

'Yes, I brought up the money boxes on that day at a quarter to ten, at half-past eleven, and at a quarter past two. There were twenty-eight boxes to come up in all. Afterwards I went upstairs to collect the boxes at half-past three and half-past four.'

'Do you remember who else was in the office at half-past four?'

'I'm not sure. I went downstairs to give the boxes to the guard of the five o'clock train, then saw the train start.'

'Did it leave on time?'

'It might have been a minute or two late, but not more. Straight after that I went home to supper.'

'When you left Mr Little's office, were you in the habit of going down the grand staircase, or the back stairs?'

'Usually the back stairs. I certainly used them when I picked up the boxes at half-past four. I left them in the luggage van with Bissett, the guard, then went to assist the other man. I kept an eye on the clock to see if it was time to collect the last lot of boxes, and went up for them before the five o'clock train started.'

'You said a moment ago that you saw it depart. Now you say you went upstairs before it left?'

McCauley looked thrown.

'Well, the first bell for departure had rung before I left the platform. I always look at the platform clock when I think it is time to go for the boxes. That clock is further from Directors' House than the clock over the gate.'

'So it takes you a few minutes to reach the offices from that end of the platform?'

'Exactly.'

'What did you find when you went upstairs?'

'I went up the back stairs opposite the audit office. Mr Little's door was shut, but not locked. I opened it and went in. Mr Little was inside.'

'Did you see anybody else there?'

'No. I don't think there could have been anyone else there. In fact I am sure of it.'

'Did you say anything to him?'

'I said, "Goodnight, Mr Little," and he said, "Goodnight, McCauley." I shut the door gently, took the boxes down the back stairs and passed out by the solicitor's clerks' offices.'

'Did you see anybody else?'

'There were several clerks in the hall ready to go home, but I could not tell you the names of any of them.'

'Go on.'

'Then I took the boxes to the parcel office, set them down, and without waiting a moment longer went home. I walked straight along the platform, under the projecting clock and out by the locomotive gate, and then . . .'

McCauley paused, having apparently remembered something.

'I must have been wrong earlier, Mr Guy, for now I recall I saw the five o'clock train start after I left the money boxes in the parcel office.'

The superintendent looked steadily at the porter, trying to gauge whether he was telling the truth.

'When you went upstairs, McCauley, are you sure you did not see Chamberlain, Mr Little's assistant?'

'I do not think I saw him after half-past four.'

'Very well. So, you say you were on the platform when the five o'clock train departed. What did you do next?'

'Yes, sir, I was standing within a few yards of the parcel van. I went home and found three or four of my children there. My daughter Anne – she's a big girl, twenty-three years old – and her sister Ellen, who's thirteen. My wife was not there and my supper was not ready, so I came back to the platform.'

'Why? You had finished work for the day, surely?'

The porter laughed.

'Oh no, sir, my work doesn't finish at suppertime. I had to inspect the water closets, which took only a few moments. Then I had five or six coal boxes to fill – they hold about three stone of coal each. So I went to the coal store underneath the parcel office and was there about half an hour. When I came out of the coal store I stood on the platform waiting for passengers who might be going off by the mail train. I heard both the bells ring, and saw the quarter-past seven mail train start. Then I inspected the water closets again, and put out the lights in the waiting rooms. I went back to the coal store to get coals and firewood . . .'

'How long were you in the coal store?'

'I cannot now be certain, but as soon as I left I went home to supper. My wife was at home by then, and all my children. I stayed there for an hour and had bread and butter and tea for supper. I think I had a piece of fish also, but can't be positive.'

'What time did you go to bed on the night of the murder?'

'At about nine o'clock.'

'What did you do the following morning?'

'I took up the boxes to Mr Little's office as usual, and Mrs Gunning was at the door. That was at about ten minutes to ten. I asked Mrs Gunning whether Mr Little had come, and she said not. I then locked the money boxes in Mr Moan's office, and gave the key to Mrs Gunning's girl.'

Mr Kemmis was very far from being convinced that they had grounds for suspecting McCauley, although Superintendent Guy pointed to the porter's equivocation about timings. They could at least agree that they needed to find a way to check his alibi.

Patrick Moan lived with his wife in an apartment owned by the railway company in Phibsborough Road, a few hundred yards from the Broadstone terminus. Their home was not luxurious, but they lived there rent free. The Moans had no children of their own, but were bringing up Patrick's nephew and niece, who had been orphaned some years earlier.

Mr Moan was a strikingly tall man with a restless, perpetually distracted manner. He had grown up in Maryborough, a town about sixty miles south-west of Dublin, and was originally destined for the Catholic priesthood. But after training at the seminary of St Patrick's, Maynooth – the largest and most prestigious in Ireland – he had abandoned his studies without being ordained, instead setting up a small private school in Dublin. Fourteen years of teaching proved more than enough, however, and in 1853 he had joined the railway company as chief clerk, having been recommended for the position by Mr Beausire.

His duties, he explained, consisted mainly of checking the accounts of the locomotive department. He kept tabs on the mileage run by every engine, ensured that the ledgers in the stores were kept up to date, and made a running tally of expenses for maintaining track and stations.

Mr Guy asked whether his work ever brought him into contact with cash.

'No, I deal with figures and not with money. In the week of Mr Little's death I prepared our account on the Wednesday. It was for two hundred and sixty-six pounds, fourteen shillings and tenpence, the sum owing to the locomotive department for wages and other expenses. I sent a duplicate to the accountants, and it went also to the finance committee, who approved it. The department was paid through Mr Christian, who must have received the cash from Mr Little for that purpose.'

'Did you know Mr Little?'

'My office is opposite his, but I was not acquainted with him, except the casual courtesy of one gentleman to another.'

'And where were you on the day of the murder?'

'I was in my own office all that Thursday, from ten o'clock to five minutes to five.'

'Did you see anybody unusual around the corridors that day?'

'No.'

'And what did you do that evening after leaving your office?'

'I went over to the goods store to meet Mr Osborne and Mr Gunning. I needed to speak to them about a dinner for Mr Wilson, an engineer who recently left the company. We were going to present him with some silver plate. We agreed to go to the European Hotel in Bolton Street to talk it over the next morning at eleven o'clock.'

The European Hotel was the largest in Dublin, a few streets away from the Broadstone terminus and catering mainly for travellers. It was known informally as Molony's in honour of the proprietor, James Molony, who ran the hotel with his wife Jane.

'And what time did you leave the stores?'

'Mr Gunning left at about twenty to six, leaving me with Mr Osborne discussing the plans for the dinner. We decided to go over to Molony's in the morning, and if they could offer us a suitable menu at eight shillings a head we would have the dinner there.'

'When is this dinner taking place?'

'This tragic circumstance has postponed it. It was to have been for sixty people. I am the secretary of the organising committee, responsible for the dinner and the plate.'

'Did Mr Little make a contribution?'

'Yes, he gave ten shillings towards the piece of plate. Mr Osborne was the treasurer; I think he said that Mr Gunning also subscribed ten shillings. It was I who got the ten shillings from Mr Little – a long time back it was, maybe last August.'

'Now, Mr Moan, would you tell me what you remember of last Friday morning?'

'I came to my own office at ten. Mr Chamberlain was standing at the end of the corridor. The door to my office was locked. I was surprised, since this was unprecedented. I sent the little messenger boy, Moore, downstairs to get the key from Mrs Gunning. She brought it up and opened it for me.'

'Why were you surprised?'

'My door was not normally locked. Mrs Gunning said the reason for it was that McCauley had put the cashboxes in my office, as Mr Little's door was locked, and he had not come in.'

'I see. And what happened next?'

'Well, I had my appointment with Osborne and Gunning at eleven o'clock, but since the cashboxes were still in my office I did not like to leave. I went out into the corridor and expressed my surprise to Chamberlain that Mr Little had not come, saying that I had an appointment. Chamberlain said he was also surprised, and that he would not be surprised if Mr Little had walked into the canal.'

'Into the canal! What did he mean by that?'

'I do not know. At that moment Mr Gunning came up to find me, and asked why I had not kept our appointment. I pointed at the cashboxes and said that I could not leave with them in my office. He told me to lock the door and give the key to his wife, which I did, but only after I had got permission from Mr Cabry and told him where I was going. Then Gunning and I got a cab round to the entrance of the locomotive department on Phibsborough Road and picked up Mr Osborne.'

'And the three of you went into town?'

'Yes, we went to Molony's as arranged. Molony produced a bill of fare which Gunning had spoken to him about on the previous evening. It was a lengthy bill, Mr Guy, a special menu indeed. That bill of fare was so good that we said nothing could beat it. We had a bottle of wine – well, all except me, Mr Guy, I had a bottle of ginger beer. So we said to Mr Molony, we'll make up our minds and send you word in the evening. And when we'd finished our drinks we got back into the cab and we all agreed that nothing could be better than that bill of fare, and that we should adopt it. And then somebody said, why don't we go to the Dolphin and have some oysters. So we did that, and then we returned together to the locomotive department about half-past one.'

'And then you went back to your office?'

'Yes.'

Moan described finding Mr Beausire and several others trying to get into the cashier's office, and his frustrating odyssey through Dublin looking for a doctor. He seemed to know nothing further, so Mr Guy thanked him and they walked back to the station.

William Millar, Mr Gunning's assistant in the goods store, was waiting for them. Although barely into his teens, William spent most of his waking hours at work: he was required to be at his post from 5.30 every morning until 6.30 in the evening, six days a week. His principal task was looking after the tools. Mr Guy asked him about the hammers: were they kept under lock and key?

'No; I keep them in a box behind the counter, and issue them to the men when they need them.'

'Is there a signing-out book, any record of who has borrowed them?'

'No, I do not keep any account.'

'Did you give one out on the day of the murder?'

'I don't know. I do not remember whether anybody took a hammer that day.'

'Was Mr Moan in the stores that day?'

'He was not inside the counter by the hammers, to my knowledge.'

'What about Mr Gunning?'

'He might have been there, but I don't recollect.'

'You have seen the hammer that was found in the canal. Does it look like one of those in your store?'

'Possibly, but engine drivers also carry a hammer similar to that one.'

'Do you remember anybody making some excuse to borrow a hammer?'

'Such a thing might have occurred, but I do not recollect it happening.'

'What time did you leave on Thursday the thirteenth?'

'I left about half-past six with Mr Osborne.'

'Just the two of you? What about Mr Gunning?'

'He had left about half-past five, so it was just the two of us.'

'Was Mr Moan there too?'

'I do not remember.'

A pattern was beginning to emerge from these interviews. A minor inconsistency would present itself, a tiny glimmer of light indicating a fruitful new avenue to explore; and just as things were looking promising, the latest clue would turn out to have led them into yet another cul-de-sac.

7

Friday 21 November
Day 7 of murder inquiry

Thomas Kemmis found Mr Gunning's wife Anne in her parlour in the basement of Directors' House. The Gunnings
enjoyed somewhat unusual domestic arrangements, with their
kitchen and living rooms below ground and their bedrooms three
floors up, in the eaves of the house. Their servant Catherine
Campbell did not even have the luxury of her own room, sleeping
on a folding bed in the kitchen. Catherine was busy in the scull-
ery when the investigators arrived, but at Mr Guy's request she
was sent away to continue her chores upstairs.

Anne Gunning and her husband were two of the longest-serving
employees of the Midland Great Western Railway Company. She
told Mr Kemmis that they had met when both were working as
domestic servants for Mr James Perry, one of the directors of the
company: she had been his cook and housekeeper, and Mr Gunning the butler. Mr Perry had recommended Gunning for a position
as clerk as soon as the company was formed, and they had moved
to Broadstone when the terminus was first built. They now lived in
their flat with their twin girls, Sarah Anne and Mary Jane.

'Mrs Gunning, when did you last see George Little?'

'At about ten o'clock that Thursday morning, as he was coming up the grand staircase to his office. He wished me good
morning. I never saw him again.'

'And that evening, where was your husband?'

'He was in a hurry for his tea, so I made it for him and he went
out at about half-past six.'

The superintendent asked her to recall her own movements around the house after her husband's departure. She gave a more detailed version of her evidence to the inquest: her walk around the building checking that the lights were out, and noticing that the gas was still lit in the cashier's office.

'Did you mention to anyone that Mr Little was still upstairs?'

'No.'

'And did Catherine tell you that she had knocked at Mr Little's door, or that he was in his office?'

'No.'

'When your husband came home at half-past eleven, he told Catherine to turn off the gas. Why did you not tell him that Mr Little was still in his office?'

'I was certain he had gone by then. The solicitor's clerk, Mr Thornton, had left at eleven o'clock, so I thought that there was nobody else in the office.'

Mr Guy asked her about the door at the foot of the grand staircase, which gave access from the ticket hall to the offices. When was it locked?

'I always lock it myself, every evening at about half-past five.'

'And did you lock it on Thursday evening?'

'Yes, and kept the key. I unlocked it again the next morning around nine o'clock.'

'Did you notice any mark, or a bloodstain, on the door frame when you unlocked it?'

'No.'

'There is a window that opens on to the platform just there, next to the door. Was it open or shut?'

'I am positive it was shut.'

Mr Kemmis thought he detected a certain reserve in Mrs Gunning's manner, and wondered whether she might be hiding something. But he had nothing specific with which to challenge her, so decided to draw the interview to a close. He thanked her for her time, and asked her to send Catherine down to speak to them. A few minutes passed while Mrs Gunning went upstairs to find her. The two men sat in silence, listening to the distant hubbub of the train shed, with Mrs Gunning's mantel clock ticking quietly in soothing counterpoint.

Three quarters of Dublin's population could read and write, but Catherine Campbell was not among them. The Gunnings' servant was seventeen, a country girl who had never been to school. Orphaned at the age of three, Catherine had been taken in by a local worthy who owned a substantial house in Ashbourne, a dozen miles north of Dublin. Her benefactor, a Mrs Woods, spent most of her time in town, and in her absence Catherine was raised by the domestic servants. As the daughter of an illiterate labourer she was not thought worth educating, and was instead prepared for a life in service.

Mr Kemmis and the superintendent had often passed Catherine in the corridors of Directors' House, and both noticed that she seemed uneasy in their presence. She was sullen and uncooperative, and it was only with difficulty that they managed to persuade her to talk with any freedom.

Catherine told them that she had been with the Gunnings for nine months, but would soon be leaving. She had given her notice and would have moved out on Friday 14 November, but then 'Mr Little's murder came to trouble us all'.

'When did you last see Mr Little?'

'I went into his office some time between noon and one o'clock with an inkstand tray that Mrs Gunning had told me to put there. I gave it to Mr Chamberlain. Mr Little was there, but I did not speak to him.'

The detective asked about her movements on the Thursday evening. She replied that she had gone upstairs to start cleaning at about a quarter to five. She began in Mr Cabry's office, and when she had finished scrubbing the grate she moved next door to Mr Moan's.

'What time was it then?'

'The clock was just striking five.'

'Did you see anybody in the offices, or in the passage?'

'I saw nobody.'

'And how long did you stay in Mr Moan's room?'

'Maybe twenty minutes. When I had laid the fire I stayed for a while looking out of the window.'

'Mr Moan's office is opposite that of Mr Little, is it not? Did you hear any sound coming from his room?'

'Yes. While I was in Mr Moan's room I heard somebody coming out of Mr Little's office. The person seemed to shut the door behind them.'

'Did they lock the door?'

'I did not hear the lock turn. I think the person went down the back stairs after that, but I cannot be positive. Afterwards I went to Mr Little's door to see if it was he that was gone. I turned the handle and found it locked.'

'Could you hear anybody inside the office? Did anybody speak?'

'No, sir. I only heard the one person leave. There was no talk or conversation in his room.'

Catherine related her lonely progress through the building, sweeping floors, cleaning grates and laying fires. Mr Kemmis interrupted.

'Did you see anybody on your way downstairs?'

'I think I met Mr Jolly when I went into the audit office. I told one of the constables that I was quite sure I had seen Mr Jolly, but the gaslight in the office was low. I think he told me that he would be away for a few minutes. But perhaps I was mistaken.'

Mr Jolly was one of the clerks in the audit office. Mr Kemmis made a mental note that they would have to speak to him. Superintendent Guy was keen to hear more about something Catherine had mentioned at the inquest: the footsteps she claimed to have heard coming from the cashier's office.

'Yes, sir. I was in the canal office, blackening the grate and making up the fire. There was no one there, but I heard Mr Little moving around in the office above.'

'How did you know it was him?'

'I felt sure it was Mr Little, on account of the creak of his boots. He seemed to be crossing the room towards the door. Then I heard the same foot coming back.'

'What time was that?'

'It was just as the first bell for the mail train rang.'

'So at about ten past seven.'

'Yes, sir.'

'And did you hear any other sound? Any more footsteps, for example?'

'No, sir, I heard nothing.'

'Did you see Mrs Gunning while you were cleaning the offices?'

'Yes, shortly afterwards I went to make up the fire in the audit office, and Mrs Gunning came in. She asked me for a box of coals.'

'Did she mention that Mr Little was still in his room, or that his light was still lit?'

'No, she said nothing of it.'

Mr Kemmis asked Catherine whether she had seen anybody else in the building after this encounter with Mrs Gunning. She thought for a moment before replying that she had seen Mr Thornton and two other gentlemen in the solicitor's clerks' office when she went up there to clean the table.

'And when you had finished your cleaning, what did you do then?'

'I went downstairs to the kitchen and took my tea.'

'What time was it then?'

'It was half-past nine. On my way to the kitchen I passed Mrs Gunning's parlour and saw the clock in the room.'

'And what did you do after that?'

'I stayed in the kitchen until the clock struck eleven. Then I lit the lamp, and went upstairs to lock all the doors.'

'When you went upstairs, was the window which looks over the platform open, or shut?'

'It was shut.'

'When you reached Mr Little's office, was his door locked?'

'It appeared to be locked. I turned the handle, and gave it a good shake.'

'Was the key in the door?'

'It was not on the outside.'

'And was there a light in the room?'

'I did not look in at the keyhole, but from outside I could not tell.'

'Did you see Mr Gunning, or Mrs Gunning, before you went to bed?'

'Yes. I went back downstairs, and about five minutes afterwards Mr Gunning came into the kitchen. Mrs Gunning was in the hall with a candle in her hand. Mrs Gunning said it was about twenty past eleven. Mr Gunning said it was time for me to turn off the gas. I went up to bolt the door on to the platform; while I was doing that I met the watchman, King, and wished him goodnight. Then I came back down and turned off the gas at the main stopcock.'

'Does that turn off all the gaslights in the building?'

'Yes, with the exception of Mr Cabry's office, Mr Moan's office, and Mr Little's office. The stopcock for those three is nearby, but I forgot it.'

'Did you say anything to Mrs Gunning about Mr Little still being in the office?'

'No, I said nothing about him to her the whole night. I thought Mr Little was gone home.'

The conversation turned to the events of the following morning. Catherine said that she had got up at 7.00, and immediately went upstairs to light fires and dust the offices. The superintendent asked whether she had visited the cashier's office.

'Yes, I went to his door and turned the handle, but it was locked and there was no key.'

'When you passed the door to the platform, did you notice whether the window was open?'

'It was shut. I am certain of that, for I was looking out down the platform.'

'Did you find it strange that Mr Little's door was locked?'

'Yes, when I saw Mrs Gunning in one of the offices I asked her if she had the key of Mr Little's office. I told her that he had been in late, so I had not had a chance to do up the fire, and that the door had been locked when I was shutting the doors last night.'

'What did Mrs Gunning say to that?'

'She said, perhaps he had papers on the table which he did not wish anybody to see, and it would not take me long to make up the fire whenever he came in.'

'And when did you hear that Mr Little had died?'

'Chamberlain has several times come down to ask for the key, and I told him that Mr Little took the key home. I said to Mrs Gunning, "That young chap that be's in the office with Mr Little was looking for the key, he's not been in," and she said, "Poor man, perhaps he's not well." About four o'clock, Mrs Gunning was ironing in the kitchen, and Mr Gunning said to me, "Kate, when were you in Mr Little's office?" I said, I was at it last night, when the door was locked, and I was at it this morning, when the door was locked. "Well," Mr Gunning said, "there is the man now found dead in his office." And he asked me why I did not turn off the gas last night. Mrs Gunning looked nervous and frightened, and she walked out of the kitchen.'

'Did she, indeed! Did Mr Gunning say how Mr Little had died?'

'No, only that he was found dead. Mrs Gunning told me to go and call Mary Jane – that's her little daughter – and not to tell her, for fear of frightening her. So I went to get her, and when I came back to the kitchen, Mrs Gunning came in and told me that Mr Little had died of apoplexy. I said, I always thought it was fat people who died of that, and Mr Little was very thin, and Mrs Gunning agreed. It was later, after dinner, when I was in the audit office, the messenger boy Doyle came in and said, Mr Little cut his throat.'

They had been speaking to Catherine for a good portion of the afternoon, and the young woman had relaxed considerably. At first the lawyer and the detective had struggled to get more than a few words from her, but now the sentences came tumbling out, a chaotic tangle of information, much of it – to Mr Kemmis's frustration – entirely irrelevant to the inquiry. After a little more inconsequential probing they thanked her for her time, and let her return to her work.

The canal was being refilled – much to the relief of the boatmen, some of whom had now been reluctant landlubbers for three days. Mr Kemmis, who had remained at the terminus until midnight on Friday, was back at seven the following morning. He did not have time to look at the newspapers, which was probably just as well. The Dublin papers were still largely supportive of the police, but the unprecedented decision not to share any details of the inquiry with journalists came in for much criticism. In the absence of solid facts, rumours were now swirling around the city. It was claimed, for instance, that the police had traced the owner of the razor, who had been arrested and charged.

It was true enough that the detectives believed that the razor might prove to be the key to the mystery. Inspector Ryan had spent a frustrating Friday afternoon trudging around the barbers, knife-grinders and cutlers of Dublin with the blade in his pocket, hoping that one of them might recognise it. It seemed the sort of task destined to end in failure, but he had returned to Broadstone with a grin on his face.

Saturday morning found Augustus Guy fighting through the crowds of Upper Ormond Quay, on the north side of the Liffey. Most were on their way to Ormond Market, one of the city's largest. On every day but Sunday its narrow seventeenth-century alleyways were packed with more than a hundred stalls, the majority of them selling meat. In every direction could be seen a joint hanging from a hook, or fish laid out in neat rows, or great slabs of fresh butter and cheese. It was a colourful scene, if not a terribly hygienic one: the cramped and airless market had been designed for a slower, less populous age, and in warmer weather the stench of rotting offal soon became too much for most shoppers to bear.

Superintendent Guy cut across the corner of the market and emerged on to Charles Street, a short thoroughfare running between the quayside and Pill Lane. For years this road had been the heart of Dublin's metal industry: of forty shops on the street, three quarters were involved in the sale or manufacture of items made from iron, zinc, copper or lead. Mr Guy's destination was number 32, a poky establishment with the words 'Flanagan – Cutler' above the door. This was a family concern, a dynasty, indeed, which had survived for more than fifty years. Its proprietors had retired, died, or – in one notorious case – been transported to Australia in chains, but the business still thrived.

The current owner was John Flanagan, an amiable fellow in his mid-forties who lived above the shop with his wife and eight children. He ushered the superintendent behind the counter and into a private room beyond. Mr Guy reached into the pocket of his greatcoat and removed the razor.

'Mr Flanagan, would I be right in saying that you have seen this razor before?'

Flanagan took it from him and examined it minutely.

'Yes, sir. About five weeks ago, to the best of my belief.'

'How can you be sure?'

'What attracted my attention to it was, I was sitting at my breakfast, as well as I can remember, when the lad – that is, my son James – brought me in a case of two razors, one of which is this one. He said they were to be ground and set. I delivered them on the Thursday evening to a man who wore a cap and a dark brown coat, and appeared to me as a working man. He paid me eightpence for grinding and setting the razors. I remember it particularly because my son joked that they looked like the razors I had given as a present to Mr Cowan, who is the foreman at the workshop where my daughter works.'

Mr Guy asked to speak to Flanagan's son James. The boy, a lad of twelve or thirteen who had been minding the shop while his father spoke to the detective, was called into the room while his father relieved him behind the counter. He looked worried, but a few gentle words from the superintendent were enough to put him at his ease.

'Now, James,' said Mr Guy, 'this razor was found at the bottom of the canal a few days ago. Have you seen it before?'

The boy turned it over in his hands before answering.

'Yes, about five weeks ago. I was in the shop, I think on a Tuesday morning, when a man came in and handed me a black case containing that and another razor. He said he wanted them both ground and set by Thursday evening.'

'You say they were in a case. What did it look like?'

'On one side it was decorated with a hound and some trees, and on the other were crosses like diamonds.'

'What about the man? Could you describe him?'

James frowned as he tried to recall the customer's features.

'He was wearing a brown frock coat with pockets in front. He had on a cap with a button on the centre of the crown. He had a dirty face, as if he had been working in a forge, and full darkish whiskers which nearly met at the chin.'

'Was he tall, or short?'

'He was not very tall.'

'Would you know him again if you saw him?'

'Yes, I think so.'

A dirty-faced man with whiskers and wearing a brown frock coat. If the Flanagans were right in thinking that the razor found in the canal was the same one they had sharpened some weeks earlier – and they seemed pretty sure of themselves – this might be a description of the murderer. That assumed, of course, that the person who had visited the shop was also the person who had wielded the blade with such merciless effect. Nevertheless, it gave them something tangible, something they might call progress.

And progress was what they needed today. Late the previous evening a messenger had been sent from Dublin Castle to Broadstone bearing an urgent memo. It informed Mr Kemmis and the superintendent that the Chief Secretary himself, Edward Horsman MP, would be pleased to inspect the murder scene and speak to the investigating officers on Saturday. A visit from the usually elusive cabinet minister – the representative in Ireland of the Westminster government – was not good news. It was an unambiguous sign of official concern, and no doubt the Chief Secretary would be making a report of his findings to the Prime Minister Lord Palmerston himself on his return to London.

For those trying to get on with the investigation, the occasion was not only an unwelcome interruption but also an absurd charade. At 4 p.m. a carriage pulled up outside the station and the lanky form of the Chief Secretary emerged, preceded by his mutton-chop whiskers. Mr Horsman was recovering from a nasty hunting accident the previous weekend, when his horse had rolled on top of him, and his movements were laboured. He was accompanied by the Lord Mayor, Alderman Joseph Boyce, clad in his chain and robes of office, and Colonel Browne, commissioner of the Metropolitan Police. It was as if some minor royal had come to lay a foundation stone or open a new building. The senior detectives dutifully lined up in the ticket hall to be introduced to the visiting dignitary, and then trailed after him as he was conducted on a tour of the premises. He made a minute inspection of the murder scene, expressing great interest in every feature pointed out to him by Mr Guy. Afterwards the VIPs were taken to the meeting room, where Superintendent Guy and the Crown Solicitor gave them a confidential briefing on the status of the inquiry. Mr Horsman declared himself 'most anxious for the discovery of the murderer', but the sentiment came across more as a threat than an expression of support.

The evening was well advanced when the deputation finally left, but for Mr Kemmis – whose appetite for work was apparently insatiable – the day had barely begun. The detectives had been warned that they were likely to remain on duty until late that night, but few had any idea quite what a marathon lay in store. It would be 5.00 on Sunday morning before they were finally allowed to go home. Few had families to go home to, for 'home' meant the police barracks, where they slept, ate and spent most of their leisure time. Only the married officers were permitted to live independently, and so exacting were the requirements for a policeman contemplating matrimony – he would have to apply to the commissioners for permission to wed, and then only if he had at least £40 in savings – that most chose to resign from the force before tying the knot.

With the official visit over, Mr Kemmis took Superintendent Guy aside and told him that he wanted the station searched again. The entire building had already been combed for evidence, but they now had good reason for thinking the murderer worked, and possibly lived, on the premises. One of the accountants had told Mr Kemmis that the stolen cash weighed somewhere between forty and fifty pounds – as much as a six-year-old child. That much money could not easily be disposed of without arousing suspicion, so it was overwhelmingly likely that it had been stashed somewhere. If the killer had any sense they might have split it between several different hiding places, or even moved it after the first sweep of the building had been completed. Mr Kemmis had another reason for wanting a second search. After the exhumation the surgeons had told him that whoever had wielded the hammer would have been liberally spattered with blood. The officers were directed to scour the building without omitting any niche or corner big enough to conceal a purse, and – a messy job, this – to rake the grates and ash buckets for any fragments of recently burnt clothing.

The Crown Solicitor decided to have another chat with Anne Gunning. He was ever more convinced that the housekeeper and her husband were hiding something from him, and possibly their servant as well. Catherine's behaviour during their interview had been strange, he thought, as if she were wrestling with her conscience, or perhaps covering up for somebody else. She might have been a willing accomplice in the business, or simply feared the consequences of telling the police all that she knew. When he went into the Gunnings' parlour for the second time, Mr Kemmis decided to find out a bit more about her.

'Mrs Gunning, I would like to ask you about Catherine Campbell. How did she come into your service?'

'She was recommended to me by Mrs Woods, who used to live opposite my sister-in-law just round the corner in Constitution Hill. Mrs Woods gave Catherine the best possible reference.'

'Did you ask others about Catherine's character before employing her?'

'No, and I have always supported her all the time she has been here.'

'Does she ever go out, or keep low company?'

'Never; the only time she goes out is on Sunday evenings, when she visits the Scotch Church in Capel Street. I sometimes see her walking with another young woman from the church.'

'Do you check on Catherine – keep an eye on her, to make sure she is doing her job properly?'

'Every morning I go after her to see that she has done her business. It is not my practice to do the same thing in the evening, but I do take particular care to lock the door at the foot of the grand staircase going into the porters' hall every evening between five and six o'clock. I always watch for the gentlemen to leave, so that I can lock that door.'

'Who keeps the key to that door?'

'I do. Mr Dolan in the accountants' office also has a key for that door, and I think my husband has another. He certainly used to.'

'Where do you keep your key?'

'In the sideboard drawer in the sitting room, and there is a spare in the cupboard in the kitchen. Nobody could get at the key to that door without going through my sitting room.'

'So you locked the door on the Thursday evening of the murder?'

'Yes, I am sure I did, at about half-past five.'

'Did you see anybody when you did so?'

'No, and I was alone. Then I went down the wooden stairs and was drying clothes after that.'

'Where was your husband that afternoon?'

'He was with me at dinner at two o'clock, then he returned to the store at about three. He came back to the sitting room, where I was, at a quarter to six by the station clock.'

'Who else was there?'

'Nobody but me and him, and the children. He told me to hurry up with the tea, as he wanted to go out on some business before the shops closed.'

'What business was that?'

'I do not know all of it, but I do know that he had to go to Mr Ireland's about some coat or other. He washed himself in the little dressing room opposite the sitting room before going out. That was straight after he had his tea, so about a quarter of an hour after he came in.'

'When did you see him next?'

'Not until after eleven. But I think it was no later than a quarter past.'

It occurred to Mr Kemmis that Bernard Gunning's alibi relied heavily on two of the other suspects: his wife, and Patrick Moan. Between them, the pair accounted for Gunning's whereabouts between 6.00 and 11.00 on the night of the murder. Could they be relied upon?

'And what did you do after he went out?'

'I stayed in the room with the children, washed up the tea things and then went to Maunders's in Church Street for bread.'

'Really! You did not tell us that before. Did you meet anybody while you were out?'

'I called in on Mrs Woods in Constitution Hill on my way back, but I did not stop there long. I came back alone, and walked into the station under the clock by the platform.'

'What time did you go out for the bread?'

'About half-past six, and I came back about a quarter past seven. Then I went up the back stairs to lower the gaslight in the offices.'

Mr Kemmis got her to repeat her account of her movements through the building, checking every detail with pedantic care. There was no apparent discrepancy.

'Mrs Gunning, was there anything you saw, or anything you did, which you omitted to tell us when first we spoke about it?'

'Well, Mr Kemmis, I told you I came downstairs after checking the offices at eight o'clock. Then I sat down here, in my sitting room, to sew. But I think I forgot to say that Mr Linskey, of the solicitor's office, and another man whom I do not know, and never saw before, came in and asked for a light. I gave them three matches to light the gas.'

'We know about that. But I meant to ask, when did you and your husband go to bed?'

'After my husband came back – that was about five past eleven – he took off his boots or shoes, whatever he was wearing, and sat for a quarter of an hour or so, and then we both went up to bed by the back stairs. When we went through the hall he told Catherine to bolt the door going out on the terminus.'

'What time was that?'

'It was twenty past eleven, by the terminus clock.'

'And when you came down to breakfast the next morning, are you sure the windows from the staircase overlooking the station platform were shut?'

'I am positive.'

As Mr Kemmis returned to his office he reflected that he had once again drawn a blank. And yet, and yet . . . Vague suspicions were starting to coalesce into something like certainty. He did not trust the Gunnings; they not only lived in the building but kept the keys to every door; and the murder weapon had been taken from the very room where Bernard Gunning worked. They might have had an accomplice, but he was becoming sure of their guilt.

His train of thought was interrupted by one of the detective constables assigned to the search. They had found something. Mr Kemmis followed him back down to the basement; not to the Gunnings' this time, but to the neighbouring apartment occupied by the stationmaster Patrick Hanbury and his family. Hanbury had already been interviewed and eliminated from the inquiry, since he had an apparently watertight alibi. On the Thursday of the murder he had remained on the station platform without a break until after 10 p.m., a fact confirmed by several of the porters. But now he looked worried, for the police had found a piece of bloody linen in the ash bucket next to his hearth.

Worse, he was entirely unable to explain what it was or how it had got there. His protestations of ignorance eventually brought his wife, who had been putting their daughters to bed, into the room. When he explained the situation to her she laughed, seem-ingly untroubled by the grave implications of the discovery made in her own home. She turned to the officers and told them that the object they had found was not clothing; it was a napkin, she said, used by their servant Mary Mitchell. Seeing that the men had not grasped her meaning, she explained, as delicately as she could, exactly what she meant by the word 'napkin'. Her husband smiled, more in relief than amusement, while a couple of the younger offi-cers shuffled their feet in embarrassment. Mr Kemmis, ever practical, merely asked whether it would be possible to speak to Mary. Summoned to the parlour, the young woman confirmed that the linen was hers and that she had burnt it.

In light of this information, Mr Kemmis thanked Mary, apologised to Hanbury and, having established that the officers had found nothing else of interest in the apartment, told them to move next door and start searching the Gunnings' home. Mr Kemmis watched this undertaking with interest. He had already noticed that Bernard Gunning owned several pieces of valuable furniture, but now he could see that he also had expensive tastes in clothes and a large wardrobe. The police also found several razors and a sword and ammunition, though no firearm in which to use it. There was no question that for a man of his apparent means, Mr Gunning owned a surprising amount of property. On the other hand, Mr Kemmis thought it possible that he had taken advantage of his position in the goods store to make money by some dubious under-the-counter method, perhaps by striking private deals with the company's suppliers.

The Crown Solicitor decided to confront him. In keeping with the conditions of secrecy under which he had decided to operate, he waited until the last detective constable had left the apartments before beginning his interrogation: only Superintendent Guy and his superiors could be party to his suspicions.

'Mr Gunning, how much do you and your wife earn?'

'My salary is one pound and sixpence a week; my wife earns fourteen shillings a week. Our house rent, light and coals are all free, but we have to meet the cost of the house servant from our own wages.'

'Have you any other source of income?'

'I make about five pounds a year in rent, from a house for which I pay the company fourteen pounds a year.'

'This is a property you let on behalf of the company?'

'That's right. I used to be a butler, you know, and until a few years ago I also drew a little extra income from working as a waiter at the Castle for parties, and so on. My present income from all sources is something like one hundred and twenty pounds a year.'

'Do you have any relations who are dependent on you?'

'There are my two little girls, the twins, who are nearly twelve. I have a sister living in England, and another who is married to a man named Reilly, who works for the company. Another used to live on Constitution Hill – her name is Bridget Nolan, and she is the widow of a guard who worked on the railway. She kept a lodging house for several years but is now a pauper in the North Dublin Union Workhouse.'

'About Mr Little. How well did you know him?'

'I knew him, of course.'

'Did you know his hours of business? When he would be in his office?'

'Yes, but I did not often go into his room.'

'When did you last go there?'

'Before he was discovered lying dead in it, the last time was on the fifth of September, when I went to get gold from him for a five-pound note.'

'Did you owe him money, Mr Gunning?'

Mr Gunning looked startled, and not a little offended.

'No. I did not owe Mr Little any money at any time.'

'But did you ever ask him for money?'

'I once asked him to lend me five pounds, but I never took it.'

Gunning was growing more agitated as he realised that he was under suspicion.

'Did you see Mr Little on the day he was murdered, Mr Gunning?'

'No!'

'That is your final word?'

'It is.'

8

Monday 24 November
Day 10 of murder inquiry

As the investigation into George Little's death entered its second week, there was no sign that public interest in the murder had in any way diminished. Letters were pouring in to Broadstone from concerned citizens offering suggestions and tip-offs. The usefulness of these communications was greatly mitigated by their sheer number, and also by the mostly anonymous correspondents' rather vague sense of what represented a clue. Some made accusations based on nothing more than tittle-tattle, and one or two even gave painstaking accounts of dreams which were supposed to explain the whole affair.

Nor were the newspapers any less obsessed with the case, despite the dearth of information available to them. A rumour that Inspector Field was about to arrive and take over appeared in print so many times that the great detective himself finally felt obliged to quash the speculation, issuing a statement to express his regret that he was engaged on another case and would be unable to travel to Dublin. But on Monday 24 November the *Evening Freeman* appeared to have a genuine scoop:

> There remains now but very little doubt as to who is the murderer of Mr Little. From a number of circumstances that have gradually transpired in the course of the investigation, the attention of the police was especially fixed on one individual. Every day's inquiry served to strengthen suspicion, which has now, we understand, become all but certainty. We have already stated

that the murderer must have been well known to Mr Little, and must have been in conversation with him at the time of the murder, and we may now add that the person on whom suspicion has fallen was well known to the unfortunate gentleman, and his business brought him into constant communication with the deceased at all hours. It is expected that an arrest will take place this evening.

Somebody had found a reliable informant, since both the Crown Solicitor and Superintendent Guy had indeed pinned their suspicions on one person: Bernard Gunning.

Even so, the suggestion that an arrest would take place on Monday evening was decidedly premature. The investigators still lacked proof of Gunning's involvement, and were uncertain whether he had an accomplice. Mr Kemmis decided to step up the inquiry, and in decisive fashion. Several railway employees including Gunning and Moan were placed under surveillance, with plain-clothes officers tailing them night and day. But the Crown Solicitor's main concern was Catherine Campbell, who he believed was being pressured by her employers to lie to the police. At Superintendent Guy's suggestion she was taken into protective custody and spirited away to another part of the city. Mr Kemmis hoped that once free of the malign influence of the Gunnings, Catherine would feel able to give an honest account of what had happened on the night of the murder.

There was another complication. Mr Kemmis had spent the entire weekend at the station interviewing and re-interviewing witnesses, and an interesting fact had emerged. Two of the audit clerks remembered a conversation in which William McCauley had claimed to be the last person to see Mr Little alive – at a quarter past five, some fifteen or twenty minutes later than he had claimed to police. Had the cash porter lied, or was he just forgetful? Mr Kemmis summoned him to the meeting room to explain himself.

'McCauley, you visited Mr Little's office several times on the day of the murder, didn't you? Would you tell us when?'

'I was there at about a quarter to ten, half-past eleven, half-past two, half-past three, half-past four and five o'clock. Six times altogether.'

'I put it to you, McCauley, that you are not telling us everything.'

'No, sir, I have a clear recollection of that Thursday. I was six times in his, in Mr Little's, office. Or it might be seven.'

'Tell us what happened on the last of those occasions. What time was it?'

'I called at five o'clock for the money boxes. There was no one in the office except Mr Little. I picked up the boxes myself, as they had been put out for me. There were six boxes, on that occasion: they were outside the railing, on a bench.'

'Was the door open?'

'It was shut, but not locked.'

'Where was the key to the door?'

'I do not remember, but my impression is that it was inside the door, in the lock.'

'How do you know that it was five o'clock when you went to his office?'

'I generally leave the platform to go to his office about three minutes to five, and I am sure it must have been five o'clock when I was there that Thursday.'

'You told us last time that you were on the platform at five o'clock, and watched the five o'clock train pull away from the station. Why have you changed your mind?'

'Well, sir, on the Friday as I was passing through the locomotive gate, I heard from the watchman that Mr Little had cut his throat – it was then about half-past one. I said I had not heard that, and that it was not possible that a man as steady and calm should do such a thing as that. The whole thing made me think over when I had last seen Mr Little alive, and having been in his office at five o'clock. At that moment, when the watchman told me about it, I believed I was the last person to see him alive. I do not believe so now, because Mr Burns from the audit office told me, maybe two or three days afterwards, that somebody else had seen Mr Little a good while after. I asked him when he was seen, and Mr Burns replied, at half-past five. Nothing else was said.'

McCauley looked nervous, and his curiously illogical answer caused the detective and Mr Kemmis to exchange a sceptical glance.

'When you were in Mr Little's office, where was he? Was he sitting at his desk, or standing?'

'He was not sitting in his usual place but moving about, with his back to me, between the counter and the table. I was there for no longer than a couple of minutes.'

'The railing in the counter has a little hatch in it, for passing money through. Was it open or shut?'

'It was shut.'

'Did you see anybody in the corridor or the offices nearby on your way out?'

'There was nobody in the passage. The door of Mr Moan's office was open and there was a light in it, though I could not hear anybody in that office.'

'What were you wearing that evening?'

'Just the usual. My corduroy suit. I always wear it, except for a few hours on a Sunday. I have had it about four months.'

'Did you wear your suit even in the coal vault?'

'Yes, I had a coat on over it.'

Did McCauley's retraction of his earlier evidence change anything? Mr Kemmis was not at all sure that it did, although he had to concede that it was a discrepancy worth investigating further.

There was another loose end to be gathered up from the previous week's interviews. Catherine Campbell had mentioned seeing one of the audit clerks, John Jolly, hanging about the office after most of the staff had left on the evening of the murder. She had not seemed sure of herself, but it was a matter that needed clearing up. Jolly was summoned from his office to see the Crown Solicitor. A bachelor in his thirties, he lodged in a cheap hotel on Capel Street.

'Mr Jolly, did you often visit Mr Little's office?'

'No, I did not usually have business there. I have not been in that office for two months, except once when I went to deliver a message.'

'Would you tell us about that Thursday evening, the day of Mr Little's death?'

'Yes, that morning I had come up to town from Mullingar, where I had been on company business. I left the office with the other clerks at five o'clock, then I went to the transfer office, where I met Magee, Green and Chamberlain. We all went out together, but I came back on my own to retrieve my railway rug, which I had taken with me to Mullingar.'

Jolly confirmed Chamberlain's story – that the young man had begged him for a donation to the orphans' charity, and that after much pestering he had eventually handed over 6d.

'And what did you do after that?' asked the superintendent.

'Went into my lodgings. There were several people in the parlour, I remember. Then I went out again, say at half-past six.'

'Where did you go?'

'To the Cornmarket.'

'What time was it then?'

'About seven, I suppose; I can't be certain. Then I walked from there to Nassau Street, just to while away the time, returned home, and went to bed about nine.'

This route would have taken Jolly past Christ Church Cathedral and Dublin Castle and as far east as Trinity College – but it seemed an odd choice for an evening stroll, particularly on a dark November night.

'It would take you only twenty minutes or so to walk from the Cornmarket to Nassau Street, surely. Is that all you did during those two hours?'

'Yes.'

'And what took you to the Cornmarket? Did you have business there?'

'No, I just felt like a walk.'

But the clerk's face told another story. Superintendent Guy pressed the point.

'Mr Jolly, if you are deceiving us, we will find it out. What were you doing there?'

'I have told you everything.'

Mr Jolly would say no more, and sat in stubborn silence. Sensing that further attempts to breach his defences would be ineffective, Mr Kemmis decided to return to the fray on a later occasion. He dismissed the clerk with a curt warning that he would soon be asked to speak to them again.

At lunchtime the investigation was interrupted by another official visit, this time from the Attorney General John FitzGerald. Mr Kemmis was only too happy to see him, since he greatly respected his superior's judgement and expertise. A member of Parliament, an experienced Queen's Counsel and the senior law officer in Ireland, FitzGerald was somebody whose opinion was always worth hearing. Mr Kemmis had been giving him regular updates, and on more than one occasion sought his advice, since taking on the murder investigation. They spent more than two hours together in the meeting room, discussing what was to be done next. Mr FitzGerald pointed out a couple of glaring deficiencies in their knowledge. They had found the murder weapon; but where was the money, or the key to Mr Little's door? If they could find these items, and associate them with a suspect, they would have a compelling case. It was also necessary to establish the route taken by the murderer in leaving the building – especially since he had done so unnoticed, despite being weighed down by a considerable quantity of cash.

The afternoon had another surprise in store. Shortly after the meeting ended, Bennett from the accountants' office came to see

Mr Kemmis. He had remembered something, he said, which he thought might be important. At the Crown Solicitor's invitation he sat down and explained.

'At the time of Mr Little's appointment I told him to keep his door shut, as pilfering was well known to have been going on. He declined, because he was worried that people would feel insulted. About a month later he came to tell me that his cash was short by fifty pounds, but that he would on no account wish the directors to know it, lest they might think him inefficient. He said that he would borrow a portion of it from a gentleman he knew in town, and that he would make up the remainder.'

'Interesting! And do you know who this gentleman was?'

'Yes, a day or two after that he said that he had borrowed twenty pounds from Mr Egan, and he showed me the cheque Egan had given him.'

'So the directors never learned of it?'

'No, not as far as I know.'

'And did you ever discover who had taken the fifty from Mr Little's office?'

'Well, a very short time afterwards Mr Moore, from the transfer office, told me that he had seen Robert Fair, George Green and James Magee, all clerks in the company's service, near Marlborough Street, quite drunk, as if they had been out all night. After hearing this I went to Mr Little and asked him for his opinion of Fair. He said he would not suspect a man without proof, but he heard that Fair was given to drink. Mr Little said that he would get Fair moved to the audit office, so that he could be alone by himself. But then he asked me casually what I thought of Collins, the railway sergeant, as he would be reassured to know that he bore a good character.'

'What did you tell him?'

'That I could not say from my own knowledge, but that I would make enquiries. Afterwards I went several times to Superintendent Hodgens's house and asked about Collins. Hodgens told me that Collins was a man of sound character, and that he would trust him with his life.'

The conversation lasted only a few minutes, but by the time Bennett left the meeting room the Crown Solicitor's head was spinning from the plethora of names thrown at him. When he considered what the clerk had told him, Mr Kemmis realised that it boiled down to three simple facts. First, a substantial sum had been stolen from George Little's office some months before his death. Second, there was circumstantial evidence suggesting that one of the clerks, Robert Fair, was the thief. Third, Mr Little had had doubts about the honesty of Sergeant Collins, the railway policeman who often visited the cashier's office to pick up the company wages. Mr Kemmis must now add these two names to his list of suspects. He went to find Mr Guy to tell him about it. They agreed that the detective should take some of his men to search Robert Fair's house and question him, and afterwards speak to the railway policemen. As for Mr Kemmis, he had an appointment on the roof.

The Crown Solicitor had no intention of venturing out on to the great iron and glass canopy himself. As soon as he realised that the detectives' supposedly top-to-bottom search of the build-ing had omitted its highest and most prominent feature he had applied to the company secretary for help. Mr Beausire was aware that there was a man who regularly went up on to the roof to look after the glazing, but he did not know the fellow's name. He scribbled a note to the chief carpenter Mr Brophy, and sent a messenger boy to take it to him in the locomotive workshop. Not long afterwards a heavily bewhiskered man in a corduroy work suit knocked at the door and introduced himself as one of the carriage painters. His manner was pleasant, and his face was handsome; but the feature most people noticed straight away was the blank patch of skin where his right eye should have been. Mr Kemmis did not catch the man's name, but recognised him from his visit to the locomotive shed the previous week. The painter was one of several labourers who had hung around the door to the storeroom during the first interrogation of Mr Gunning, hoping to pick up some fragment of gossip.

The Crown Solicitor explained that he needed somebody to inspect the roof and look for anything unusual: marks, discarded items or indications that it might have been used as an escape route. They went upstairs to the cashier's office, opened the gate in the wooden counter and approached the window by Mr Little's desk. Mr Kemmis asked the man about his work, and learned that he had originally been employed to caulk the roof, which needed constant maintenance. Over the years he had evolved into the Broadstone handyman, fitting windows, painting door frames and doing minor repairs around the place. By way of illustration he pointed at the security screen, recently installed at Mr Little's request, and explained that he had varnished it. The pleasantries over, the painter opened the window and climbed out on to the roof. Mr Kemmis watched him pick his way carefully over the duckboards that provided a safe route across the fragile glass panes, examining every inch as he went. He disappeared from view for a few minutes, eventually returning the way he had come. When he had clambered back into the room, Mr Kemmis asked what he had found.

'Nothing, sir. I looked closely but could make out no traces of anyone going over the roof or down the wall.'

The Crown Solicitor thanked him for his time. The man made as if to leave, but hesitated.

'There's one other thing, sir. The detective officers spoke to me last week, but afterward I remembered something I did not tell them. My wife and I live in a cottage nearby. We were at home on the evening of the murder, but late that night we went out to buy food. As we returned, about ten o'clock, we saw the girl Catherine Campbell on the platform talking with a police constable.'

'Did you recognise him?'

'Yes, sir. I believe his name is Hobson.'

'Thank you for telling me. But I'm afraid I have forgotten your name.'

'Spollin, sir. James Spollin.'

It was late when the Crown Solicitor finally had a chance to sit down and make a note of the various conversations he had had that day. Either fatigue or a lapse in memory caused him to record that he had gleaned this important piece of evidence from 'Smollen, the painter'.

Early the following morning an exclusively male crowd gathered at the front of the Broadstone terminus. Most wore brightly coloured clothes, while others were dressed in the overalls of labourers. Abruptly they split into groups of three and scattered in every direction, like gaudy shrapnel from a slow-motion explosion. This exhibition was the brainchild of Augustus Guy, who had decided to conduct a search of the entire Broadstone estate, looking for money and the elusive key. He had requested the assistance of every available officer from all seven divisions of the Metropolitan Police, and their striking apparel was intended as an aid to identification, each division allocated its own colour. Each pair of officers was accompanied by a railway worker to act as guide. During the course of the morning they would explore every outbuilding, every cupboard and cellar – without the slightest hint of success.

Tuesday also brought news from Liverpool, where for a few thrilling hours it appeared that the murderer of George Little had been captured. Late the previous week a man had arrived in the city on a boat from Ireland, and took a room at a hotel a short distance from the docks. He was travelling without luggage, but appeared to have plenty of cash. His conduct was erratic, so much so that it attracted the attention of hotel staff, who kept an eye on his movements. He ate expensively and drank heavily. His manner was strange, and a general sense that all was not right with him was strengthened when he summoned the hotel boot boy and gave him £60 in cash, asking him to take care of it for him.

Things came to a head one evening in the dining room when the Irishman, who had been muttering to himself, shocked the other guests by leaping up from his chair and shouting wildly, 'I did not kill him, I did not kill him! I only gave him two blows of a hammer in the back of the head. I did not cut his throat.'

Somebody ran for a policeman, who arrested him. When questioned he was barely coherent, saying again and again that he had 'not cut the man's throat', adding that the police had tracked him down in Athlone, but he had managed to elude them. The Liverpool detectives believed that they had caught the Broadstone killer, but one of the officers began to wonder if their suspect was in fact an alcoholic in the grip of delirium tremens. A doctor was called to examine him, and confirmed that their prisoner was not a wicked criminal, but simply suffering from acute alcohol poisoning.

After medical treatment his symptoms were relieved, and it emerged that the Irishman, who was genuinely from Athlone, had been experiencing psychotic episodes for some days before his departure. During the voyage over the Irish Sea he had been reading newspaper reports of the murder, and developed the extraordinary delusion that he was the actual murderer. Subsequent inquiries established that he had in fact arrived on a steamer from Belfast, not Dublin; and though he was travelling with a suspiciously large sum of money he was able to explain its provenance to the satisfaction of the police. That brought the inglorious tally to four suspects arrested and four released without charge, since the police had concluded that the Cullens, the couple from the Stoneybatter pub who had been brought before the magistrate a few days earlier, were also innocent.

Augustus Guy had no particularly startling news to offer Mr Kemmis that morning. Inspector Ryan had interviewed Robert Fair, the young man suspected of pilfering money from the cashier's office, and searched his residence. Nothing had been found, and Fair hotly denied any suggestion of wrongdoing. When asked about his whereabouts on the night of the murder he claimed to have been drinking in Carroll's, a public house in Great Britain Street which was the usual haunt of the junior clerks. Few alibis are as straightforward to check as one involving a pub, and it took very little time for the inspector to find a saloon bar's worth of witnesses prepared to confirm Fair's story. Similar results followed Mr Guy's conversations with Superintendent Hodgens and Sergeant Collins, the railway policemen. They were both in the clear, as far as he was concerned. Still, this was not necessarily bad news, since it served only to strengthen suspicions against Bernard Gunning.

And there was one positive development. Mr Guy had also spoken to Abraham Hobson, the railway constable who had been on duty on the night of the murder. Hobson had returned from his supper break shortly before the arrival of the 10.00 'up' train. He was standing by the gate watching the locomotive draw into the station when Catherine Campbell approached him. She asked the constable to look out for Mary Mitchell, Mrs Hanbury's servant, if she was on the 10.00 train, and pass on a message to say that Catherine wanted to see her. Mary had not been on the train, and the constable had not thought the incident of any importance; but it disproved Catherine's claim that she had spent the entire evening in Directors' House. What else might she have lied about?

Finding out would have to wait. The pressing business of the day was a second interview with Patrick Moan, who was suspected of providing a false alibi for Bernard Gunning – and perhaps of being his accomplice in the murder. Mr Kemmis, the superintendent and a small contingent of detectives went to his house in Phibsborough Road. While the two senior investigators interrogated the clerk, the other officers subjected his apartments to what was euphemistically referred to in the Crown Solicitor's notes as a 'close search'. By the time they had finished, his living quarters looked as if they had been ransacked by a horde of marauding Vikings.

Mr Kemmis began by asking Moan to account for his movements on the evening of the murder.

'I left my office about five minutes before five o'clock. I went down the grand staircase . . .'

'Did you meet anyone, or see anyone in the corridor?'

'I did not see anyone from when I left my room until I reached the platform, to my knowledge.'

'Did you see Mr Tough, or Mr Chamberlain, or McCauley the porter?'

'No, none of them.'

'Did you notice whether Mr Little's door was open or closed?'

'No.'

Moan repeated his account of his meeting with Gunning and Osborne at the equipment stores, and their discussion about the planned dinner at the European Hotel. Superintendent Guy interrupted.

'Did Gunning tell you that he was planning to go to Molony's that evening?'

'No, it was later that I learned he had been there to apprise Molony of our visit, so that he could have the menu ready for us.'

'What time was it when you left the storeroom?'

'I remained there for a time talking with Osborne. I think it was after six o'clock when I left. I then went home through the locomotive yard. My wife was there with the servant girl, Margaret Lowry, and my nephew Michael Burke, who is about eleven.'

'Did you go out again afterwards?'

'Well, my dinner was not ready, so my wife went to get it ready. About half an hour later I ate it and had a tumbler of punch. I did not go out at all that night, but went to bed.'

'Mr Moan, are you telling us the truth? Were you really at home on Thursday night?'

'I am quite certain I was at home on Thursday night. I went home direct from the goods store and did not go out at all.'

'Do you often see Mr Gunning? Do you know any of his friends?'

'Yes, very often, but I do not know any of his friends.'

The superintendent asked Mr Moan to show him any shoes or boots he might own. The clerk looked rather startled.

'I have none, except those I am wearing. Oh, and there is one old pair of boots which used to belong to Mr Wilson, the engineer who left.'

Superintendent Guy asked him to fetch them. The clerk went away and soon returned with a dusty pair of boots. A cursory inspection was enough to satisfy the detective that they had not been worn for many months.

'What about those you are wearing? Take them off, please; I should like to examine them.'

Mr Moan obeyed, but the detective noticed that he seemed anxious. When the policeman turned the boots over to examine the soles, Moan offered what sounded very much like an excuse.

'Recollect, Mr Guy, I was in the room near the body.'

'I am examining the heels, Mr Moan, but not for blood. Nobody said anything about blood.'

Both Moan's wife and his young nephew confirmed the clerk's claim that he had not left home that Thursday night, but the encounter served only to strengthen Mr Kemmis's suspicions. Moan had looked genuinely frightened when the superintendent asked to look at his footwear, and his strange reaction was not obviously that of an innocent man. It was not long before his troubles grew deeper.

The Moans lived on the first floor of a building near the locomotive workshop. The stairs to their apartment came down directly to the 'locomotive gate', which opened on to Phibsborough Road. At the bottom of the staircase was a cubicle not much bigger than a sentry box, from which a bored watchman spent most of the day observing the railway employees come and go. As Mr Kemmis and the superintendent walked outside, this gentleman was in residence, stamping his feet to ward off the cold. A thought occurred to the Crown Solicitor. He introduced himself to the watchman, a man in his late forties named Edwin Moore. Mr Kemmis asked him if he knew Mr Moan.

'Yes, I know him.'

'What time does he generally come home in the evening?'

'Usually about ten o'clock, sometimes later.'

'Did you see him the night that Mr Little was killed?'

'Yes, I saw him that night. The other watchman, George Slack, and I take it in turns to be on duty, night and day. On the night of the murder I came on duty at eight o'clock. Mr Moan came in by the locomotive gate at nine o'clock, or thereabouts. I remember the time because I had a toothache, and was walking up and down with a hand to my jaw, and because I thought of the time when I heard next day that Mr Little was murdered.'

'What was he wearing? Was he alone?'

'He had no top coat on, I remember that. There was nobody with him when he came to the gate.'

Mr Kemmis thanked the watchman, and set off back towards the station building with the superintendent. It was only by happy accident that they had discovered a flaw in Mr Moan's story, but now they must regard his entire alibi as unsafe. The fact that his wife and nephew had backed him up suggested that this was not a simple oversight, but that he had persuaded them to collude in his deception. It was tempting to go straight back upstairs and challenge Moan with this new information, but Mr Kemmis had a better idea. He trotted back to the gate where Edwin Moore was standing in his little box, and had a quick word with the watchman. Returning to Mr Guy, he answered the detective's quizzical look by explaining that he had told Moore that he should not feel bound to keep the fact of his encounter with the police to himself. Moan would soon hear about it, and realise that the truth of his story was in question. It would be interesting to see how he reacted. If he had any sense he would approach the detectives to explain the discrepancy before they came looking for him. But if he had anything to hide, Moan might easily panic and do something stupid. At least he was now under surveillance: if he started to behave strangely, or even decided to abscond, the police would soon know about it.

Back in his temporary HQ a little while later, Mr Kemmis asked one of the detective sergeants to fetch the audit clerk John Jolly from his office at the other end of the corridor. When the clerk walked into the room he gave every sign of wishing he could turn round and go straight out again. Jolly's refusal to be frank during his previous interview had convinced the Crown Solicitor that greater incentives would be needed to make him talk, and at his request several of the railway company directors had agreed to sit in on this second encounter. Jolly eyed them warily as he sat down. Mr Kemmis did not bother with preamble.

'Mr Jolly, we asked to see you again because we believe you have not told us everything about the evening of the murder. You said that you had been for a walk to "while away the time". But that isn't true, is it? Where did you go?'

Jolly did not answer, evidently unable to deny the charge. The Crown Solicitor let him sweat for a minute or two before repeating the question.

'I am sorry, sir, I had rather not say.'

'You must tell us, Jolly.'

The clerk regarded Mr Kemmis unhappily.

'I cannot tell you, sir. It will stop my chance of promotion.'

One of the directors intervened.

'Jolly, a man is dead, and you are worrying about your promotion! We –' he waved a condescending hand in the approximate direction of his fellow directors – 'are here today because the chairman has promised that all company staff will cooperate absolutely with the police. You have some secret which you do not wish us to know. That may harm your prospects, or it may not; but if you wish to continue working here at all, I insist that you answer the Crown Solicitor's question.'

Jolly was cornered, and he knew it.

'All right, sir, I will tell you. I was at a pawnbroker's – Halbert's, on Cornmarket.'

'And what were you doing there?'

'Redeeming a pair of trousers. I had pawned them for twelve shillings, as I wanted some cash to go down to Mullingar Fair.'

This was certainly an embarrassing admission for a respectable clerk to make in front of his superiors, but Mr Kemmis was not convinced that it was what he had been trying to hide.

'We can easily check that, Mr Jolly, and we shall. Now you have admitted misleading us, would you tell us where you were at half-past five that evening? You were in the audit office, were you not?'

'No, sir, I was not there.'

'You were. The maid is positive that she saw you there.'

'If she says that, she must be mistaken. I did not see her that evening.'

Superintendent Guy turned round and exchanged a few words with the policeman standing next to the door. The constable left the room and returned shortly afterwards, accompanied by Catherine Campbell.

'Now, Catherine,' said Superintendent Guy, 'is this the man you saw in the audit office?'

'Yes, sir, I believe it is.'

Jolly looked shocked.

'It is not true! Superintendent, Mr Kemmis, I swear to you, she is mistaken. I was not there.'

They were at an impasse, since Catherine Campbell and John Jolly were equally adamant that the other was wrong. Seeing no point in continuing the conversation, Mr Kemmis sent Catherine away and allowed Jolly to return to his office. Superintendent

Guy instructed several of his officers to search the clerk's accommodation. They returned an hour or two later, empty-handed. The other residents of the hotel in Capel Street where Jolly lodged could not say what time he had come home that evening, and there was nothing suspicious in his room. The officers had then visited the pawnbroker, who confirmed that Jolly had come to collect a pair of trousers pawned a few days earlier. This corroboration went some way to clearing him, although there was also the question of whether Catherine could really have seen him. It was not until several days later that the point was finally cleared up to everybody's satisfaction. Another of the clerks came forward to say that the man in the office had not been Jolly but a former employee, recently returned from military service in the Crimea, who had dropped in to visit his old colleagues. Desultory efforts were made to trace this person, but without success; it did not matter, for the police had by now realised that he was not the man they were looking for.

9

I f Dublin rumour was to be believed, an arrest was merely hours
away. His name was not mentioned in print, but it was widely
known that Bernard Gunning was the man suspected of the crime.
Both the Crown Solicitor and Superintendent Guy accepted,
however, that the case against him was flimsy and purely circumstantial. Until they unearthed some damning piece of evidence – or
Gunning unwittingly led undercover officers to the place where
he had hidden the money – an arrest would be premature.

On Wednesday Mr Kemmis had arranged to pay a visit to
George Little's home in Ballsbridge. Intruding on the family's
grief was no small matter, and he had thought it best to leave a
decent interval before calling on them. But it was also essential.
The dead man had been such an intensely private person that his
colleagues knew little about him. Unlikely as it seemed, it was
possible that he had financial troubles, or that his placid exterior
had concealed some personal turmoil. If he had secrets, perhaps
he had shared them with his closest relatives.

It was late morning when the carriage containing Mr Kemmis
and the superintendent drew up in front of 58 Waterloo Road.
The door was opened by one of George's female cousins, who
was there to look after his sister and elderly mother for a few
weeks. The two investigators were shown into the parlour while
the cousin went upstairs to announce their arrival. A few minutes
later George's sister Kate entered the room, dressed in mourning.
It was now ten days since she had braved the November wind to

stand in Mount Jerome, the local Protestant cemetery, watching her brother's coffin being lowered into his grave. Now he was gone, she stood to lose everything. What little savings she and her mother had would soon be exhausted, and then they would have to give up their comfortable home.

The future must have seemed bleak, and yet Kate Morton conducted herself with a stoical dignity which could not fail to impress. She accepted the Crown Solicitor's condolences graciously, and submitted to his questions without complaint. Mr Kemmis began by paying tribute to her brother's character; all who knew George Little, he said, seemed to have liked and admired him.

'George had a very peculiarly conscientious mind,' said Kate. 'He was a member of the Exclusive Brethren, and because of his religious beliefs he would not say anything unkind, or allow anything unkind to be said in his presence – he would not even tolerate anybody to be accused of a misdeed without the clearest proof.'

Mr Kemmis asked about his daily habits. Kate mentioned that he often returned late, but had not expected to do so on the day of his death.

'And, apart from you, who resides in this house?'

'There is our mother, who is so deaf that people must write to communicate with her; and her sister, Mrs Walker, who is in delicate health and often confined to her room.'

'Had George any property, or insurance on his life?'

'None apart from this house, which belongs to my mother.'

'So nobody stood to gain financially from his death?'

'No one.'

'Have you heard him speak of the people who worked with him in the office?'

Kate answered in the affirmative, so Mr Guy ran through a few names. When he mentioned the Gunnings she suddenly became animated.

'I have frequently heard him mention Gunning; indeed, within four or five weeks of his death I am certain, most positive, that he mentioned Gunning coming into his office, but I could not say for what.'

'Are you quite sure? Mr Gunning told us that he has not been in your brother's office since September the fifth.'

'If he says that, it is simply false. My brother was a very accurate man.'

Mr Kemmis shot Superintendent Guy a meaningful glance before continuing.

'It now appears that a great deal of money was stolen from your brother's office. As far as you know, was anything taken from his person?'

'He had a small wallet or pocket-book, with a rubber band around it, which he used to keep in his pocket. He kept a few documents in it, notes for some money owed him by some of the clerks. After his death I was sent his watch and spectacles, which were found in his room, but not the pocket-book, which is still missing.'

'You say that some of the clerks owed him money. Do you know which ones?'

'Young Moore owed him a pound, and begged him not to mention the debt to anybody. Burns, a clerk in the audit office, also owed a pound, but had paid half of it back. And he had lent a man called Hodgens two pounds, but I think he had paid back one pound already.'

'And was there anything else in the pocket-book? Any money, for instance?'

'I believe he may have had some banknotes, perhaps ten pounds, which was what he said he had left until his salary was next due.'

Mr Guy asked whether he had any enemies at the terminus. There had been stiff competition for the position of cashier earlier in the year; had anybody resented his appointment?

'I believe my brother thought that all the officials and clerks were pleased that he had won the position.'

'The company secretary, Mr Beausire, told us that some

money had gone missing from his office a few months ago. Did he say anything about it to you?'

'Yes, I recollect it. When he told me about it I alluded to the person generally suspected of taking it, and he interrupted me, saying that until there was proof I was not to mention any names. He never told me who he suspected, but I feel certain that he believed that Mr Fair took the money.'

If they had only been investigating the theft of the £50, Superintendent Guy felt sure that they would have little difficulty proving that Robert Fair was their culprit. It was unfortunate that he was demonstrably innocent of the crime they were actually trying to solve.

Afterwards Mr Kemmis and the superintendent agreed that they had picked up at least one interesting new fact. There was the clear suggestion that Gunning had been a much more frequent visitor to the cashier's office than he claimed. But it was George Little's informal role as the station moneylender that most surprised them, and the disappearance of the wallet in which he had kept the IOUs recording these loans seemed significant. Kate had mentioned three of his 'clients', who included the former Metropolitan Police officer, Superintendent Hodgens. The latter had already been ruled out as a suspect, but Mr Kemmis was interested in finding out more about the other two. Superintendent Guy had not heard of 'young Moore' but had met Burns, an audit clerk.

Once they were back in their incident room at Broadstone, Mr Guy sent a constable to fetch Richard Russell, the railway company's audit superintendent. The six clerks who worked for him in the audit office included George Burns – now known to have borrowed money from Mr Little – and Isaac Christian, who since the murder had taken over as acting cashier. As Mr Russell reeled off the names of his six employees he let slip that Mr Christian was the brother-in-law of Mr Nugent. Mr Kemmis was intrigued.

'Do you mean the Nugent who was formerly cashier? The embezzler?'

'Yes, that is correct. Mr Nugent is at present living at Killucan. He left last March, having stolen large sums from the company. Mr Christian was appointed temporary cashier when he left.'

'Really! Rather a strange arrangement.'

'Yes, he acted as such for ten weeks, but on account of his connection with Nugent he could not get a recommendation for the permanent position, so Mr Little was appointed instead. Christian has been with us about six years.'

'And how about the other clerks?'

'I got Landy in, about three years ago. Mr Jolly joined a year and a half before that, as did Burns. Kelly came to us from the goods store three months ago to replace a man named John Henry Moore, who I had dismissed.'

Mr Kemmis inferred, correctly, that this was 'young Moore', who had owed Mr Little money. He asked Mr Russell why the youth was sacked.

'Inattention to business, and coming in with drink on him. On one occasion Fair's mother visited the office and complained to me that Moore was in the habit of taking her boy to brothels. Moore's father still works here, in the transfer office.'

'Have you ever lent money to your clerks?'

'Yes, on occasion. I have lent to Burns and young Moore – say a pound, or thirty shillings.'

'And have you ever borrowed money from Mr Little?'

'I once borrowed a pound from him, but I repaid it, of course.'

Conversation turned to Mr Russell's role in the company. He was one of the officials responsible for checking the cashier's accounts, and he confirmed that they had been in order up to the week of his death. He told Mr Kemmis that he had been the last person in the office on the evening of the murder, since he liked to stay until the last of his clerks had finished work.

'What did you do on leaving the office?'

'I went straight home. I was on my own, and stayed at home the whole night. I came in the next morning at half-past nine.'

This was no sort of alibi, but the audit superintendent was not regarded as a suspect. He was an old and trusted servant of the company, and there was something about his stolid, dependable presence that inspired confidence. Mr Kemmis was much more interested in his former subordinate John Henry Moore, the inadequate clerk, daytime drinker and corrupter of youth. He asked how he could get in touch with the young man, and was pleased to learn that his father was at that moment in the building. Archibald Moore turned out to be Mr Russell's counterpart in the transfer office, the department that oversaw the issue and exchange of shares in the company. Mr Russell was excused, and after a short discussion with Mr Guy, the Crown Solicitor sent for Mr Moore.

The superintendent of the transfer office was in his early fifties, and lived in respectable prosperity in a large house in south Dublin. He and his wife had a son and two daughters, and shared their home with three lodgers and a servant. Mr Kemmis was quite clear about his reasons for summoning him.

'Mr Moore, I would like to talk to you about your son. He used to work with you here, I believe?'

'Yes, sir; John Henry is his name. He was a clerk in the audit office, but it is now two months or so since he was dismissed.'

'And why was he dismissed?'

'He was inattentive to his duties.'

'Where is he now?'

'At home, in all probability.'

'Cast your mind back to the day of Mr Little's murder, if you will. What time did you leave the office that day?'

'I left at close to five o'clock and walked out through the front door of the station, then went straight home.'

'Did you meet anybody on your way out? Your son, perhaps?'

'Nobody. I did not see my son anywhere near the station that day, or when I went home either, as I was displeased with him and avoided him. But I believe I saw him go out through the hall door at about half-past seven.'

'What time did he return?'

'I did not see him again that evening, and do not know when he came in. I did not see him again until Friday night. When he came in then I was in bed, and called out, "John, have you heard of that sad catastrophe of poor Little's?" And John said, "Oh yes; the Lord be praised it was not you."'

That was all that Archibald Moore could tell them. Mr Guy went in search of Inspector Ryan, and eventually located him in the coal cellars underneath the station platform. Ryan was supervising yet another search for the stolen money, and around him constables equipped with oil lanterns and shovels were sifting through piles of coal. They performed this task with vigour but manifest lack of enthusiasm, as it was not the first time they had been asked to do so. Most of the men were already contemplating the long washroom queues and tepid water that awaited them when they returned to barracks, filthy with soot, many hours later. The superintendent told Ryan briefly what he had learned, and asked him to speak to the other audit office clerks, establish whether any had borrowed money from Mr Little, and check their alibis. First of all, however, he was to find and interview John Henry Moore.

Exactly a fortnight after George Little had walked briskly over the Liffey, through the crowded streets of central Dublin and towards a violent and lonely death, Thomas Kemmis retraced his route towards Broadstone. It was a glorious, cloudless morning, and the stroll would have been an uplifting experience were it not for thought of the melancholy two-week landmark. Since being brought in to advise on the case ten days earlier he had thought of little else, and now minor oddments of information gathered during the inquiry constantly rearranged themselves inside his head. Occasionally this animated mental collage would threaten to fall into some sort of neat order; but however hard Mr Kemmis tried to wrestle it into a portrait of the murderer, the picture obstinately remained a chaotic abstract.

No matter how early the Crown Solicitor arrived at Broadstone, there was always some new piece of intelligence waiting for him – although many of the reports he received told him simply that there was nothing to report. The detectives placed on surveillance duties had endured a tedious night watching Gunning and Moan go about their usual business: neither had done anything more interesting than buy groceries or visit a local pub. Inspector Ryan had been to see John Henry Moore, who turned out to have been drinking with Robert Fair and his pals on the evening of the murder, and whose alibi was therefore unassailable. After that Ryan had spoken to the remaining audit clerks, several of whom admitted to borrowing money from Mr Little. All had repaid the sums in full or in part, and all could account for their whereabouts on the night of his death.

The main business of the day would be speaking to the legal clerks who worked in the solicitor's office, two of whom had been working late on the night of the murder. Given that they had, in all probability, been in the building at the time of George Little's death, it was strange that he had not got round to speaking to them sooner. Their boss was the solicitor himself, Walter Kirwan, who told Mr Kemmis that his six clerks had all left the building at about 5.30; he had stayed a little longer to finish his work and lock up. Three of the clerks – Thornton, Kearney and Linskey – had returned to the building later in the evening to do some urgent drafting.

Henry Thornton, who was next to be shown into the room, confirmed that he had come back to Broadstone at about 7.00 and remained till 11.05. He and his colleague Mr Kearney arrived and left together, and spent the entire four-hour period ensconced in their office. The Crown Solicitor asked whether he had seen or heard anybody else during this period.

'Yes: Linskey, another clerk, came into the office about eight, and remained about two or three minutes. Shortly afterward the female servant –' by which he meant Catherine Campbell – 'came in, and washed a large office table.'

'At what time was that?'

'About half-past eight, as I best remember.'

'When you returned to work at seven o'clock, the main door at the foot of the grand staircase would have been locked, would it not? How did you reach your office?'

'Yes, we descended to the basement floor, and up the back staircase to the first floor, and into the office.'

'Was there anybody there when you arrived?'

'No, I found it vacant.'

'Did you see anybody on the staircase, or in the corridor, as you left the building?'

'Not as far as I remember. I did not see even a policeman or porter when I was leaving at eleven o'clock.'

Kearney's statement was a virtual facsimile of Thornton's. Things became more interesting when Michael Linskey came to talk to the investigators. It was Linskey who had visited the basement to get a light from Mrs Gunning. His evidence on that point was disappointing. He had been in the building only briefly, and noticed nothing worthy of mention. But the following day, shortly after the discovery of Mr Little's body, he had met Patrick Moan just outside the terminus building. Moan, who had been searching in vain for a doctor, was in a strangely excited state. He had asked whether Mr Little was dead, and did not react when Linskey told him that yes, the cashier's throat had been cut. Linskey had then bumped into Moan a little later in town, and noticed that he was still in the same agitated condition.

This in itself was not especially noteworthy: who would not be upset by the savage murder of a colleague? But, as Linskey explained to Mr Kemmis, a subsequent encounter with Moan had made him think again about his behaviour on that awful day.

'On Monday last, November 24, I went into Harris's Hotel in Upper Dominick Street for a meeting with Mr Mason, who works for the railway company's parliamentary agents. On entering I had my top coat on, and I saw Mr Moan, who at first I did not recognise, in conversation with Mr Mason, who was quite ignorant that Mr Moan had any connection with the company. We then got into conversation, and Mr Moan – who, I believe, had previously ordered a treat for Mr Mason and himself – asked me what I would drink. I refused, said I had a cold, and took no drink. I then said to Mr Mason, "Remember all the business you have to do tonight; you won't get to bed before five, so we had better commence at once." Mr Mason then opened his maps, and I took my reference book, and we were engaged about twenty minutes or more, during which time we were frequently interrupted by Mr Moan chatting to us, and we were obliged to stop.'

'Was it your impression that Mr Moan had been drinking?'

'I would say so. When we sat down at the table, Mr Moan brought Mr Mason a glass of what I supposed to be spirits, and during the time that we were at work he frequently asked me to have something to drink from him, and at length I accepted a glass of punch.'

'Go on.'

'Well, then he commenced to speak about the murder, and asked if I recollected meeting him outside the station, and I said yes. After we had stopped working he produced a plan of the interior of the terminus, and began to explain to all present – there were one or two whom I did not know – the mode of egress, by both staircases, from the scene of the murder, and also the mode of concealment in case a person should wish to conceal themselves. When he was describing this I interrupted him, and pointing to the plan, said, "Could a person not get out this way –"

meaning the back stairs – "or lie concealed behind the door, at five o'clock, as the passage is then quite dark?" '

'What did he say to that?'

'I don't recollect him saying anything else. Mr Mason and I packed up our work and went upstairs to the sitting room.'

Was Patrick Moan a killer tormented by his own guilt, or a man of fragile temperament who dealt with his anxieties by getting drunk on a Monday? Mr Kemmis considered that either interpretation was, for now, equally valid. He was mulling over the question of Moan, about whom the evidence was so suggestive and yet so equivocal, when the clerk himself appeared at his door. He was sober, but in something of a state. When Mr Kemmis had done his best to calm him down, he asked what the matter was.

'Well, sir, I think I said something in my previous examination that was not correct.'

'Really? And what was that?'

'When I said I did not go out on the evening of the murder. I now recollect that my brother-in-law, Mr Joseph Burke, was in the house dining with us, and playing his flute to the birds . . .'

Mr Kemmis let this strange detail go without comment.

'. . . and I think perhaps I may have gone out for a bit of tobacco.'

'Well, Mr Moan, if you wish to make any alterations to your earlier account you must write it down in your own hand . . .'

'Certainly, sir, I shall.'

'But I must remind you that I gave you a very deliberate examination before, and I am surprised that you did not remember all the particulars at the time. You asserted most positively that you had not been out, and that no one but your wife and nephew and niece was with you on Thursday the thirteenth. Can you explain yourself?'

Mr Moan could not. The Crown Solicitor found it impossible to get anything more out of him, and allowed him to go. Mr

Kemmis was perplexed by this six-foot bundle of nerves. Moan had none of the defiance or braggadocio one expected from somebody capable of beating a man's head to pulp and calmly cutting his throat, and yet his demeanour was that of a guilty man. Mr Kemmis wondered whether he, like John Jolly, had some other secret which he did not want the world to know.

Later that afternoon the coroner and Mr Porter were summoned to the station in the vague hope that further discussion of the crime scene, and the post-mortem findings, might reveal some detail previously overlooked. Elsewhere in the building, detectives were speaking again to witnesses they had already interviewed, repeating entire dialogues like repertory actors in some tedious and inconsequential play.

There was still no sign that surveillance would produce useful results, and Catherine Campbell, though still under police protection, was refusing to cooperate. To add to the detectives' woes, there were ominous signs that even their staunchest supporters in the press were losing faith. The *Evening Packet* was the first local newspaper to express the frustration that many Dubliners were feeling:

> From an early hour in the morning till late at night the detectives are engaged in consultation and action; and yet with all this labour they have, we believe, been unable to find the slightest clue to the assassins. Everything seems a perfect puzzle to them in connection with the murder. The variety of their suppositions, and the indecisive way in which their suspicions are shifted from one party and place to another, lead to the surmise that they are entirely at fault. To say the least of it, they seem totally guided by chance. Every day that passes makes the likelihood of the murderer being caught less probable.

If there had been any doubts that the investigation was in crisis, they were dispelled by the sudden arrival of the Chief Secretary,

Mr Horsman. This was no mere courtesy call; the senior representative of the British government in Ireland meant business. For more than two hours he, the Crown Solicitor and Superintendent Guy were holed up in the meeting room, their conversation subject to the sort of secrecy normally associated with a papal conclave. When Mr Horsman left, late in the afternoon, it was clear that he intended to make some important intervention in the case, although nobody was quite sure what it would be.

They did not have long to wait. On Saturday morning Mr Kemmis received a courteous note inviting him to a meeting with the Attorney General. Overnight the weather had suddenly taken a severe turn: a hard frost had descended on Dublin, and the park in the middle of Merrion Square looked as if some celestial baker had sprinkled it liberally with icing sugar. Within twenty minutes of leaving home, the Crown Solicitor was warming himself by the fire of John FitzGerald's study, being thanked for the unstinting effort he had put into his inquiry, and learning that his involvement in the case was now at an end.

Mr Kemmis felt as if a great weight had been lifted from him. He was sorry to have been taken off the case, but sleep had been a rare commodity in the fortnight since he started work at Broadstone, and he was approaching total exhaustion. His friend Mr FitzGerald assured him that no doubt was being cast on his competence. The Chief Secretary retained every confidence in his abilities, but now believed that the Crown Solicitor had completed the task assigned to him.

With the initial phase of the inquiry staggering to its conclusion, Mr Horsman believed it was time for a fresh approach to the problem. In a move calculated to increase his stock in Westminster, but unlikely to win many friends in the Dublin Metropolitan Police, he had appealed to Scotland Yard for help. If a cabinet minister requested assistance from Scotland Yard they got it, and quickly. Within hours, two inspectors from the detective division were packing their bags, and by Sunday evening they had already checked into a hotel in central Dublin. A local newspaper alluded to the arrival of 'two of the most distinguished of the London detectives', and for once this was not hyperbole. Scotland Yard had sent two of their finest: Detective Inspector Jack Whicher and Detective Inspector Henry Smith.

When Charles Dickens first became infatuated with the romance of undercover police work, he invited seven London detectives for drinks at the office of the journal he edited, *Household Words*. Whicher and Smith were among his guests on that memorable evening, an account of which was published in July 1850 under the headline 'A Detective Police Party'. Jack Whicher, a member of the detective force since its establishment eight years earlier, appears as 'Sergeant Witchem', short and stocky, with a face scarred by smallpox. Dickens describes him as having 'something of a reserved and thoughtful air, as if he were engaged in deep arithmetical calculations'. His colleague 'Sergeant Mith' was a newer recruit, 'a smooth-faced man with a fresh bright complexion, and a strange air of simplicity'. By 1856 Whicher and Smith were experienced and highly regarded detectives; both had been promoted to inspector earlier in the year.*

It would have been excellent publicity for Scotland Yard if the pair had been welcomed to Dublin as saviours and left it in a blaze of glory, but the reality was rather more prosaic. Their stay in the capital was low key, and coincided with a period when the investigation seemed to have ground entirely to a halt. In the week of their arrival one newspaper published a four-word bulletin that stated simply: 'There is nothing new.' There were even rumours that the police had given up hope of catching the killer. This was all rather dispiriting for Augustus Guy, who following the departure of Mr Kemmis was now in sole charge of the

---

* Jack Whicher is best known today for his involvement in the 1860 Road Hill House investigation following the murder of a three-year-old boy in Wiltshire – the subject of Kate Summerscale's celebrated book *The Suspicions of Mr Whicher*.

murder inquiry. It ought to have been an opportunity for Dublin's most experienced detective to shake things up, but the superintendent had run out of ideas.

The public responded to the apparent standstill with a variety of novel suggestions. One proposed the use of mesmerism to put witnesses in a trance and thus enable them to reveal the identity of the killer. Another recommended exhuming the body for a second time and examining the dead man's eyes, in case an image of his murderer had been imprinted on his retina. This macabre idea – a process known as optography – would receive a great deal of attention in later decades, though it proved to be without any forensic value.*

On the evening of Tuesday 2 December Dr Richard Robert Madden, secretary of the Loan Fund Board, caught the night train from Dublin to Cork. Dr Madden was, by any standards, an eminent Irishman. A prominent anti-slavery campaigner, he had served as a senior diplomat on three continents and was equally well known as a writer and historian. It was late when Dr Madden arrived at the Victoria Hotel, where he went straight to the coffee room. There he met a man of whom he was immediately suspicious. This person could talk of nothing but the Broadstone murder, as if it consumed his every waking thought. Stranger still, although he ordered a room for the night he did not use it, remaining in the coffee room until a quarter to six in the morning. The man then announced that he was leaving by the morning train, and when paying for his drinks he produced an enormous bundle of notes, amongst which the waiter thought he saw a pawn ticket.

Dr Madden was disturbed by this encounter, and as soon as the man had left he went to the nearest police station to report it.

---

* This letter is notable as one of the first on record to propose the use of optography to identify a murderer. A similar suggestion was made in an American journal the following year, but I have been unable to find any example that predates this one.

The inspector to whom he spoke was sufficiently concerned to telegraph the detectives in Dublin, and immediately issued orders to his own officers that the man should be arrested on sight. The following day he was spotted in central Cork, detained and taken in front of magistrates. He gave his name as Joseph Hale, and said that until recently he had been employed as an auctioneer in Dublin. He admitted leaving the capital after getting into financial difficulties, and because he feared being arrested for debt he had been anxious to conceal his presence in Cork. These goings-on were picked up by the newspapers, which gleefully reported the arrest of the 'murderer' – but the episode ended in anticlimax, as once the man's identity had been established he was released without charge.

That was not the only false alarm, for on the very same day a man named James Robinson actually confessed to the murder. Robinson seemed a plausible suspect. He had worked in the Broadstone locomotive works as a fitter until his dismissal a few days earlier. He was arrested by two of the Dublin detectives and locked up in the cells of the police station at Chancery Lane. But his account was incoherent, and he veered unpredictably from professing his own guilt to accusing others. When the police surgeon Dr Richard Ireland examined him he swiftly pronounced him insane. The unfortunate James Robinson was released into the care of his family, the sixth person wrongly arrested for a crime whose perpetrator still seemed far out of sight. Half a dozen was quite a tally for an investigation barely into its third week – but, to be fair to the detectives, the figure reflected public anxiety more than police incompetence. Dubliners were terrified of the undiscovered killer, and hypervigilant for any potential sign of guilt. If the investigators received a credible tip-off they had little alternative but to bring the suspect in for questioning.

Some sort of nadir was reached the following week when one of the senior railway officials – his identity was never revealed – decided to call in a clairvoyant, in the hope that intercourse with the spirit world might reveal crucial clues that had hitherto eluded the detectives. Three seances were held, and, according to one of the attendees, a number of remarkably specific details about the crime were elicited, including the route by which the murderer had entered and left the building. During one of these sessions the medium even gave instructions which she said would lead to the apprehension of the killer. Unfortunately the versions of events recounted in the three seances differed so irreconcilably that everybody present soon concluded that corporeal sleuths were preferable to their supernatural counterparts. The police regarded these unofficial activities with disdain, and Augustus Guy felt moved to write to the newspapers publicly distancing himself from the affair.

With little actual news to report, journalists belatedly remembered the other victims of this terrible crime. On Tuesday 9 December the *Freeman's Journal* drew public attention to the plight of Mr Little's 'aged mother and helpless sister', stating that they faced financial ruin, and appealing for corporations and individuals to help them:

> The Midland Great Western Railway Company, which has thus lost an able, honourable, and faithful officer, may succeed in securing the services of another equally devoted to their interests; but to the afflicted mother and sister the loss is irreparable – aggravated, too, by its adding poverty and privation to the grievous suffering in which they have become involved by the sudden and appalling misfortune of their family.

Thomas Kemmis's final contribution to the murder inquiry, once he had handed over his leading role to Superintendent Guy, was a written report of his findings. This document, together with more than a hundred pages of interview transcripts, was forwarded to Edward Horsman, the Chief Secretary for Ireland. The Crown Solicitor's ten-page analysis of the case is a snapshot of the investigation as it stood in early December, three weeks after Mr Little's death. Mr Kemmis began by exploring possible motives for the crime. He argued that nobody had stood to gain from George Little's death, and that there were no grounds for believing that revenge or malice had been behind it. That left only robbery, and the circumstances suggested that it was opportunistic. 'It would appear to have been done *in haste*,' he wrote, 'as much gold and silver was left untouched.'

But the Crown Solicitor devoted most of his confidential report to a discussion of the possible suspects. He was convinced that George Little's killer was somebody already known to him:

> Being nervous he was not likely to open the door except to someone he knew well after office hours . . . The doctors consider his throat was cut after his head was battered. Was that not to stop his telling the name of his assassin with perhaps a dying breath?

This, Mr Kemmis suggested, was a good reason for suspecting those who actually lived on the premises.

> The parties who were the most familiar with the office, the house, etc., and who had an exact knowledge whether clerks were in or out, were Mrs Gunning, her husband and servant . . . It is true Mr Hanbury the station master, his wife and family live on the basement floor, but they do not seem on any intimate terms with the Gunnings, and had no recourse to the upper part of the house at any time. Hanbury was at his office to a late period of night and early in the morning.

Mr Kemmis believed that the cash porter William McCauley must also be considered a suspect, since he was one of the most frequent visitors to the cashier's office, though out of business hours he did not have such easy access to the building as the Gunnings. The Crown Solicitor noted that McCauley was probably the last railway employee to see Mr Little alive, and that when questioned his evidence had been strangely contradictory. The cashier's assistant William Chamberlain also had to be included, given his intimate knowledge of the office, but Mr Kemmis concluded that the young man's alibi was rock solid: 'I cannot believe that Chamberlain has any knowledge [of the crime], directly or indirectly.'

The next two people on the Crown Solicitor's list were the railway policemen, Superintendent Hodgens and Sergeant Collins. Both were often in the office to pick up the wages they distributed to railway staff every week, and both knew that there was more money there than usual that Thursday because of the Mullingar Fair receipts. Again, Mr Kemmis felt there were grounds for suspicion: 'Some accounts of Collins's character were not good. When the hammer was found in the canal Hodgens, who brought it to me, was extraordinarily excited.' But, Mr Kemmis added, he and Mr Guy had been satisfied with the alibis given by both men.

Then there were the clerks from the solicitor's office, Thornton, Kearney and Linskey. 'They were in the house late that night,' the Crown Solicitor observed. 'We took no detailed examinations but were satisfied that they had pressing business belonging to the office and were in so engaged.'

Mr Kemmis next turned to the staff of the audit office, some of whom had owed money to Mr Little. Alluding darkly to the fact that 'persons of loose character' had worked there, the Crown Solicitor picked out two. John Henry Moore, a 'very young man of loose habits', seemed a tempting suspect, but Mr Kemmis concluded that his alibi was satisfactory. The name of Robert Fair, on the other hand, he underlined twice. The audit clerk was suspected of having stolen £50 from Mr Little on a previous occasion; although Fair had supplied what seemed to be a good alibi, Mr Kemmis declared himself 'not quite satisfied' of his innocence.

Finally, there was Patrick Moan. Mr Kemmis had several reasons for suspecting the engineering clerk: his strange demeanour on the day of the discovery of George Little's body, his unsatisfactory alibi, and the fact that his story kept changing.

That made fourteen suspects – some of whom seemed remote possibilities, though the Crown Solicitor could not entirely rule them out. One or two clearly had more to tell than they had so far admitted to the police: 'Mr Moan ought to explain more satisfactorily,' Mr Kemmis wrote. But there was no doubting who he regarded as the prime suspect. There was something decidedly fishy about the behaviour and circumstances of Bernard Gunning, whose 'clothes, furniture and habits of living greatly exceed what he could afford', while the Crown Solicitor was also sceptical about the 'extraordinary accuracy' of the assistant storekeeper's alibi. He believed that Catherine Campbell was still protecting her employers, and that her evidence – if she eventually decided to cooperate with police – would be crucial in securing a conviction.

But all of this was now Superintendent Guy's concern – and within days an important discovery would turn the entire case on its head.

10

Tucked away to one side of the cathedral-like space of the Broadstone locomotive works, separated from the factory floor by a wooden partition, was the carpenters' workshop. The amiable dictator of this dominion of timber and sawdust was James Brophy, foreman of the carriage department. His office was noisier but less foul-smelling than that of the painters, who occupied a smaller, fume-filled workshop next door. It was 2 p.m. on Thursday 11 December, and Mr Brophy had just returned from his lunch when he had an unexpected visitor. It was Mrs Cabry, wife of the chief engineer, and she had a favour to ask.

She was about to embark on some major domestic undertaking – perhaps having the chimney swept – and needed something to protect her furniture and carpets from dust. A couple of years ago, she explained, her husband Joseph had deposited an ancient wicker hamper in the loft above the boiler shed, intending to use it for kindling. There it had languished, forgotten, until now. But she had just remembered the hamper contained an old oilcloth that she had been loath to throw away, and she wondered whether Mr Brophy might be kind enough to get it for her.

James was happy to oblige. Mrs Cabry waited in his workshop while he left the building by a side door, walked past the boiler shed and climbed a rickety wooden staircase at its side. He soon found himself in the half-light of the roof space, surrounded by spiders' webs and mouse droppings. It was an unappealing part of the building, little frequented and used mainly for storage.

He did not spot the basket immediately, as it had been placed on some rafters above the doorway through which he had entered. Mr Brophy heaved it down and took it into the next room, which was larger and cluttered with discarded junk. Throwing the basket carelessly down on to a table, he noticed that it jingled on impact. When he opened the lid he was surprised to find a large canvas bag, apparently saturated with water, sitting on top of the oilcloth. Mr Brophy's intention had been to remove the oilcloth and replace the hamper where he had found it, but he realised that this discovery required further investigation. He took the basket back down to his workshop and placed it on his workbench, in front of the uncomprehending Mrs Cabry. Without opening it, he examined the bag. It was dirty and large and heavy, soaking wet, and filled with something that chinked and rattled like a pocketful of loose change.

And it was then that he made a disastrous mistake. For a few fleeting moments there had been every chance that the police would catch George Little's killer, that they would identify him and obtain such conclusive proof of his guilt that he would certainly hang. All these things were not just possible but likely, until James Brophy told a workshop full of craftsmen what he had found.

It was only a few minutes later that he realised he ought to notify the police, but by then it was too late. Half the station already knew about a bag of money Brophy had unearthed in the boiler shed, and all had leapt to the same conclusion. It must be the cash taken from Mr Little's office, concealed in a corner of the Broadstone estate where not even the police would think to look.

Superintendent Guy came hurrying to the carpenters' workshop, accompanied by several of his officers. When he lifted the bag out of the hamper a considerable amount of water slopped on to the table. A crowd of carpenters and painters, as well as various locomotive fitters who had sidled into the room, watched as he tipped up the bag and a bright metallic shower poured out on to the bench. When it had surrendered its last coin, one of the officers was given the unenviable job of counting them all, and he eventually announced that the total was £43 17s 6d – all in silver.

Mr Guy's elation at the find was tempered with disappointment. He was sure that this must be part of the robber's haul, but he was also pricked by knowledge of an opportunity missed. If he had been told about this discovery in confidence, he would have ensured that it remained a secret, replaced the bag in its original hiding place and set a watch on the boiler shed. Then it would only have been a matter of time before they caught the murderer in the act of handling his plunder. Still, the breakthrough gave them several new clues. The fact that it had been concealed on railway premises indicated that the killer was an employee of the company, someone who knew every inch of the estate and could walk around the terminus and outbuildings without arousing suspicion. And he must have been there that day: the bag appeared to have been kept totally immersed somewhere else, and moved to its latest hiding place within the last couple of hours. Augustus Guy realised with a thrill of certainty that George Little's killer was somebody that he had already met, somebody who knew and worked with the people now surrounding him. One of the faces now gazing in silent fascination at the pile of coins in front of him might even be that of the killer.

They had recovered £44, less a few shillings, but that left close to £300 still unaccounted for. Where was the rest? Mr Guy wondered whether the robber had split his hoard into several smaller sums dotted around the estate, or had one large cache hidden elsewhere, from which he was surreptitiously removing the money bag by bag. He ordered an immediate search of the surrounding area, telling his men to start with anything that contained a large volume of water. They began with the tank that supplied the central-heating boiler, which was immediately underneath the loft where Brophy had found the cash. There was nothing else inside it, but several of the policemen assumed that this was where the canvas bag had been stowed until its removal upstairs. Superintendent Guy was not so sure. Once the tank had been drained he pointed out a layer of sediment lining the bottom. It was undisturbed; surely an object as heavy as that bag would have left an impression? He told the detectives to keep looking.

Cisterns, culverts, rainwater butts: all were emptied and peered into with lanterns, and all proved equally void of cash. It was suggested that the money might be hidden in the canal, but Mr Guy dismissed this as implausible – and they had already drained it once. Late in the afternoon he was visited by the railway company chairman, Mr Ennis, accompanied by the Lord Mayor and Colonel Browne, the police commissioner. After viewing the money and the container in which it had been found, they dutifully went to inspect the dusty loft space and the boiler tank beneath. Afterwards they retired to the meeting room and discussed what to do next.

Superintendent Guy told his audience that he was increasingly confident of catching the killer. The latest development greatly strengthened his suspicions against two company employees: Mr Moan, who lived a few minutes away from the locomotive works; and Mr Gunning, whose office was actually in the building. Mrs Gunning was, he thought, possibly an accessory to the crime. He intended to maintain surveillance of this trio for as long as necessary. His interest in McCauley was waning, the minor inconsistencies in his evidence now appearing to be defects of memory rather than honesty. Mr Guy also announced his intention to find out precisely who had access to the loft, and whether any unfamiliar faces had been seen around the locomotive shed. Almost as an afterthought, he observed that there was, as yet, no proof that the money originated in the cashier's office.

That proof was not long in coming. The following day Superintendent Guy went to see George Little's sister Kate. He showed her the cloth bag in which the money had been found, and she identified it as one she had made some months earlier. George had mentioned that he wanted something to keep coins in, she recalled, so she had run up several of these bags from strong linen. After totting up his cash he would place the silver in the bags, exactly £10 in each one. Mr Guy concluded that the robber had swept up as much silver as he could carry, using a nearby bag as the most convenient receptacle.

It was not, on the face of it, a great advertisement for the competence of the police that the money had been found quite by accident, and by an employee of the company, in a building so close to the scene of the crime. On the other hand, it was reasonable to assume that the murderer was aware of the detectives' movements and so had been able to relocate his stash periodically so as to avoid its discovery. Either way, he managed to outwit them again. For the next four days the police went to extraordinary lengths to scour every inch of the terminus. They dismantled entire locomotives to check that money had not been hidden in their boiler tubes. They entered the room of a desperately ill child and searched her bedding; and when she died they searched her coffin. But they found not a farthing more. Augustus Guy concluded that the remaining cash had been removed from the Broadstone estate entirely.

On Monday 15 December the celebrated London detectives Inspectors Whicher and Smith left the inquiry and boarded a steamer back to England. It is tempting to speculate what exactly they achieved. The answer may be nothing, because the heroes of Scotland Yard left barely any trace on the historical record during their stay in Dublin. Beyond the fact of their arrival on 30 November, and their departure two weeks later, their names did not feature either in government records or press coverage of the case, and they slipped out of the country virtually unnoticed. It seems that they were just as flummoxed by the mystery as anybody else.

A month had passed since the death of George Little. Crisp winter sunshine was succeeded by bitter cold, followed by a deluge that turned the back streets of Dublin into a sea of mud. The latest meteorological indignity was a week of violent gales that pounded the Atlantic seaboard, capsizing cargo ships and drowning fishermen. Even inland the damage was severe. In Tipperary an impoverished labourer and his family lost their home and every possession when the storm reduced their cottage to rubble. In a stark illustration of the priorities of contemporary newspaper editors, this dreadful event was given less prominence than the mild inconvenience suffered by the Earl of Donoughmore, whose carriage was forced to take a detour because of a fallen tree.

In the capital the wind ripped tiles off roofs and pushed over elderly chimneystacks. It whistled through the streets and tugged at the bills haphazardly pasted to walls and lamp posts. Among the flyers for theatrical entertainments, concerts and political meetings were posters appealing for information about the Broadstone mystery. They were illustrated by engravings of the hammer and razor, and asked any member of the public who recognised them to speak to Superintendent Guy. The implements themselves could be viewed by anybody who cared to drop in to the detective headquarters at Dublin Castle, and hundreds of people took advantage of the opportunity. Soon there was barely a Dubliner who did not know what the razor looked like, but without any useful consequence. The man with the dirty face and the distinctive whiskers who had walked into Flanagan's shop with a razor he wanted sharpening remained unidentified.

Private expressions of dissatisfaction at the progress of the inquiry were spilling over into very public criticism, and the detectives were losing the support of even the Dublin journals. One evening newspaper published an excoriating leader headlined 'The Broadstone Farce'; another observed scornfully that the police were 'strong fellows, no doubt, and can smash heads with their batons; but a little more power of mind – a little more skill, acuteness, and sagacity in detecting the authors of ingeniously planned crimes – would render them more useful to the public'. It was left to the *Freeman's Journal* to defend their conduct and point out the dangers of pursuing an investigation with unwarranted haste. It was better to act slowly and methodically, an editorial argued, than to charge ahead and risk letting a suspect walk free through lack of proof. The article concluded by alluding cryptically to some new facts that made the police more certain than ever that they would catch the killer. The source of this information was said to be Catherine Campbell, although the newspaper did not 'deem it prudent to enter into more details at present'.

However they got hold of it, there is no question that the *Freeman's Journal* correspondent had access to information of the utmost sensitivity. After weeks of taciturnity, Catherine Campbell had finally decided to help the police. Moreover, she had changed her story, and the allegations she now made on oath were so incendiary that they would never be allowed to appear in print.

11

It was late November when Catherine Campbell was declared a Crown Witness, and for months afterwards she lived under virtual house arrest. Her guardian during this period was John Ward, a sergeant in Augustus Guy's 'C' division, which policed an unruly area in the east of the city. Ward and his wife lived in a tenement building in Mecklenburgh Street, a short walk from the divisional headquarters. By day the road was a bustling commercial thoroughfare, but at night the place came alive with an entirely different clientele. Since the late eighteenth century, Mecklenburgh Street and its environs – known as the Monto – had been notorious for its brothels, and its location near the docks and army barracks ensured a steady supply of clients. After dark, prostitutes loitered on every corner, hoping to attract the attention of the many young men who made this their regular haunt.

Catherine cannot have enjoyed witnessing these nightly scenes of depravity, as she was a devout Catholic. She was rarely allowed into the outside world, but an exception was made for her regular trips to church. She never missed High Mass on a Sunday, and once a week she went to confession, chaperoned by Mrs Ward. It was on the way back from one of these outings that the policeman's wife noticed a change in Catherine's demeanour. The girl was fretful but would not explain what was worrying her, saying only that she would have to speak to Mr Ward. When the sergeant returned from his shift that evening, Catherine told him that she would like

Dublin's Broadstone Terminus as it appeared in 1860,
showing the pontoon bridge over the Royal Canal.

A contemporary engraving of George Little's office, the scene of his murder.
A counter and railings that divided the room in two were dismantled shortly after his death.

Bernard Gunning, the assistant storekeeper, in later life.
For much of the murder inquiry he was the detectives' prime suspect.

The railway company cottage occupied by the painter James Spollin and his family in the grounds of the station.

James Spollin, in his first public appearance since his arrest, hears the charges against him at the police court.

1624

To His Excellency

The Lord Lieutenant of Ireland
your Memmorialist humbly
Showeth he is a Prisoner in Richmond
bridewell Charged with Robbery
from the midland. Great western
railway Co. of Ireland.

your Memmorialist not haveing
Sufficient money to fee Council for
His defence Humbly Prayeth

your Excellency will Order my
furniture & Beding & to be Given up
to me that I may Sell the Same
It is Now detained by the Crown
Soliciter in the Cottage I occupyed on
the Company's Premices Broadstone Terminus
Dublin

and your Memmorialist will ever Pray

I am with Great respect
your Humble Servant

James Spollin

September 5th
1847

Memorial (petition) written by James Spollin from his prison cell to the Lord Lieutenant of Ireland, requesting the sale of his furniture to pay for legal representation.

Frederick Bridges, the Liverpool phrenologist who helped James Spollin and his son to emigrate.

Portrait of James Spollin taken a few weeks before his departure from Liverpool.

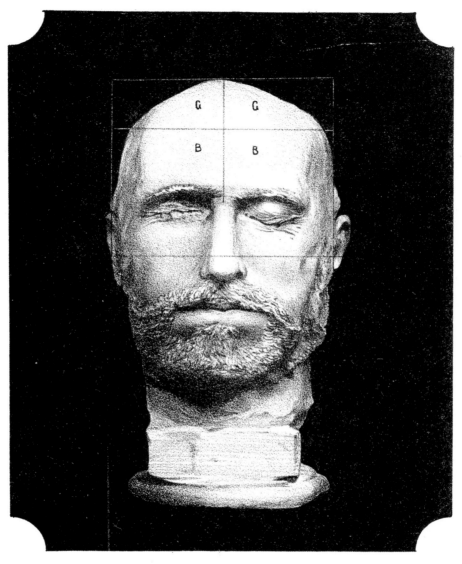

FRONT VIEW OF HEAD OF SPOLLIN.
Diagram N.º 2.

Plaster cast of James Spollin's head, made by Frederick Bridges for phrenological study.

to make a statement on oath. She had lied at the inquest, she said, and there were certain facts that she had deliberately concealed. Mr Ward was curious to know why she had waited for more than a month before deciding to recant her evidence. Her priest had persuaded her, she explained, telling her in the confessional that the murder would hang over her until she declared the truth. Mr Ward listened to her story, and quickly realised that he had to pass it on to his superiors as soon as possible.

On Sunday afternoon Superintendent Guy and Inspector Ryan took a stroll through the mean streets of the Monto. Their faces were well known in the fleshpots of east Dublin, and figures – many of them dressed with scant regard for the prevailing temperatures of mid-December – scuttled into doorways at their approach. As they walked along Mecklenburgh Street they passed respectable businesses: grocers, a sweetshop, a piano tuner's. But around half of the buildings were tenement blocks, substantial Georgian houses subdivided by unscrupulous property speculators into apartments of various sizes and degrees of squalor. Their destination, number 77, was one of these tenements. John Ward and his wife lived in a cramped apartment, sandwiched between a dairy and the Female Penitents' Retreat, a Magdalene laundry which provided accommodation for thirty-five former prostitutes.

Catherine Campbell seemed relieved to see them. She had been to Mass that morning, and she was tormented by the knowledge that she had committed a sin that no amount of prayer could expiate. She could atone only by telling the truth, an absolution gained by talking to the police rather than to a priest. She needed to admit what she had done, and her confessor would be Superintendent Augustus Guy.

Mr Guy had a good idea of what she was going to say, but needed to hear her say it. He knew the mental anguish that had precipitated her decision, and had no desire to exacerbate it. Gently he guided her through her statement, asking what she had to tell him.

'Well, sir, on the evening that Mr Little was murdered, I saw Mr Gunning going up the back staircase which leads to the top of the house and to his bedrooms.'

'What time was this?'

'Between six and seven o'clock.'

'This is the same staircase that leads up to the passage in which Mr Moan's and Mr Little's offices are situated?'

'Yes, sir.'

'Where were you when you saw him?'

'I was passing through the corridor on the ground floor, by the canal office. The door to the stairs was open and I saw him going up.'

'And what happened next?'

'I went into the canal office to clean it. I was there some little time and I heard a footstep over my head, which I am sure was Mr Gunning's.'

'Mr Gunning's! At the inquest you said it was Mr Little's tread that you heard.'

'Yes, sir, but I am positive it was Mr Gunning.'

'Could he have been in a different office – Mr Moan's, for example?'

'I am positive he was in Mr Little's, as his office was over the one I was in.'

'In your previous statement you said that you saw Mrs Gunning a little after hearing the footsteps. Did you?'

'Yes, I left the canal office and went to clean the audit office. Shortly afterwards Mrs Gunning came in and said, "Oh! You are here, Kate." "Yes, mum," said I. She asked where she could get a coal box.'

'Where did she go after that?' asked Mr Guy.

'I saw her get an empty coal box from the canal office and go up the back stairs with a candle in her hand, which was not lit. I did not see her any more until she was going to bed.'

'And how about Mr Gunning? Did you see him again?'

'Not until about eleven o'clock, when he passed the kitchen door with his hat on. A little later he brought me his shoes to clean.'

Sergeant Ward, who had been listening intently, intervened.

'Tell the superintendent about the keys, Catherine.'

'Yes, sir. I always used to keep the key to the door that leads from the back staircase to the corridor outside Mr Little's office, but on the evening of the murder Mrs Gunning told me to leave it in the door.'

'Did she explain why?'

'She said she would take the key herself on her way up to bed, and also that she wanted to go into Mr Cabry's water closet in the morning to get some water for the flowers.'

'Do you know what happened to this key?'

'At about eleven o'clock that night I saw it in the door leading from the back stairs to the corridor outside Mr Little's office.'

'Which side of the door was it on?' asked Mr Guy.

'On the same side as the stairs.'

'And was it locked then?'

'No, the door was open. I locked it and left it in the door, according to Mrs Gunning's orders.'

'If she had not given those orders, what would you have done with the key?'

'I would have locked that door, and using the same key would have locked the door which leads from the upper landing to the boardroom. Then I would have taken the key out of the door and kept it in my pocket till the morning.'

'Was the key still there the following morning?'

'No. At about nine o'clock the morning after the murder I went through the door near Mr Little's office and it was unlocked and the key gone. About an hour later I saw the key hanging on a nail in the kitchen. During the hours of business the keys are always removed from the doors and hung on this nail.'

'Do you have anything else you wish to tell us, Catherine?'

'Well, sir, on the Thursday evening, I was struck by the circumstance of Mrs Gunning's children not coming near me, which they were normally in the constant habit of doing. I would usually see them go to bed, but on the day of the murder I did not see them at all between five o'clock until ten the next morning, when I saw Sarah. The other child did not get up until one o'clock that afternoon.'

That was all that Catherine had to tell them, and she completed her statement with the look of one who had managed to ease a troubled conscience. Daniel Ryan had been taking down everything she said, and he now took a blank piece of paper and wrote it out in longhand, tidying up the grammar and inserting sentences here and there to clarify the meaning. When he had finished the statement he read it aloud for Catherine's approval, and handed her the pen, indicating the place at the bottom of the document where she was to sign. She took a deep breath and with two quick strokes drew a cross. The inspector took back his pen, and on either side of her unlettered autograph wrote 'Catherine Campbell, her mark'.

Catherine's change of heart created problems for the detectives as well as opportunities. Yes, she had given them a vital link in the chain of evidence: they could now put Gunning at the scene of the crime, finally breaking what had appeared to be a bulletproof alibi. Motive, means, and now opportunity: the evidential trinity was complete. On the other hand, what use was this information? They could not ask Catherine to testify, even in a police court. By her own admission she had lied under oath at the inquest, and repeated those lies to the detectives. The evidence of a perjurer was worthless, and a competent magistrate would throw out any case that relied on it. Deciding that he needed advice, Mr Guy sought it from one of his superiors.

When Robert Peel established the London Metropolitan Police in 1829, he decided that running such a novel organisation required a range of skills that could not be found in a single person. So he appointed two police commissioners, equal in rank and status, but picked from quite different professional backgrounds. One was an experienced barrister, the other a soldier. The lawyer would deal with policy and administration, while the military man looked after operational matters. This division of labour seemed to work well, so when Dublin gained its new police force seven years later the government decided to adopt the same arrangement.

In 1856 the two commissioners of the DMP were Colonel George Browne and John More O'Ferrall. Colonel Browne was a cantankerous British Army officer in his late sixties, a veteran of the Napoleonic Wars whose flair was for recruitment and discipline. Mr More O'Ferrall was ten years his junior, but had been in post since the creation of the police force two decades earlier; he was a consummate administrator and diplomat, and his barrister's eloquence made him the ideal spokesman for the force. It was Colonel Browne who had most often visited Broadstone during the inquiry, but this time it was to Mr More O'Ferrall that Superintendent Guy went for advice. He explained his dilemma, and gave an outline of the statement offered by Catherine Campbell. The commissioner thought for a while, and then made a suggestion. He would visit the girl, he said, and speak to her for himself. If he agreed with Mr Guy's assessment that she was now telling the truth about what had happened on 13 November, Mr More O'Ferrall proposed to put the matter to the Crown Solicitor. Christmas was only a few days away, so they would reconvene to discuss the matter the following weekend.

For George Little's family the first Christmas without their beloved son, brother and cousin was always likely to be a festival without cheer. But on the morning of Christmas Eve, just when the contrast between public celebration and personal grief was at its starkest, an announcement in the newspapers brought a welcome reminder that Dublin had not forgotten them:

> We have much pleasure in being able to state that a highly influential committee is in progress of formation that will shortly give the public an opportunity of testifying their sympathy for the bereaved family of Mr Little, whose case forms so remarkable and melancholy a contrast to those of the railway officials who have been prominently before the public within the past year. The Midland Railway Company have headed the subscription list with a donation of £200, and we are satisfied that had they made it £400, they would receive the cordial approval of their shareholders for this effort to alleviate the sad consequences which must ensue to the family of Mr Little from the melancholy bereavement they have suffered . . . Public policy, as well as the desire to lighten domestic sorrow, suggest that this subscription list should be filled promptly and generously. We may add, that several gentlemen of the highest respectability, both in the city and country, have intimated their desire to serve on the committee; and our new Lord Mayor will signalise his accession to office by placing himself at the head of this excellent body.

The aim of this public-spirited initiative was to raise enough money to buy an annuity, which would provide an income sufficient to support Mrs Little for the rest of her life. The timing of the announcement was no accident, for during the festive season Dublin's establishment traditionally made ostentatious gestures of charity. Thomas Arkins, who held the ceremonial title of Sword-Bearer to the City of Dublin, spent Christmas Eve performing an exhausting tour of almshouses and orphanages, distributing several hundred pounds of beef and loaves on behalf of the Lord Mayor. The following day, more than three thousand inmates of the South Dublin Workhouse sat down to a meat dinner paid for by private subscription; at its counterpart in north Dublin, a short distance from the Broadstone terminus, a similar celebration was in full swing, attended by various magistrates, retired army officers and other local dignitaries who took a benign interest in the institution.

The station itself was deserted on Christmas Day, apart from the residents of Directors' House; for the first time in more than six weeks, not a single policeman crossed its threshold. The constables were in their barracks, tucking into roast beef, while Augustus Guy was enjoying the relative calm of a family Christmas at The Hermitage, his cottage in the grounds of the Meath Hospital in south Dublin. Like the rest of the city, Mr Guy and his officers were simply observing a religious festival, but when they downed tools for the holiday it was as if the investigation were not merely suspended but in abeyance.

There was, in fact, a distinct possibility that it would not be resumed. That Sunday the Attorney General chaired a confidential meeting of Ireland's most senior law officials. There were just three other people present: his deputy Jonathan Christian, the Solicitor General; the Crown Solicitor; and Mr Kemmis's clerk Mr Rae. The purpose of the conference was to decide whether the police inquiry should be abandoned, and, if not, what further steps ought to be taken.

They began by reading a statement provided by the police commissioner Mr More O'Ferrall, who had visited Catherine Campbell on Boxing Day. It confirmed the account she had already given to Superintendent Guy, alleging that she had seen Bernard Gunning going upstairs towards Mr Little's office on the evening of the murder, and thus putting him at the scene of the crime. Catherine had told Mr More O'Ferrall that when she gave evidence at the inquest she had not properly understood the obligations imposed by swearing an oath. She had been in a state of confusion, she told him, with her master sitting behind her, and her mistress at her side. She did not see how she was expected to tell the whole truth in front of them – especially as she was fond of their daughter Sarah, and could not bear to deprive her of her father.

The discussion that followed focused on the evidence: how much did they know, how much of it was admissible in court, and what more would be needed in order to make a prosecution viable? The three senior officials agreed that the investigation had reached a dead end. But they also felt that it was far too soon to be giving up all hope of catching the killer. Mr Kemmis's superiors concurred with his view that the prime suspects must be the Gunnings, but the police still lacked any proof of their guilt. How could they remedy this deficiency?

A consensus quickly emerged in favour of decisive action. The following day, and with the wholehearted support of the Attorney General, the police would apply for warrants for the arrest of Bernard and Anne Gunning. As soon as the couple were in custody their apartments, and every part of the Broadstone estate to which they had access, would be subjected to a fingertip search. Then they would be examined in front of the magistrate, and the evidence of Catherine and others put to them.

This otherwise admirable plan of action fell to pieces within a matter of hours. Mr Kemmis and his clerk went straight to Mecklenburgh Street to take yet another statement from Catherine, which would form the basis of their application for an arrest warrant. It will never be known exactly what was said during their encounter, but Mr Rae – who had not met the young woman before – immediately smelt a rat. He told Mr Kemmis that he did not trust her, and a subsequent memorandum referred to 'certain peculiarities in conduct and discrepancies in statement' which caused them both grave concerns. They were sufficiently alarmed by Catherine's behaviour to notify the Attorney General, who called another meeting.

After Mr Kemmis and his clerk had given an account of their conversation with Catherine, the legal officers came to the conclusion that no confidence could be placed in any allegation the young woman had made. Under such circumstances there was no justification for arresting the Gunnings, although it was decided that the search of the Broadstone terminus should go ahead. The surveillance of the main suspects would continue – strangely, one of those being shadowed by detectives was William Chamberlain, who nobody seriously suspected of the crime.

It was just as well that the press did not get wind of these developments. Any last vestige of optimism about the case, or support for those investigating it, had vanished. The newspapers were united in their anger, and differed only in their analysis of who was to blame. The detectives, the law officers and the government all came under sustained attack. One commentator railed against the decision to withhold details of the inquiry from the public, thus restricting the problem to 'half a dozen stale official minds' rather than opening it up to 'a thousand inquisitive brains actively at work thinking and reflecting'. Another demanded wholesale legal reform, and the adoption of a system of public prosecutors like that in France. One paper of high Tory sympathies, the *Daily Express*, even suggested that the investigation had failed because too many Catholic officials had been promoted beyond their talents. After one last paroxysm of fury the great beasts of Abbey Street – Dublin's equivalent of Fleet Street – fell silent, their passion spent. There was no news to report, no cause for hope, nothing more to say.

The first day of 1857 was also the forty-ninth since George Little's death. The arrival of the New Year coincided with the delivery to Dublin Castle of a package whose contents aroused intense interest. It was a razor.

The sender of this intriguing object turned out to be Joseph Rogers Wiseman of Whitechurch in County Cork. A few days later a letter from this gentleman arrived on the desk of the Under-Secretary, Colonel Larcom. It was forwarded to

Augustus Guy with a covering note making clear that the colonel believed the matter worthy of further investigation. Mr Wiseman was a retired land agent who lived on a substantial country estate. In his letter he explained that he suspected one of his former labourers, Michael Owens, of being the Broadstone murderer. Ten years earlier Owens had been dismissed and imprisoned for stealing from his employer; after his release from jail he had been a 'known robber' around Cork, the letter alleged, before moving to another part of the country. Owens's father Denis still lived in Whitechurch, and word had got round that he had money to lend. The source of this cash was said to be Michael, who had supposedly arrived in Cork in mid-November bearing gifts for his father: a razor, and £7 in gold (around £750 today).

According to Colonel Larcom the evidence was 'very persuasive' and the circumstances 'very suspicious', though to Mr Guy's mind the accusation was flimsy. But he could not ignore the wishes of government, and for more than a week precious resources were squandered on pursuing yet another false trail. Detectives were dispatched to Cork to liaise with local police, and Inspector Ryan was given the task of tracking down Michael Owens, whose whereabouts were not known. The inspector eventually found him in Tallaght, south-west of Dublin, where for the last eight years he had made a living as a rag-and-bone man.

Owens admitted to the detective that he had been in prison, but said that his only crime had been stealing food at the height of the Great Famine. Since then, he insisted, he had lived an honest life. Inspector Ryan soon found this claim borne out in his conversations with everybody from the local constable to the parish priest: all agreed that he was a fellow of exemplary character. Moreover, there was abundant proof that he had not left the town since six months before the murder. Mr Ryan concluded a characteristically thorough report with the assessment that 'there are no grounds, at present, either directly or indirectly, to suspect Owens of being in any way connected with the murder of the late Mr Little'.

This was enough to satisfy his superiors in the Metropolitan Police but not, apparently, their masters in government, since the matter dragged on for several days more. After almost a fortnight of wasted effort, Augustus Guy wrote a peevish, long and wilfully pedantic letter, addressed to Colonel Browne but clearly intended for those in authority above him, laying out in excruciating detail why Owens could not be a suspect.

It was an ill-advised gesture, because the superintendent was not in good odour with the people who mattered. A few days earlier he had submitted a detailed report on the case, offering his own analysis of the evidence gathered to date. It contained nothing that had not been stated by Mr Kemmis a month earlier, except the statements of Catherine Campbell which had already been discounted. But Mr Guy's crowning misjudgement was his covering note, a shameless attempt to gain preferment:

> If the Commanders should think it necessary to forward my report I beg respectfully to ask of them to remind the Chief Secretary of a kind promise which he made to Mr Inspector Ryan and myself during the late investigation. The Chief Secretary was gracious enough to say to us as follows: whether you succeed or not in this inquiry, recollect I will treat you and Mr Ryan handsomely.

The Attorney General was unimpressed. In a confidential memo to the Chief Secretary he described the superintendent's work as 'a very poor production: contains many inaccuracies and is not free from mischief'. Mr Horsman agreed, replying that it was 'an imperfect and defective report, and had better not be sent out'. The document was quietly suppressed, and a black mark entered against the name of Superintendent Augustus Guy.

Once again the detectives were beating their heads against a brick wall. They needed another lead, and out of the blue they got one, from a most unlikely source. It is a delicious irony that the breakthrough came from a new allegation made by Catherine Campbell, barely a week after the most senior law official in the land had declared her evidence worthless. Her latest claims were so specific and so obviously incriminating that any competent investigator would wonder why she had not mentioned them sooner. It is surprising that the police even bothered to investigate further; presumably it was only desperation that prompted them to do so.

On Monday 5 January Catherine told her guardian Sergeant Ward that on the day after the murder she had seen Mrs Gunning ripping off and removing the lining of the coat worn by her husband on the evening of Mr Little's death. She also watched Mrs Gunning wash a black crêpe shawl which she believed had been used by Bernard Gunning while he committed the murder. Catherine claimed that the shawl had been washed a fortnight previously, and only worn on two occasions since. She concluded that Mrs Gunning had washed it to remove the bloodstains. The young woman became emotional as she made her allegations, declaring that if Gunning were arrested she could confront him with facts which he could not deny. Catherine was convinced that Mr Kemmis suspected her of taking part in a conspiracy to murder Mr Little, and added that it was 'a monstrous thing' to allow the real murderer to walk free.

The sergeant wasted no time in passing this new information on to Superintendent Guy. Two constables were sent to Broadstone to talk to Bernard Gunning, with instructions to examine his coat for any sign of alterations. What might have been a mundane visit turned into something far more interesting when they walked into his office and found him with a bottle of turpentine in one hand and a cloth in the other, in the act of cleaning stains off a blue overcoat.

The constables leapt to the obvious conclusion: they had just caught the prime suspect in the act of destroying evidence. They confiscated the coat and bore it back to headquarters in triumph. Mr Guy examined it minutely, and noticed some dark stains on the sleeves. Could they be blood? He could not tell, but maybe an expert would be able to. It was undeniably a valuable piece of evidence, but there was one glaring anomaly about the garment in front of him: it was not the coat described by Catherine Campbell. This was a heavy winter overcoat, but she had spoken of an office coat, something he would wear indoors.

Accompanied by Superintendent Finnamore, Mr Guy went back to Broadstone to speak to Bernard Gunning. The working day was nearly over, and they found him shutting up the stores in anticipation of his supper. They asked him to take off his coat, which they then examined and found that the linings of the cuffs had been removed, exactly as Catherine had said. Mr Finnamore asked him to explain. Gunning told them that his wife had done it while making alterations about eighteen months earlier. The two detectives decided to check this statement with Mrs Gunning, warning him that he was not to intervene while they were questioning her.

A few minutes later the three men were in the Gunnings' kitchen in Directors' House. Mr Finnamore showed Anne the coat and asked when she had removed the lining from the cuffs.

'It was about three months since, sir.'

'Are you sure it was not longer ago than that?'

'I am not sure, but it might be four months.'

Superintendent Guy noticed the Gunnings exchanging anxious glances.

'Come, Mrs Gunning, it is not a difficult question to answer. Was it three months, or four, or longer?'

'I think it might have been five. No, six. I forget. Perhaps twelvemonth.'

'Could it be two years ago, Mrs Gunning?'

Mrs Gunning, whose face betrayed panic, was rescued by her

husband's sharp instruction not to answer the question. Mr Finnamore glared at him, furious that the assistant storekeeper had disobeyed his instructions.

'This matter is not over, Mr Gunning. We shall need to speak to you again.'

The following day Mr Guy took Gunning's coat to a tailor, who said he thought the lapels had recently been sponged clean. For a second opinion the superintendent then went to a dyer who was more ambivalent, suggesting that chemical tests might reveal the presence of blood even if the superficial staining had been removed. The two coats were sent to Dr Thomas Grace Geoghegan, a pioneering professor of forensic medicine who had a laboratory at the Royal College of Surgeons. The doctor wrote back by return of post, assuring the detectives that he had already begun performing his tests, although 'a preliminary inspection of them . . . renders me very sceptical as to any positive result'.

His doubts proved well founded. Both chemical analysis and microscopic examination failed to reveal any traces of blood, ending all hope that the coats would yield important forensic evidence. But there were plenty of questions still unanswered, and numerous ways in which Bernard Gunning might incriminate himself. The following Monday the two superintendents returned to Broadstone. This time they were under strict instructions to speak to the two suspects separately. Colonel Browne had been infuriated by their lapse in allowing Bernard Gunning to sit in on his wife's previous interview, a mistake which might have jeopardised their chances of learning anything useful.

They went first to the locomotive department, where they found Bernard Gunning in his office. Mr Finnamore explained that the detectives were there to talk about coats. In particular, which had he been wearing on the evening of the murder?

'When I left my office at half-past five I was wearing my new office coat, and took my blue outside coat with me.'

'Were you wearing your overcoat, or carrying it?'

'I cannot recall.'

'And when you went out again after tea, which were you wearing then?'

'Both. The new office coat, and over that the blue outside coat.'

'And what about the old office coat, the one we took away for examination?'

'I generally wear it in the morning, from when I get up until breakfast. But I cannot tell you whether I wore it that Thursday.'

'Tell us about the cuffs of that coat. When were the linings taken out?'

'My wife replaced them about twelve months ago.'

'Your wife did not seem so sure of that when we spoke to her. She seemed to think that it was much more recently.'

'I have been thinking over the circumstances since that occasion, and now I wish to state that it was fully twelve months ago that the cuff linings were renewed.'

'And yet you said to us last week that it had been eighteen months ago. Come, Mr Gunning, which is it? Three months, or twelve, or eighteen?'

'No, sir, I did not say eighteen months. I said that it was *twelve or eighteen* months.'

Mr Gunning was adamant on this point, although the truth could not be proved either way.

'How long have you owned the older of the office coats?' asked Superintendent Guy.

'I bought it new more than three years ago, I think, from a tailor called Robinson.'

'And when was it last cleaned?'

'Not lately. I always clean my coats when they require it, but I cannot recollect when I last cleaned that old office coat.'

'Have you cleaned it since the murder?'

'I can say positively that I have not.'

'Or had it cleaned by somebody else?'

'No.'

'Two constables who called on you last week say that you were dabbing your blue overcoat with turpentine when they walked into the office. Why were you doing that?'

Mr Gunning shrugged.

'I was simply cleaning it. I cleaned the collar, principally, or anywhere that I noticed a stain.'

'What about the stains on the cuffs: were you trying to remove those also?'

'No, I did not on that occasion see the marks on the cuffs.'

'And can you confirm that this blue overcoat is the one you wore on the night of the murder?'

'Yes, the same.'

Leaving Bernard Gunning to sweat it out in solitude, the two detectives went to speak to his wife. There was only one question they wanted to ask her, but a crucial one: when had she replaced the lining of her husband's coat? Her answer was oddly specific: between Christmas of 1855 and New Year's Day of 1856.

'Why those particular dates, Mrs Gunning?'

'I know the time from Mrs Butler, the schoolmistress. A few days ago she told my child Sarah that she was present when I did it.'

This seemed an unlikely circumstance, but the detectives let it go.

'Last week when we asked you seemed most uncertain, telling us three months, then four, then six . . . And when Mr Guy asked if it might have been two years ago, you refused to answer. Why?'

'I do not know, but I recollect Mr Guy rebuking my husband for some interruption. I'm sorry that I did not answer, but I cannot tell you why.'

'Which coat was your husband wearing on the day of the murder?'

'I cannot recall.'

'And when were Mr Gunning's coats last cleaned? Have you cleaned them?'

'I do not know about his office coat, but my husband himself cleaned the blue overcoat in his office – I heard him tell you both that he had done it. About three weeks ago he left the blue coat with me to make some repairs, but he took it away before I had time to do it, and it was after that that he cleaned it.'

The superintendents compared notes as they walked back to the divisional headquarters at Castle Yard. They both agreed that the circumstances surrounding the two coats gave grounds for suspicion, but what could they actually prove? It amounted to disappointingly little. Gunning had recently cleaned one coat, and at some unspecified time in the past his wife had repaired another. Their prevarications were of no evidential value, although they provided a useful hint to the detectives that there might be some substance to Catherine's allegation.

The affair of the coats had turned into another frustrating dead end. Where could the inquiry go from here? Augustus Guy and Joseph Finnamore were convinced of the Gunnings' guilt. The official line was that the police knew the identity of the killer, and lacked only the final proof necessary to send him to the gallows. Half of Dublin was aware that their suspect was Bernard Gunning, and the assistant storekeeper could not leave his basement apartment without enduring hostile stares and muttered insults. But just when the detectives had ruled out all other lines of inquiry, events took a turn which briefly shook them out of their complacency.

On Friday 16 January Patrick Moan was dismissed from his position as clerk to the engineering department of the Midland Great Western Railway. For two consecutive days he had turned up at his office drunk and incapable, and his superiors decided that enough was enough. It is possible that his drinking was an attempt to deal with severe anxiety, which seems to have affected him repeatedly during the course of the inquiry. The police interpreted it as evidence of a guilty conscience, because within hours he was under investigation again. In a letter to his superiors Augustus Guy wrote that 'I have considered it advisable to place constables in plain clothes to watch the motions of Mr Moan, in consequence of the statement of Sir Percy Nugent'.

Unfortunately the letter gives no hint of whatever allegations this statement contained. Sir Percy was a director of the railway company, an influential landowner and former MP who sat on the committee raising funds for George Little's family. He was somebody whose views the police would take seriously, and after speaking to him they hauled in Mr Moan for questioning once more. They were instantly rewarded for their tenacity when the former clerk admitted that he had lied about his movements on the night of the murder. When first interviewed he had claimed that he spent the evening at home with his family, later conceding that he might have gone out for tobacco. The story he now told was quite different. After leaving work he had gone to the house of a friend in Capel Street, where he remained for an hour. At 7.30 p.m. he walked round the corner to Mary Street, where he spent some time consulting a surgeon and apothecary called Edward White before returning home at 9 p.m.

The strangest aspect of this volte-face was that Mr Moan's latest alibi seemed perfectly sound. Both the friend in Capel Street and Mr White the surgeon confirmed his claims; even Mr Kemmis, who was shown a copy of the statement, admitted that it had 'the appearance of truth'. So why had he lied? The Crown Solicitor speculated that Moan 'considered that a perfect alibi completely covering the whole of the evening was preferable to stating he was out at all'. Perhaps it was another manifestation of the former clerk's anxiety that the prospect of being considered a suspect was too much to bear. Persuading his wife and adopted children to lie on his behalf seemed a simple way of avoiding such stress, but when his deceit was uncovered it rebounded against him, with disastrous results. Moan remained under surveillance for a little while longer, but subsequent events must have made it obvious that he was not the guilty man. Having lost his job he was also evicted from the apartment that came with it, a calamity for a man who had several dependants and no other source of income. His decline into unemployment and poverty was the ultimate proof of his innocence.

PART THREE

The Suspect

12

Saturday 14 February 1857
Day 92 of murder inquiry

A couple of months after the Broadstone murder the Dublin correspondent of an English periodical, the *Press*, described a recent visit to the scene of the crime:

> The building in which Mr Little was assassinated stands at the terminus of the Midland Railway and the Royal Canal. Built of granite, pierced with few windows, its architectural aspect is at once gloomy and handsome, and its simple massiveness suggests the idea of an enormous sepulchre. The internal arrangements of the station are in the usual style of great railway buildings. A winding stone staircase conducts to the corridor which traverses the upper floor. On turning to the right, after ascending the staircase, the visitor passes three or four rooms at either side, and sees a padlock loosely driven into the doorway of the last room at his right hand. On opening the door an apartment, about fourteen feet by twelve, presents itself to his view. It is lighted by two windows. A great bass* mat is cast on the floor, exactly on the spot where the corpse of the murdered man was found. Large black patches discolour and darkly stain the mat all over, and are by a practised eye at once recognised as human blood. By the mat and around the floor are torn and trampled envelopes, addressed to various officials of the railway. The room is unswept and uncleaned.

* A type of matting made from the bark of the lime tree.

It's the minor details in this almost cinematic passage that are the most telling. The padlock, the discarded envelopes, the dusty floor: they paint a picture of dereliction, as if George Little's employers had decided that the memory of his violent death could be expunged by locking it behind a stout oak door.

To contemporary readers the description of the abandoned office would have had a metaphorical significance. Mr Little's relatives had been failed by the authorities, and now the world seemed indifferent to their plight. Despite the support of luminaries including the Lord Mayor and the brewing magnate Benjamin Guinness, the charitable appeal to raise funds realised a disappointing £1,300. The original aim had been to guarantee the Littles an annual income of £100, approximately what an experienced clerk might earn, but in the event they received less than £80 per annum – enough to keep them from penury, although they would not be living in any great comfort. Many people felt that ensuring the Littles' financial security was the moral responsibility of the railway company directors. Their contribution of £200 was seen as an insult to the memory of a devoted employee who had given his life in the discharge of his duties, and miserably stingy for an organisation with an annual turnover in excess of £150,000.

Ordinary Dubliners also had good reason to feel let down. Despite its poverty, cramped tenements and petty theft, their city had always seemed safe; it was not London, whose streets were stalked by cut-throats, garrotters and poisoners, all waiting for an opportunity to kill in broad daylight. The failure of the police inquiry did not simply mean that a murderer was still at large. It was a sign that the government had failed in its single most precious duty, that of keeping its citizens secure.

As far as the public was concerned the affair was at an end. Any discussion of the subject focused not on what should be done next, but on what had gone wrong and who was to blame. 'That there has been mismanagement in the whole inquiry is lamentably certain,' thundered one editorial, 'and on a retrospective view of the whole case we are surprised at the utter incompetency shown by the officials.' The Dublin Castle administration observed a wary silence, apparently hoping that the less that was said on the matter, the sooner it would be forgotten. Weeks after making a very public intervention in the case, the Chief Secretary Edward Horsman had lost all interest. In late January, when the police sent him a dossier on their investigation, he replied from his country house in Northamptonshire, two hundred miles away, with a single sentence: 'I have no remarks to make on these papers.'

The heavy police presence at Broadstone had long been withdrawn. The notebook-wielding constables who for weeks on end had been accosting passengers and staff indiscriminately, getting under the feet of porters and making businessmen late for meetings, were now assigned to other duties. But although uniforms were rarely seen inside the station, the police were not entirely absent, since plain-clothes officers still tailed several railway employees night and day. A confidential note written by Augustus Guy on 14 February gives some idea of the kind of intelligence his spies were gathering:

I beg to report that Bernard Gunning has not left his house, after office hours, since the 7th inst. until the 10th when he left his residence at 7.30 p.m. and went to a private house, No. 5 Rathmines Terrace, where he remained an hour and a quarter. I have not been able to ascertain the motive of his visit as yet. He then went to a tavern No. 69 Rathmines Road and remained half an hour, and left accompanied by a female: they both went to the Clarence Hotel at 6 Wellington Quay. Gunning came out, after the lapse of 40 minutes, and returned to his residence, at which he arrived by 11.30 p.m.

Was this a clandestine liaison? If so, the police did not bother to pursue this line of investigation. After all, they were trying to catch a murderer, not a lothario. The detectives needed evidence of Gunning handling piles of gold sovereigns, or trying to dispose of blood-smeared clothing. Instead, the best they could manage was a suggestion of marital infidelity.

The cost of this operation must have been astronomical. Even the cashier's clerk William Chamberlain – who had been effectively ruled out as a suspect before Christmas – remained under observation until mid-February. The invasion of Bernard Gunning's privacy was even more disturbing, since Superintendent Guy was still filing weekly reports on his movements more than six months after the investigation had begun. On 26 April, for example, he recorded the details of several innocuous-sounding outings Gunning had made after work – to a city councillor's house, a gentleman's club, and a respectable hotel bar. On two occasions the undercover officers followed him home after 1 a.m., prompting the police commissioner Colonel Browne to scribble in the margin, 'He appears to keep very late hours.'

Intriguingly, this is the last such report to have survived in the archives. How much longer the surveillance continued is anybody's guess, but a sudden gap in the documentary record suggests that the entire inquiry may have been suspended some time in May 1857, six months after it had begun. The subject of George Little's murder had not even been mentioned in the newspapers since March, when an Irish MP announced his intention to raise the matter in Parliament. For one reason or another, he never followed through on this promise. By now public attention was elsewhere. Another sensational murder case was gripping the nation: Madeleine Smith, a twenty-two-year-old from a wealthy Glasgow family, stood accused of killing her lover Pierre Emile L'Angelier. Her story contained all the elements likely to thrill a Victorian audience: forbidden love, blackmail and death by arsenic – not to mention a cache of scandalous billets-doux. But in late June, as Miss Smith languished in prison awaiting trial, a sensational piece of news

from Dublin turned George Little and Broadstone into household names once more.

Thomas Kemmis was at his home in Kildare Street early on the
morning of Wednesday 24 June when one of the servants entered
the room to tell him that he had a visitor. The Crown Solicitor had
not been expecting anybody, and realised that there was something unusual about the situation as soon as the caller was shown
into his study. The woman who sat down opposite him was a
stranger. She was in her early forties, rather stout, and dressed as
smartly as the constraints of a meagre income would allow. Her
appearance was that of a shopkeeper or manual worker's wife – a
member of the class then known as Dublin's labouring poor. But
the first thing that Mr Kemmis noticed was not her clothing or
her accent, but the way her hands shook and her eyes darted
around the room. He could tell at once that she had some matter
of great importance to tell him, something that was causing her
deep distress.

The woman introduced herself as Mary Spollin, and informed
Mr Kemmis quite straightforwardly that her husband was the
Broadstone murderer. The Crown Solicitor was dumbfounded.
He had been aware of the progress, or lack of it, in the faltering
police inquiry, but he had not been personally involved since
Christmas – and now the solution to this mystifying case was
being revealed to him in his own house! Once he had recovered
his composure he asked her to explain. Mrs Spollin told him that
she and her family lived in a cottage on the Broadstone estate,
where her husband James worked as a general handyman. On the
evening of 13 November she had been at the door of their cottage
when she saw him returning from the direction of the station,
carrying a bucket. It was about 8.00, she recalled, and the bucket
looked heavy. When he came closer she realised that it was full of
gold and silver, and in the lamplight she noticed that her husband's clothes were spattered with blood. He told her that he had

killed Mr Little, and that the money came from the cashier's office.

Mary Spollin then watched as her husband did his best to destroy any evidence of the crime, burning a pocket-book and the cravat he was wearing before covering up the bloodstains on his clothing with dabs of paint. As he did so he gave a brief account of how he had gained entrance to the cashier's office and afterwards escaped across the station roof. Seeing that she was now complicit in this awful secret, Mrs Spollin had then helped her husband conceal the money, and agreed to lie about his whereabouts if questioned by the police. This crude alibi had been accepted without hesitation.

As Mr Kemmis listened to this extraordinary tale, he realised with a shudder why the name was vaguely familiar. Spollin was the amiable workman with the whiskers and the missing eye who had inspected the roof for him, and who had given him a tip-off about Catherine Campbell. He asked Mary why, seven months after the murder, she had finally decided to tell the truth. She could not cope any longer, she said; it was impossible for her to live with the knowledge of what her husband had done.

If she was troubled by her conscience, she was also terrified of her husband. Mary told Mr Kemmis that she believed he was trying to kill her. About ten days earlier she had fallen ill with stomach spasms and violent retching, and spent a miserable night in agony. Spollin refused to summon medical help, and threatened violence to his family if they dared to disobey. The next morning, with their father at work, one of the children defied his orders and ran for a doctor. The physician hurried to the cottage and was so alarmed by Mary's condition that he administered chloroform, concluding that she had been poisoned. His patient later told him that her husband had got up in the night, and his behaviour had been so wild that she and the children became convinced that he was going to cut their throats.

Mr Kemmis asked what she knew about the money and the

weapons. Mary said that the hammer found in the canal belonged to her husband, but doubted that the razor was his: he had thrown a razor into the water, she added, but he had first put it in its case. She had also watched him toss a key over a wall into a field not far from their home. As for the money, she promised to show Mr Kemmis where she and her husband had hidden it.

The Crown Solicitor decided that for the moment, at least, he did not need to hear any more. He was satisfied that the woman's allegations were credible, and that her life might be in danger. His immediate priority was ensuring her safety and that of her children; after that, the most important thing was to arrest her husband, and to secure any evidence that might remain on station premises.

He rang for his carriage, and within a few minutes he and Mrs Spollin were at the detective headquarters in Exchange Court. They held a hurried conference with Superintendent Guy and Inspector Ryan, and agreed a plan. The two officers went straight to Broadstone, where at 9.30 they strode into the locomotive works and found their suspect, brush in hand, painting a window frame. The industrious hubbub on the shop floor quietened as the workmen realised that something out of the ordinary was about to take place. Tools were downed, conversation ceased, and every face turned towards one end of the workshop where Superintendent Augustus Guy stepped forward and said:

'James Spollin, I arrest you on suspicion of being implicated with the murder of George Samuel Little at the Broadstone terminus on the evening of the thirteenth of November, 1856.'

And then they were gone, the detectives with their prisoner, leaving behind a ferment of speculation and a workplace where little was likely to be achieved for the rest of the morning. Their destination was the nearest police station in Frederick Lane, where they handed Spollin over to the duty sergeant, with instructions that the suspect was not to be left on his own at any time. With their suspect safely under lock and key, the detectives separated. Inspector Ryan was expected in court to give evidence in an unrelated trial, but Mr Guy returned to Broadstone to get on with the search.

As soon as Mary Spollin showed them where the money was stashed the detectives saw why it had remained undiscovered for so long. The hiding places were not only difficult to find but dangerous, too, and it almost beggared belief that the Spollins had managed to reach them at the dead of night. The first spot that Mary pointed out was at the south-western corner of the Broadstone estate, near the canal basin and on the other side of the goods yard overlooked by Mr Little's office. Trains carrying freight or livestock would end their journey here, and unload their cargo on to two broad and unsheltered platforms. Behind the platform used for cattle, a pair of parallel walls a short distance apart marked the boundary between railway land and the grounds of the North Dublin Workhouse. When the police officers peered over the wall on the Broadstone side they found themselves looking into a murky trench, a good fifteen feet deep, its bottom covered with rocks and gravel. A series of brick buttresses divided the channel into compartments, each about twelve feet by four.

Mrs Spollin could not recall which of these partitions was the right one, so it was decided to search them all in turn. It was not until the fourth compartment that the officers found anything. James Meares, one of the detective constables, noticed a pile of stones in one corner, with a hefty piece of rubble on top. On removing this rock he found himself looking at a piece of calico, damp and rotten, which had been used as a makeshift wrapping material. It was dark at the bottom of the trench, but he could tell straight away that the parcel contained money. Yelling up to the superintendent that he had found something, he carefully slid his hands under the decaying cloth, placed the parcel in his own handkerchief and carried it up to Mr Guy. Meares was eager to see what he had found, but the superintendent thought it prudent to wait until they were indoors and could examine it without any danger of losing valuable evidence. The constable was told to take his precious burden back to the station building and put it somewhere under lock and key. Superintendent Guy then hurried over to a different part of the estate, where a second search party was embarking on an even more hazardous operation.

A few hundred yards from the cattle platform was a latrine used by the labourers who worked in the goods yard. It was not connected to a sewer but drained into a stream – officially a river, known as the Bradogue – which ran along one edge of the Broadstone site, partly underground. Mrs Spollin claimed that her husband had managed to hide some of the money inside this channel by crawling through a culvert, but the officers could not squeeze their bulky frames through the tiny aperture. Instead they took up the floorboards of the latrine, revealing a chasm with water rushing past some twenty feet beneath. One of the constables, James Donnelly, gamely volunteered to descend a ladder into the foul-smelling void. After splashing around blindly for a few minutes he advanced into the tunnel that took the stream underneath the railway line, and it was then that he found it. Groping in the darkness his hands brushed against a cylindrical object which had been placed on a brick ledge to one side of the main channel. It was heavy, and Donnelly had some difficulty in carrying it back up the ladder.

Back in the daylight, when he heaved it down on to the gravel he could see that it was a workman's bucket, made by sawing an old wooden cask in two. Inside was a rotten canvas bag which burst when Donnelly tried to lift it out, showering the ground with coins – more than £67 in silver and copper. But that was not the only thing in the bucket. Underneath the bag was a mass of some substance that looked like clay and which one of the policemen recognised as red lead, used by painters as an undercoat for metal surfaces. In the damp air beneath the latrine it had hardened like concrete, and it was only after several violent blows from a sledgehammer that they succeeded in breaking it into pieces. Embedded in the middle of this mass the constable found another clue: a small brass padlock.

Augustus Guy was now quite certain that Mary Spollin was telling the truth. Only a person with first-hand knowledge could have led him to these hiding places, and accurately described where the money was to be found. The case against her husband was far from complete, but the specific details she had offered matched so perfectly with observation that he felt they had overwhelming evidence with which to charge him. Without stopping to think the matter through he hurried to the police court at Capel Street. Less than a quarter of an hour later he was in the office of the sitting magistrate, Mr Joseph O'Donnell, asking him to preside over an examination later in the day. After listening to Mr Guy's detailed account of the circumstances, the sudden arrest and the discovery of the money, the magistrate asked whose evidence the police intended to rely on for their charge of murder. The superintendent, assuming that Mr O'Donnell had misunderstood, told him that they would be calling Mrs Spollin.

The magistrate was astonished. It was quite impossible, he said. He then explained a basic point of law that Mr Guy should already have known: a woman was not permitted to give evidence against her own husband, unless the wife was herself the victim of the crime. The reason, which Mr O'Donnell no doubt might have quoted verbatim had he chosen to, could be found in the standard textbook on common law, William Blackstone's *Commentaries on the Laws of England*:

> By marriage, the husband and wife are one person in law: that is, the very being or legal existence of the woman is suspended during the marriage, or at least is incorporated and consolidated into that of the husband.

The difficulty was obvious. Legally speaking, Mrs Spollin was indivisible from her husband.* She could not speak out against him, any more than she could sue herself for libel. Augustus Guy was furious, although it was the antiquated common law – rather than the blameless official standing before him – that was the principal object of his ire. When his protestations failed to convince the magistrate to make an exception to a six-hundred-year-old legal doctrine, the superintendent asked what they should do instead. Mr O'Donnell told him that the police could make an application for the prisoner to be remanded in custody, giving them a week or so to build a case that did not rely on the evidence of his wife.

It is not difficult to imagine the frustration felt by Superintendent Guy as he returned to Broadstone that June afternoon. Since reporting for duty that morning he had arrested a likely murderer and been given what appeared conclusive proof of his guilt. Now he had to start all over again, because every shred of evidence provided by Mrs Spollin was inadmissible. There was nothing for it but to carry on as if this setback had not occurred. But one useful thought occurred to him: while Spollin's wife was, legally speaking, *persona non grata*, the rest of his family could still testify against him. Mr Guy would have to see whether they had anything useful to tell him.

The Spollins lived in a company property a few minutes' walk from the Broadstone terminus, a setting so conspicuously lacking in charm that even the most shameless of estate agents would struggle to make it sound appealing. The only approach to their home was through the goods yard. Visitors had to pick their way cautiously over the railway lines, pausing repeatedly to check that they were not about to be run down by a locomotive, and

---

* Augustus Guy really had no excuse for not knowing this. The ancient legal principle had recently been reaffirmed in the 1851 Evidence Act, which states unambiguously that 'nothing herein contained shall render . . . any wife competent or compellable to give evidence for or against her husband'.

over a stony wilderness unrelieved by any sort of vegetation. By the boundary wall, in the forbidding shadow of the North Dublin Workhouse, were a few derelict buildings, and next to them an incongruous sight: a neat, well-maintained cottage with a pretty front garden.

If James Spollin was a vicious killer, he also had a genuine appreciation for nature and tranquillity. In the most unpromising of surroundings he had succeeded in creating something lovely, a miniature idyll of neat flowerbeds and carefully trimmed shrubs. In a small vegetable patch the peas were just coming into blossom and runner beans climbed rustically up their poles, while at the centre of this picturesque composition was a rockery, an elegant arrangement of stones, moss and foliage. Hanging outside the front door was a brass cage containing a canary, and a pet rabbit sat impassively in its wooden run. None of this was new to Superintendent Guy, since the police had searched the cottage and its surroundings three times during the early weeks of the investigation; still, it seemed a very different place in midsummer, with the roses in bloom and the air scented with forget-me-nots and sweet williams. Mr Guy paused on the threshold of the cottage and turned round. In front of him was the station building; and, directly in his line of sight, the window of Mr Little's office.

The sitting room of the cottage was just as tidy and thoughtfully arranged as its exterior, with prints of Kew and other great gardens in gilt frames. Several officers had been at work for a little while already, and at the superintendent's arrival they broke off to show him a suit of tough cotton overalls which Mrs Spollin claimed were those her husband had worn during the murder. There were numerous stains, but nothing that was necessarily out of the ordinary for a painter's clothing. Mr Guy asked for it to be packaged and sent to Dr Geoghegan for analysis. Another item of interest was a fitter's hammer, similar to the presumed murder weapon but with a broken head, which one of the constables unearthed in a drawer.

It was late afternoon when Mr Guy decided that they had exhausted the possibilities of the tiny cottage. He was keen to find the key to the cashier's door, which James Spollin – according to his wife – had thrown over a wall and into the Bradogue. The superintendent instructed one of the sergeants to organise a search of the stream, concentrating on a section which ran through the neighbouring grounds of the workhouse. He and Inspector Ryan were off to make their second arrest of the day: it was a strangely familiar routine, for again their destination was the locomotive workshop, and again their prisoner would be a railway worker named James Spollin.

This was not Mary's husband, but her son. The Spollins had four children: James, aged sixteen; Joseph, thirteen; Lucy, ten; and George, six. The three younger children were all at school, but James had recently joined the company as an apprentice fitter – an enviable opportunity, and one that had been awarded partly because his father's work was held in such high regard. The teenager was surprised to see the detectives back in the workshop, and astounded when he learned that this time they were there to arrest him. The superintendent did his best to reassure the lad that his detention was only a matter of routine, but as James watched the heavy door of his police cell swing shut a little later he knew that he had embarked on a journey which might end at the scaffold.

Superintendent Guy's reasons for detaining the younger James were twofold. He thought it likely that the lad had witnessed some of what had happened on the night of the murder, and knew of his father's involvement. If that was so, and he could be persuaded to admit as much, the detectives' problems were at an end. There was no legal obstacle to a son giving evidence against his own father, and as long as he confirmed his mother's story they had a powerful case. He was potentially their star witness, and it was therefore essential that he was kept in isolation, away from friends or family who might try to influence him in any way.

But Mr Guy also wondered whether James was personally implicated in the murder. He had noticed that Mary deflected any question about her eldest son, and seemed a little too eager to emphasise that he knew nothing of what had gone on. For the time being, at least, he must be regarded as both a witness and a potential suspect.

Shortly after 6.00 that evening a small party gathered in the Dublin Castle office of Police Commissioner John More O'Ferrall. As well as the commissioner himself, the gathering consisted of Superintendent Guy, Mr Kemmis, Constable Meares and Mr Little's clerk William Chamberlain. On Mr O'Ferrall's desk, placed there as reverently as if it was some holy relic, was the parcel discovered by Meares next to the outer wall of Broadstone. Mr Guy had postponed this moment because he wanted the Crown Solicitor to be present at the opening of this most crucial piece of evidence. The first thing they noted about the package was its wrapping. On closer inspection the piece of calico looked like a scrap of clothing; had it belonged to one of Spollin's daughters? The superintendent carefully folded it, intending to show it to Mary at their next interview.

That the parcel contained money was obvious, but nobody had expected it to yield quite so much. It was packed with gold, silver, copper and banknotes, many of which had begun to decay during the seven months they had spent buried in damp rubble. Meares sat in silent concentration for some time, gradually taming the unruly mass of coins into neat stacks, before finally announcing that the total was £130 0s 8½d. But the parcel contained something else of interest. Some of the coins had originally been wrapped in paper, and although much degraded by damp, several fragments still bore signs of handwriting. These were passed over to William, who identified his own writing on two scraps of paper, and George Little's on one. To put the origin of the money beyond any doubt, another piece of paper had the words 'Midland Great Western' printed on it.

The commissioner asked how much of the missing money had been found, and how much was still outstanding. After a brief silence of furrowed brows and hurried mental arithmetic, Mr Guy was the first to supply the answer. The bucket recovered from underneath the latrine had contained £67 5s, and £43 had been found in the hamper six months earlier. Mrs Spollin claimed that her husband had retained £65 in gold for his own personal use. That all added up to £296 5s 8½d, and the railway company now said that £341 7s 6d had been stolen from the cashier's office. That left a further £45 1s 9½d still unaccounted for.

The entertainment was at an end. Mr O'Ferrall announced that he needed to write to the Chief Secretary, and his guests took the hint and left. Chamberlain wandered off homewards, but for the others the working day was far from over. Superintendent Guy returned to the Frederick Lane police station, where Mary Spollin was waiting for him, accompanied by two of his officers. The superintendent learned from the duty sergeant that the elder Spollin had spent the day in almost total silence, refusing to engage with the officers guarding him. Once or twice he had muttered something about his wife and children, but nothing worthy of note. On Mr Guy's instructions he had not been informed of his son's arrest, or that it was his wife who had accused him of murder. The superintendent asked for the prisoner to be brought down to see him. Spollin was about to have the shock of his life.

When the painter arrived at the front desk, flanked by two constables, his face was a picture of studied indifference. That changed as soon as he caught sight of his wife. His marble-white complexion suddenly flushed with colour, but he managed to control his emotions as he worked out what was going on. Mary was less restrained. She yelled at him.

'You villain! You murdered the man for his money – you murdered him! Confess your guilt, you unfortunate man. What I have done was to save your soul, so that you may repent of your crime.'

Spollin brushed off this outburst, responding, 'Oh, you foolish woman,' and then moved towards Mary as if to speak to her. She screamed out to the officers to hold him back, apparently worried that he meant to hurt her. Once calm had been restored, Superintendent Guy told Spollin that he was to be charged with murder, and the theft of £300 of railway company money.

'I deny it in toto,' he said.

The superintendent told Spollin that he would now be searched, and Mary again intervened.

'Search him well! Leave nothing with him. Give him a fair trial for his life, for I know his words when he was on his sickbed. He is determined not to confess it.'

'Confess what?' retorted Spollin.

'You know you murdered him. You told me all about it at a quarter to nine the Friday morning after. You said to me that he would tell no tales.'

Spollin ignored her. A detective sergeant called Hughes then went through his pockets, finding nothing of interest except a penknife and three keys. He asked what they were for.

'This one is for a chest in my workshop,' said Spollin. 'These others are my property, and you have no right to take them. It is too bad to have one's private affairs interfered with in that way.'

Sergeant Hughes took the keys and told the superintendent that he would investigate further. Spollin said nothing more as two officers took him back to his solitary confinement. A little later the door of his cell opened and one of the constables handed the prisoner a prayer book. 'Your wife wanted you to have this,' he said, stepping back into the corridor and locking the door behind him.

13

The three Spollins – James, Mary, and their eldest son – spent that night in three separate police stations in different parts of the city, each isolated from outside contact. Mary was under the protection of officers at the Sackville Place police station, a short walk from the General Post Office in central Dublin. So why had she been present when her husband was charged at Frederick Lane?

The police did their best to make it look like a chance encounter, but it was a trap – and a decidedly underhand one. The uncomfortable fact was that once they had arrested James Spollin they were not allowed to interview him. If the prisoner chose to make a statement – such as a confession – after he had been formally cautioned, that would be admissible as evidence; but until 1864 officers were not permitted to elicit information by questioning, a rule intended to protect the suspect from making admissions under duress. However, the police could submit as evidence anything the prisoner had said in conversation with other people. Mr Guy hoped to use this loophole to trick Spollin into saying something incriminating. That was why he arranged for Mary to be present at Frederick Lane, and when she harangued her husband she was acting on the superintendent's instructions. However genuine the rage underlying her accusation, the confrontation was mere subterfuge. It was also a failure, since Spollin refused to be provoked.

News of the arrest had come early enough to make the evening papers, so by Thursday morning most of Dublin was aware that the police believed they had caught the killer. Superintendent Guy had told the press – prematurely, as it turned out – that they intended to bring the prisoner before the magistrate at noon, and long before that hour Capel Street was thronged with crowds hoping to catch a glimpse of him. A groan of disappointment went up when an officer appeared on the steps of the police court and bellowed an announcement to the effect that there would be no examination of the suspect today; but so many people remained on the street exchanging gossip that constables had to be sent out to disperse them.

Augustus Guy hoped that he would be ready for a public hearing the following afternoon, but there was a great deal of work to be done before then. His first task of the day was to sit down and compare notes with Ryan and the other detectives on what they knew about their prime suspect.

His name was James Spollin – although officials and the newspapers insisted on spelling it 'Spollen'.* He was forty-three, married with four children, and had only one eye. This disfigurement was not the result of violence but had been caused in his youth by an infection. He was Irish and a Catholic, born and raised in the town of Ferns, fifty miles south of Dublin. In his twenties he had started working at the Hammersmith Works, an iron foundry in Ballsbridge, to the south of the capital. The proprietor, Richard Hamilton, was a celebrated engineer who specialised in designing conservatories and hothouses. In 1844 Hamilton won the commission to build the Palm House at Kew Gardens, and Spollin was one of the employees he took with him to London to work on the project. The construction of this horticultural temple of glass and wrought iron – at the time the largest greenhouse ever built – lasted four years, and by the time the

---

* Even allowing for the fact that there was often a degree of flexibility in the spelling of family names at this date, it is strange that almost every source renders the name incorrectly. He invariably signed his name 'Spollin'.

Spollins returned to Ireland they had added two more children to their growing family.

Richard Hamilton's next major project was a roof for Dublin's new rail terminus at Broadstone. Once it was complete the railway company directors decided that they needed somebody to maintain it, and at Hamilton's recommendation James Spollin was offered the position. He proved so reliable and versatile in his skills that it was not long before his role was expanded to include glazing, painting and general repairs. He became indispensable, in fact, and when the detectives looked into his eight years' service at Broadstone they found that he was known as quiet, amenable and a hard worker – a model employee. He was not attached to a single department of the company but went wherever he was needed, so had access to every part of the premises, night and day.

James Spollin earned £1 4s a week, and his son's apprentice wage added an additional 6s to their household income. This was important, because late on Wednesday night a significant amount of gold had been discovered in their kitchen. After confiscating the prisoner's keys, Sergeant Hughes had gone to the cottage and used them to open a chest of drawers in which he found eight gold sovereigns. Not only was this a suspiciously large sum for a man of Spollin's means to have in cash; two of the coins appeared to be smeared with mud, as if they had been buried or stored underwater.

It was easy to see how Spollin, with his impeccable record and tastefully furnished home, had not leapt out as a potential suspect. But Mr Guy was curious to know exactly what he had said when the detectives first spoke to him in late November. Inspector Ryan read out his notes of the brief conversation. Spollin claimed to have left work at 5.30 on the evening of the murder and gone straight home. He had then eaten tea with his family, spent several hours reading and then gone out shopping with his wife and eldest son at 9.00. Spollin said that they had not returned to Broadstone until 10.30, and it was as they were passing through the station on their way home that he saw Catherine Campbell talking to the policeman. Superintendent Guy wanted to know why this account had not been challenged at the time. Ryan told him that Mrs Spollin had given an identical statement, and that since there was no way that she could have conferred with her husband since his interview the police had concluded that they were both telling the truth.

There was little in his subsequent behaviour likely to raise suspicions. He never showed any disinclination to talk about the murder, frequently discussed it with colleagues when the subject cropped up, and always expressed his disgust at the crime. The only thing that struck a jarring note was his admiration for the 'nerve' displayed by whoever had committed it. One workman recalled that when the first cache of money had been discovered in the wicker hamper, Spollin was noticed spying on the police through the keyhole of an adjacent office. Another told the detectives that a few days before Spollin's arrest a few of them had been speculating about the identity of the killer, and it had been suggested that he might be one of several employees recently laid off by the company.

'No,' replied Spollin, 'I am certain he is still amongst us and laughing at us.'

Policemen were once again turning the station upside down, in a fruitless hunt for the missing money: though it was possible that Spollin had spent the outstanding £45, it seemed unlikely that he could have disposed of such a large sum without attracting unwanted attention. The search also extended into the grounds of the workhouse, whose boundary wall passed close to the Spollins' cottage. Mr Guy had ordered the nearby field to be mown, and the underground sections of the Bradogue to be dug up, in the hope of finding the missing key, but despite all these efforts it would never be found. The superintendent himself was not in attendance, but spent most of the day with the Crown Solicitor taking a statement from Mary Spollin.

She was much calmer than on the previous day, when the gravity of the situation had quite overwhelmed her. In a conversation lasting several hours she retold her story in greater detail, elucidating several matters that had perplexed the detectives. Among these was the method used by the murderer to enter Mr Little's office. Mary told the investigators that her husband knew the cashier was often alone after business hours, and since he had recently varnished the new security screen he was intimately familiar with the layout of the room. On the evening of 13 November he had hidden himself in a corner of the darkened corridor, waiting for a suitable opportunity. At some point George Little had emerged from his lair to use the lavatory opposite, leaving his door unlocked. Spollin had slipped inside and concealed himself behind the counter. It was only a minute or two before the cashier reappeared, turning the key in the lock behind him. The room was dimly illuminated by the gas lamp on the table, and Mr Little did not notice the intruder as he sat down to resume his work.

'There was nothing then for it but to finish him,' were the chilling words Mrs Spollin attributed to her husband. After bludgeoning his victim to death and cutting his throat, Spollin gathered as much money as he could carry in his bucket and climbed through the window of the back staircase on to the roof. He then walked along the duckboards and clambered down a ladder he had placed there earlier, which took him into the lavatory provided for third-class passengers. It contained a urinal, a deep trough of continuously running water which he used to wash the blood from his hands before exiting to the platform. The station was still busy but dimly lit, and nobody paid much attention to the solitary workman, dressed in overalls and carrying a bucket, as he strode purposefully through the terminus.

Spollin was clear of the building and crossing the goods yard when he realised with a thrill of horror that he had left his pocketbook on Mr Little's desk. If it was found he was finished, because it contained his name and the details of his work around the building. He had no alternative but to retrace his steps, climb the ladder and return to the office to retrieve it. He must have smeared blood on the covers, Mrs Spollin suggested, because this was the pocket-book that he burnt shortly afterwards.

She also claimed that the money had not been placed in its final hiding places straight away. Near the cottage, empty and almost derelict, was an old forge. Spollin had fetched a tall ladder, propped it against the wall of this building and climbed on to its roof. He had then driven an iron spike horizontally into the inside of the chimney and hung the bucket from it. This made his haul invisible from the ground, but something about this ingenious solution seems to have worried him, since a few nights later he retrieved the bucket and separated its contents into packages of silver and gold.

This was when the Spollins had deposited the parcels by the workhouse wall and under the latrine. But most of the silver was placed in a canvas bag which they concealed in a water tank – the one used by the engine drivers to top up their locomotive boilers – a short distance from their cottage. In early December, alarmed by incessant police searches, Spollin had remembered the empty wicker basket in the loft above the carpenters' shop: he knew that it had been lying unused for two years, and had not been disturbed by the detectives. Realising that he could keep the money there and safely remove small sums from it whenever he needed to, he had taken the bag out of the water tank at 6.00 one morning and succeeded in stashing it in the basket without being seen. It was sheer chance that Brophy happened to stumble across it just two days later.

That was the version of events told by Mary Spollin, and though inadmissible in court it gave the detectives something to work with. There were details in her statement that might jog the memory of a witness, or that might be corroborated by one of her children. Later that afternoon they spoke to the couple's daughter Lucy, a bright ten-year-old who had been carefully insulated from outside influence ever since her father's dramatic arrest the previous morning. Lucy gave the investigators another vital link in their evidential chain. Mr Guy showed her the piece of calico found with part of the money and asked if she recognised it. The girl did not hesitate: yes, it was a bonnet that her cousin Julia had given her. But Lucy had decided she did not like the material, so instead her mother had used it as a duster. Julia was duly tracked down and confirmed that the piece of cloth was the one she remembered giving her cousin.

Attempts to talk to Lucy's elder brother James proved less rewarding. The sixteen-year-old did his best to keep up a facade, but incarceration proved a brutal reminder that he was a child in an adult's world. By the end of the day he was distraught, crying out for his mother and refusing to speak to police unless she was brought to him. This was deemed impossible, so the young man was left alone. Meanwhile his father – at least, according to the *Freeman's Journal* – spent most of the day 'in one position, with his head resting on his hand and apparently impressed with the fearful character of the charge brought against him'.

The atmosphere in Dublin had become unpleasantly febrile in the forty-eight hours since James Spollin's arrest. An audience that had revelled in every detail of this lurid case now sensed that it was approaching its apotheosis. Curiosity was turning into obsession, and the crowd that had kept the Capel Street police court under siege now gained satellites across the city. Newspaper offices were surrounded by people so impatient for the latest information that they could not wait for it to appear in print. A mob descended on the Frederick Lane police station, demanding to see the prisoner. There was a hint of anarchy in the air, and the police did not like it. If many people simply wanted to see justice done, there was also a faction that hoped for something not seen in Dublin for many years, the theatre of a public execution: thousands of spectators in front of Kilmainham Gaol, the condemned man emerging in a white cloak and hood, the anticipatory silence before the trap opened and the murderer was launched into eternity.

Mary Spollin had been allowed home after her interview, although she now had an uninvited house guest, a police constable who watched her every move. She spent Friday engaged in her usual domestic activities, and a journalist who went to see her found her watering the garden, walking about 'with very little apparent concern or trouble of mind'. Later she sat by an open window to darn stockings, pointedly ignoring the railway employees and other interlopers who came to stand and stare.

Her son James, meanwhile, was being interrogated by Superintendent Guy and the Crown Solicitor. The boy claimed that on the evening of the murder he had been out with his parents to buy black puddings, and that they returned home at about 10.00. His mother had then cooked the puddings for their supper, but would not touch any herself. His father asked why she was not eating, and she replied that they reminded her of a story she had read about a man who had committed murder, and who came home 'with sweetmeats in his hands, which were all covered with blood'. Like Lady Macbeth, Mary Spollin was starting to see her husband's crime in every mundane detail of her life.

Mr Guy asked James whether he had seen his father climb the roof of the old forge. He admitted that he had, but added a somewhat unlikely explanation: a labourer called Magill often worked late in the building, lighting a fire in the hearth when he did so, and James's father liked to play a prank on him by pouring water down the chimney to put it out. But this was all they could get out of the boy, who proved a reluctant witness. As subsequent events would show, he was fiercely loyal to his father. Afterwards Mr Guy and Mr Kemmis remained in conference, preparing their case for the hearing in front of the magistrates, which had been fixed for that afternoon.

A little before 4.00 the prisoner was removed from his cell in Frederick Lane and taken to a waiting cab, accompanied by two policemen. A line of officers was needed to hold back the crowd, which then followed the vehicle as it set off on its ten-minute journey. It had got no further than the next street before it was brought to a sudden halt by a constable who stepped into the road in front of it. He told the driver to turn round; the magistrates had postponed the examination. Bodies swarmed around the stationary cab, faces pressed to its windows in the hope of catching a glimpse of the villain. Spollin sat hunched in his seat, his features concealed by a peaked cap pulled down low.

The person responsible for the delay was Mr Kemmis, who had been concerned to discover that the accused had no legal representation. After securing a postponement he sent an urgent message to Superintendent Guy, instructing him to speak to Spollin about engaging a solicitor. The superintendent went straight to Frederick Street, informed the prisoner of the change of plan, and at his request wrote letters to two Dublin barristers, requesting their presence at the police court the following morning. Then the detective went home, satisfied that he had discharged his responsibilities. Alas, he had not.

If a James Spollin were charged with murder today, the chances are that he would appear at one of Dublin's district courts within a day or two of his arrest. At a brief hearing the judge would simply ask how the accused intended to plead, and then refer the case to the Central Criminal Court for trial at a future date. By contrast, the legal procedures required to commit a murder suspect for trial in Victorian Ireland were tortuous and slow. At the heart of this process was the preparation of documents known as 'informations', statements made by witnesses under oath. Each witness appeared in front of the magistrates and was examined – and often cross-examined – by counsel. Once a written record of their evidence had been prepared by the clerks it would be read back to them, and amendments made if necessary. After hearing all the evidence the magistrates would decide whether there was a case for the defendant to answer, and if so commit them for trial.

One of the drawbacks of this laborious system was that a hearing intended as merely preliminary could easily turn into a long-winded and chaotic dress rehearsal for the actual trial. In the case of James Spollin, committal proceedings took almost three weeks to complete, entailing five days in court and more than twenty witnesses. The prosecution team overseen by Thomas Kemmis was happy for it to go on for as long as possible, as every delay meant more time for the police to gather evidence. And they needed it, for most neutral observers soon came to the conclusion that the case against Spollin was distinctly flimsy.

The long-awaited hearing finally got under way on Saturday 27 June, but few Dubliners were lucky enough to witness it. Most of those eventually admitted to the courtroom were newspaper reporters, who had arrived in unprecedented numbers from every part of Ireland. Mr O'Donnell, the presiding magistrate, arranged for folding tables to be set up at the front of the room so that the court artists could get the best possible view. With him on the bench was another police magistrate, Frank Thorpe Porter, whose brother George was the surgeon who had performed the post-mortem on Mr Little seven months earlier.

The sun shone from a cloudless sky, and by mid-morning conditions inside the courtroom had become so unbearable that men were sent on to the roof to remove the glass panes from the skylights. It made little difference. For much of the day, faces were mopped with handkerchiefs and papers used as fans. Sitting near the front of the court was a sizeable contingent from the railway company – notably Bernard Gunning, whose relief at seeing suspicion shifted on to someone else must have been intense. The examination was due to begin at 11.00, and as the hour approached there was a brief commotion when bags of the stolen booty were brought into the room and placed prominently on an exhibits table by the police. At a quarter past eleven Superintendent Guy asked whether the court was ready for the prisoner, and shortly afterwards Spollin himself appeared in the dock. The reporter for the *Freeman's Journal* described him as:

> a man about five feet eight inches in height, wiry, muscular, and active, slightly bald, with red hair and whiskers, which come round the chin and nearly meet. His face is thin and angular; his nose prominent and aquiline; his mouth and chin well formed, and his complexion pale. His forehead is rather high, and indicative of considerable powers of thought. There is nothing of the usual criminal type about his head, but the loss of the right eye imparts a slightly sinister aspect to a face which otherwise would be the reverse of repulsive. Certain hard lines about the mouth, the habitual compression of that feature, and the broad strongly defined chin, give an unmistakeable expression of sternness and determination to the prisoner's countenance. The back of the head is massive, and the general bearing of the man and the intelligent expression of his countenance indicate a class of mind superior to what might be expected from the position of life occupied by the prisoner. He was dressed in a blue pilot cloth overcoat and a white fustian working jacket, with mother-of-pearl buttons, and trousers of the same material. His demeanour was quiet, cool, and composed, and he answered the questions put to him in a clear, firm voice, and in a manner that proves him to be a man of high intelligence, if not of education.

The hearing got off to the worst possible start when it emerged that the prisoner still had no lawyer. The blame for this lay squarely with Superintendent Guy, who had made the elementary mistake of trying to engage a barrister, when he should first have approached a solicitor. The magistrate decided to hear some petty cases while officials ran around trying to assemble a legal team.

A solicitor hurried to the police court from nearby Stafford Street, and by a stroke of luck walked straight into an experienced defence barrister who had just concluded a case with another client. John Adye Curran was a fiery advocate who had acted in some of the most high-profile cases in recent Irish history, and he leapt at the chance of defending the infamous James Spollin. Though virtually unprepared, Curran immediately made his presence known.

'Your worships, my client wishes to register his objection to the railway officials sitting so near the defence, since he may have communications to make to his attorney and myself which it would not be advisable for those gentlemen to overhear.'

And after the gentlemen alluded to had moved to a different part of the court the proceedings were finally under way. John Richard Corballis QC, counsel for the Crown, gave an opening speech outlining the case against Spollin, and then began the examination of witnesses. Most of the nine who appeared on that first day were railway staff or police officers, who described events around the time of George Little's death and the recent discovery of the money. The undoubted highlight of the afternoon was the first public appearance of Lucy Spollin. Her father was visibly affected by the ten-year-old's arrival in the witness box, and as the clerk stood up with the Bible for her to swear on, Spollin appealed to the magistrates.

'That is my child, and I don't think she understands what she is saying; she does not know the nature of an oath.'

Mr Porter took this intervention seriously, and halted proceedings so that he could test the girl's religious knowledge. Only when he was satisfied that she understood the grave moral consequences of lying did he allow prosecution counsel to question her. Lucy confirmed that the piece of calico found with the money was the bonnet she had been given by her cousin, a revelation that caused a ripple of excitement in the public seats. But she said something else that was potentially still more damaging for her father. On the evening of the murder, she said, she had seen him climbing the roof of the forge next door, with 'something like a pot', which he proceeded to drop into the chimney. Lucy burst into tears when this account was challenged by Mr Curran, who – perhaps ill-advisedly – told her that by giving such evidence she was 'coming against your own father's life'. She wept bitterly for several minutes, but after recovering her composure stuck doggedly to her story.

After a long day of mostly unremarkable evidence, the hearing was adjourned and James Spollin remanded in custody. Crowds continued to block Capel Street for some time after the hearing was over, and it was late in the evening before the police felt that it was safe to take Spollin out of the building. He was spirited away in the back of a cab to Richmond Bridewell, the south Dublin prison that was to remain his home for several weeks.

Monday brought grave news from abroad. Indian soldiers in the garrison town of Meerut had risen up against their British commanders, beginning a rebellion that quickly spread to Delhi and beyond. Scores of civilians had been killed, and there was no sign of an end to the bloodshed. It was a national humiliation,* something that threatened to put a permanent end to the British imperial dream. Even so, newspapers on both sides of the Irish Sea devoted more space to James Spollin's first appearance in court than to the catastrophe unfolding in India.

While the wheels of Irish justice turned at their usual glacial

---

* The official term. Queen Victoria subsequently declared a national Day of Humiliation on 7 October 1857, when shops were shut and people went to church in extraordinary numbers to pray for peace in India. It was not until the following July, after numerous atrocities had been committed by both sides, that a peace treaty was finally signed.

pace, the police were working frantically to gather more evidence. Back at Broadstone, Superintendent Guy had arranged for the canal to be drained for a second time, in the hope of finding the missing key. At first light on Wednesday 1 July an army of volunteers jumped down into the empty channel and started to shovel mud out on to the towpath, where others were waiting to sift through it, oozing handful by oozing handful. They soon found something, but it was not a key. One of the labourers gave a yell, and handed the object to Daniel Ryan. A patina of sticky mud still clung to it, but the inspector could tell instantly that the thing was a razor. Its blade was chipped, apparently damaged by some violent impact. When he wiped the handle clean he saw that somebody had scratched a name in crude block capitals: SPOLLIN.

It was difficult to know what to make of this discovery: if this was the murder weapon, why had it not been found the first time the canal was drained? And whose was the first razor, if not the killer's? Superintendent Guy believed he knew the answer. The badly paid workmen drafted in to scour the canal bed seven months earlier had been told exactly what they were looking for, and promised a hefty reward if they found it. It really would not be surprising if one of them had planted a razor in the mud and 'found' it shortly afterwards. As for the second razor, there were two possibilities: either the murderer had thrown it into the canal after the completion of the original search, or it had been buried quite deeply and simply overlooked first time round.

At noon James Spollin returned to the police court for the resumption of his committal hearing. Again the surrounding streets were thronged, but the few members of the public who managed to squeeze inside the building must have found it a tedious affair. The witnesses who had already given evidence were read their informations by the clerk, and then asked to correct any errors before signing them. The proceedings came to life only briefly, when it emerged – thanks to forensic probing from Mr

Curran – that the prosecution was deliberately withholding some of the evidence against Spollin, hoping to spring it on him during his trial. Mr Curran was furious.

'I call upon you, in the name of justice and of fair play towards the prisoner, that you now produce that evidence. I have the authority of one of the most learned and upright judges on the bench to sustain me in this application, Mr Justice Perrin, who has always said it is contrary to the spirit of the law, and an act of injustice towards the prisoner, to withhold from him the knowledge of what the evidence against him is; and afford him an opportunity of examining it and inquiring into its credibility.'

Today, Irish defendants have the right to see a summary of all the evidence against them in advance of the trial, but in 1857 there were no clear-cut rules. After some discussion the magistrates ruled that Spollin had the right to cross-examine every witness who might appear against him – effectively siding with Mr Curran. This was a blow to the prosecution, who now had to produce several new witnesses, and at their request James Spollin was remanded in custody again – this time for another eight days. The hearing concluded with an appeal to the press that would not be out of place today. Mr Curran said that he did not object to the fair and impartial reports that newspapers usually published, but his client felt that a number of extraordinary and unfounded rumours about the case had begun to circulate, and if disseminated in print they might prejudice the mind of the public against him.

As if to illustrate the need for such a warning, on Sunday it got about that Mary Spollin had deliberately taken poison and died the previous night. The police quickly dispelled this rumour, although the half-hearted manner in which they did so implied that there was more than a grain of truth to the story. They did confirm that Mary had been seriously ill and confined to bed for several days, and was 'very weak and depressed in spirits', but refused to comment any further. There is no doubt that Mrs

Spollin was under intolerable pressure. The two breadwinners in the family, her husband and eldest son, were both in police custody, and it would not be long before the railway company asked her to move out of the cottage. But perhaps most difficult for her was the realisation that many people regarded her as complicit in the crime, her husband's accomplice rather than his accuser. She found an ally in the Crown Solicitor, who appreciated that without her they would have had no case. He made a point of speaking to Mary every day, ensuring that she and her children had everything they needed. Above all, he realised that he had to give her hope, to reassure her that after this ordeal was over she would not be abandoned but given every chance to build a new life.

Although few people noticed it, a second court case related to the Broadstone murder took place in early July. Jacob Moses Braun, the Jewish pedlar who had visited George Little's office a few hours before the cashier's death, was suing John Cashel Hoey, the twenty-nine-year-old editor and proprietor of the nationalist newspaper the *Nation*, for libel. At issue was an editorial published in the newspaper in January, at a time when the police inquiry had stalled. It referred to 'a Jew, whom the police have overlooked, who penetrated [Mr Little's] seclusion shortly before the murder, doubtless with the view of *setting* the place'. Casing the joint, in other words. In casually antisemitic terms the article went on to accuse the blameless rabbi of being accomplice to a notorious band of pickpockets – one of whose members, it suggested, had murdered George Little. Mr Braun wanted £2,000 in damages, but the jury awarded him just £25.

Understandably, the libel case was overshadowed by events elsewhere. On Thursday 9 July, after a riveting nine-day trial in Edinburgh, Madeleine Smith was sensationally acquitted of poisoning her lover Pierre Emile L'Angelier. There was news of a terrible disaster in Canada, where two hundred and fifty Scottish immigrants had been killed when a fire swept through the steamship *Montreal*. But in Dublin, at least, there was only one story that mattered: the third day of the Spollin committal hearing. The prisoner's whiskery face was by now familiar to anybody who had walked through central Dublin and seen the prints, reproductions of sketches made in court, that could be bought in every stationer and newsagent from the docks to the Guinness brewery. Startling rumours were flying around: Spollin had confessed; his entire family was implicated in the murder plot; the police had made some conclusive but unspecified discovery.

There was no truth to any of these, especially the suggestion that the detectives suddenly had access to evidence that would seal Spollin's fate. To avoid the inevitable crowds the prisoner now had to be conveyed to the police court at the dead of night, twelve hours before his hearing. Having endured his first week in the harsh conditions of Richmond Bridewell, Spollin 'looked better in health than was expected, although his features were a shade sadder', as one reporter put it. After hearing evidence relating to the razors and Mr Little's accounts – much of which was ruled inadmissible – the magistrates once again remanded the prisoner in custody. The news was greeted with dismay by those waiting outside, although they also had something to look forward to. It had emerged that Spollin's son James would be appearing as a witness for the defence; was this a sign of a schism within the family?

The final evidence in this protracted hearing was heard the following Monday, and it did not disappoint. Two of the Spollin children were examined, and as expected they gave rather different versions of events. The statement of Joseph, aged thirteen, appeared damning. He claimed to have watched his father dropping some solid object down the chimney of the forge, and suggested that he had seen both the razor and hammer in the family home in the days before the murder. He also alleged that his father had told him to say that he knew nothing if questioned by police. His elder brother James then contradicted much of what Joseph had said. He stated that his father had been at home by 6.00 on the evening of the murder, and had only ventured out on to the roof in order to play a joke on a colleague.

But the most surprising thing that he said in the witness box was not even part of his evidence. In answer to a question from one of the magistrates, James mentioned that he had been in custody since the day of his father's arrest, almost three weeks earlier. This was challenged by the prosecution counsel, who claimed that James had remained in the Chancery Lane police station voluntarily. The truth, when it finally emerged, was troubling. Mr Kemmis admitted asking the teenager to stay at Chancery Lane for a few weeks to help with inquiries. But when James told the constable looking after him, and later Superintendent Guy, that he wished to leave, they told him that he could not.

John Adye Curran began his closing speech by suggesting that the prosecution had failed to present any meaningful evidence against his client. But he was resigned to the fact that the magistrates had already decided to commit James Spollin for trial, so instead of arguing the case he chose to attack the conduct of the police. Mr Curran pointed out that an arresting officer was obliged by law to bring a murder suspect to a magistrate for examination as soon as reasonably possible, but Superintendent Guy had waited for twelve hours before even charging him. Then the detective had manufactured a confrontation between Spollin and his wife, in a failed attempt to trick him; and, worst of all, had held their son in illegal custody for three weeks. The barrister was furious, and with good reason.

'With respect to the detention, come what will of this case I shall to the end complain of it, because neither life nor liberty will be safe in this country while such traps can be laid for any man.'

The magistrates agreed wholeheartedly. Mr Porter appealed to the government to ensure that nothing like it was ever allowed to happen again. Today such a serious abuse of process would result in the entire case being thrown out of court, but there was no question of that happening on this occasion. All the evidence had now been heard, but since several of the informations had not yet been prepared the magistrates remanded Spollin in custody yet again.

The final hearing two days later was a formality. Once the remaining statements had been read and corrected, the police magistrate Frank Thorpe Porter addressed the prisoner.

'We deem it our duty to send you to trial at the next Commission for the wilful murder of Mr George Samuel Little at the Broadstone terminus on the thirteenth of November last. You are not bound to say anything that may tend to criminate yourself, but anything you do say will be reduced to writing, you will be asked to sign it, and it may be made use of against you. Now if you wish to say anything, at your peril, we are ready to hear you.'

James Spollin looked the magistrate straight in the eye, and without a hint of anxiety informed him that he would be reserving his defence until his trial.

PART FOUR

The Trial

14

Thursday 16 July

Shortly after learning that he was to stand trial for murder, James Spollin wrote a letter from his prison cell.

> To Lieutenant-Colonel Thomas H. Larcom,
> Under-Secretary of State for Ireland.
> The Petition of James Spollin a prisoner under
> remand in Richmond Bridewell charged
> with the murder of the late Mr Little

Humbly Sheweth

That your petitioner is totally bereft of means necessary to defend himself against the above mentioned charge in consequence of all his furniture and effects being detained from him which he estimates of the value of about thirty pounds, and which if he were allowed to dispose of could be made available to that extent at the least.

Wherefore your Petitioner most humbly supplicates that the Crown, if not disposed to permit him so to do, would advance thereon a sum sufficient for the purposes of his defence, which must be attended with considerable cost, and for which if conceded to him he hereby authorises Thomas Kemmis Esq, Crown Solicitor, to dispose of his said furniture and effects as he may think proper to recoup any advance made him thereon, and which may be given to his solicitors Mr Fitzgerald and Mr Cane of No. 28 Stafford Street.

And your Petitioner as in duty bound
Will ever pray

James Spollin

Deprived of his liberty, estranged from his wife and children, James Spollin was also penniless. The implications were serious, because he could not mount an effective defence without experienced counsel to represent him. Barristers were expensive, and there was no formal legal aid system in nineteenth-century Ireland. But the idea that anybody should stand trial for their life without representation was virtually unthinkable. If necessary, judges could assign a barrister to the defendant, and if the case was a particularly difficult one the government might agree a suitable fee in advance.

Spollin's letter was forwarded to the Chief Secretary, who responded from his office at the House of Commons. He refused the prisoner's request to be allowed to sell his furniture, on the obvious grounds that it belonged to Mary Spollin as much as to her husband. But Mr Horsman authorised the Crown Solicitor to supply Spollin with £20 from the public purse to fund his defence, adding sternly that this was 'not to be considered or dealt with as a precedent'. The caveat was justified, for £20 was a generous sum, reflecting the fact that this was a case of exceptional seriousness and complexity. It was common for the defendant in an Irish murder trial to be represented by a single counsel, but Spollin was able to engage three. John Adye Curran, who had done an excellent job at the police court despite minimal preparation, was retained to lead the defence. He was joined by two rising stars of the criminal bar, both future silks: William Sidney and James Coffey.

This trio faced formidable opposition. The Crown would be represented by six of Ireland's leading criminal barristers, four of them QCs – and led by the Attorney General himself. The prosecution had another advantage, since counsel were being instructed by Thomas Kemmis, who knew more about the case than anybody. He was assisted by his seventy-nine-year-old father William, Crown Solicitor for Dublin, who had been involved in every significant murder trial that had taken place in the city in the last sixty years. This army of lawyers did not have much time to prepare. All the most serious criminal trials in the Irish capital were heard at the Dublin Commission, whose regular sessions lasted a week and took place six times a year. The prosecution made a half-hearted attempt to buy more time for inquiries by applying to have the trial deferred until the October session, but their request was rejected. It was announced that James Spollin would stand trial in early August, barely three weeks away.

The Dublin Commission of Oyer and Terminer* – to give it its full name – sat at the Green Street Courthouse, a brief stroll from Capel Street and ten minutes from the north bank of the Liffey. Sandwiched between two jails – the grim, dilapidated Newgate Prison, and the scarcely more inviting debtors' prison – the court-house was a grand Georgian edifice, with six columns of Portland stone supporting a massive granite portico. On the morning of Friday 7 August the surrounding streets were packed with excited crowds. Many were hoping to secure a place in the public gallery, but they would be disappointed. Admission to the trial of James Spollin was strictly by ticket only, and this was the hottest ticket in town.

For the lucky few who were able to push through the throng and show their precious slip of paper to the top-hatted constable at the gate, this would be an experience like no other. The doors of the building had been thrown open at an unusually early hour, and the courtroom was full of spectators long before the hearing was due to begin; among them, reported one newspaper, 'a

* From the Norman French, meaning 'to hear and determine'.

considerable number of ladies'. Much of the space normally available to the public was taken by journalists, who had travelled not just from every corner of Ireland, but from all over England, Wales and Scotland as well. It was only four weeks since Madeleine Smith had been acquitted of murder at the High Court of Justiciary in Edinburgh, but there was already every sign that public interest in this case could eclipse hers.

The interior of the Green Street Courthouse offered a pleasant contrast to its rather forbidding exterior. Daylight flooded in through tall, east-facing windows to illuminate an airy double-height chamber, all white walls and oak panelling. Its layout was almost theatrical, with two public galleries curving around the upper part of the room like balconies. The jurors were accommodated in a sort of royal box, elevated and to one side, and the judges sat under a heavy velvet canopy that at first glance resembled a proscenium arch. The stalls in this theatre of justice were occupied by the lawyers, who sat around a great oak table – the barristers wearing wigs and gowns, the solicitors in morning dress. There were rather more of them than usual this morning. To judge by the sea of horsehair visible from above, every barrister in Dublin with nothing better to do had donned court dress and wandered over from their quarters in King's Inns. More remarkable than who was sitting around the table, however, was what was sitting on it. Four elaborate wooden models depicted the Broadstone terminus and its surroundings in meticulous detail. The largest of them, a replica of the entire station premises, was a magnificent thing, several feet long; but there were also miniature versions of Mr Little's office, Spollin's cottage, even the latrine where the money had been found.

The temperature inside the court was stifling, the atmosphere electric. One eyewitness later recalled the 'feverish anxiety' felt by the spectators as they waited for proceedings to get under way, as though it were James Spollin's execution rather than his trial. At a quarter past ten the expectant chatter fell abruptly silent, chairs scraped and benches creaked as lawyers and public alike rose to their feet. The judges were making their entrance.

Judges sat in pairs at the Dublin Commission, and for this case the presiding justices were two of the most senior in Ireland. The Lord Chief Justice, Thomas Langlois Lefroy, was joined on the bench by James Henry Monahan, Chief Justice of the Common Pleas. Monahan, the most senior Catholic among the Irish judiciary, was widely admired across the political spectrum for his erudition and impartiality. While he generally managed to maintain his composure in court, he was a volatile character with a weakness for salty language. He once lost his temper with a magistrate and shouted, 'God damn it, sir, it's all stuff and nonsense!' – an outburst that prompted parliamentary questions about his behaviour.

Monahan, then in his mid-fifties, was a mere tyro compared with the eighty-one-year-old Thomas Langlois Lefroy. The descendant of Huguenot immigrants, Lefroy was a Protestant, and devoutly religious. At home in Dublin he began and ended every day with an act of worship which the entire household was expected to attend, and when travelling around Ireland to preside at the assizes he whiled away the interminable coach journeys in close study of the Scriptures. It was difficult to believe, but this pious elderly judge with the aquiline nose and full-bottomed wig had once enjoyed a youthful romance with Jane Austen, and may even have come close to marrying her. In 1796 the 'very gentlemanlike, good-looking, pleasant young man' became an intimate friend of the novelist, who in a letter to her sister confided that she expected to 'receive an offer' from him. The proposal never materialised, although he seems to have left his mark on Austen's fiction: depending on which literary scholar you believe, she based the characters of either Elizabeth Bennet or Mr Darcy on her witty Irish friend.*

---

* Their relationship is the subject of Jon Hunter Spence's *Becoming Jane Austen* (2003), which suggests that Lefroy was the model for the character of Elizabeth Bennet. That book inspired the (largely fictional) 2007 film *Becoming Jane*, in which the young Lefroy is played by James McAvoy.

Once the judges had taken their place and all had resumed their seats, the Lord Chief Justice ordered the prisoner to be placed at the bar. Opposite the bench, on the other side of the lawyers' table, was the dock, a small enclosure with a narrow staircase leading to the holding cells beneath. A door opened and up the stairs came James Spollin, climbing with great deliberation. He looked well, apparently unaffected by the privations of more than a month in prison. Instead of his rough work clothes he now wore a smart blue frock coat, with a dark waistcoat and a black silk neckerchief. It was clear from the outset that he was taking a close interest in every aspect of the case.

The proceedings began with the selection of the jury – often a laborious process, since both prosecution and defence could dispute the appointment of any person they deemed unsuitable. More than fifty were rejected before the lawyers succeeded in identifying a dozen men that everybody was happy with. And they had to be men; in addition, the law required that jurors were aged between twenty-one and sixty, and owned property to a minimum value that effectively excluded all but a privileged minority. The jury appointed to try James Spollin was dominated by Dublin's prosperous mercantile class. The foreman, William Trevor, was a successful rag, skin and iron merchant, while his colleagues included manufacturers of buttons and agricultural equipment, an importer of eau de cologne and an auctioneer. The latter, Charles Bennett, begged the judges to excuse him, as he 'had a sale today, and the public will be considerably disappointed if it be postponed'. His request was denied.

With the composition of the jury now decided, the jurors took the oath one by one, holding a Bible and looking directly at the prisoner as they did so. The clerk of the Crown then shouted, '*Contez*' ('count them') to the crier, who asked the jurors to confirm that they had all been sworn. 'Twelve good men and true,' he declared, 'stand together and hear the evidence.' The clerk turned to the dock and instructed Spollin to raise his right hand.

'Gentlemen of the jury,' he said, 'look on the prisoner, and hearken to his charge. James Spollin stands indicted by the Crown, charged that on the thirteenth November last he did kill and murder the late George Samuel Little, against peace and statute. Upon this indictment he hath been arraigned, and thereunto hath pleaded not guilty; and for his trial hath put himself upon God and his country, which country you are. Your charge therefore is to inquire whether he be guilty of this felony, in manner and form as he stands indicted, or not guilty. Hear your evidence.'

It was not often that the opening speech in a murder trial was given by Ireland's most senior legal officer. John David FitzGerald, the Attorney General, was barely half the age of the judge sitting opposite him, but already regarded as the leading advocate in the country. His rise to the top had been meteoric. Called to the bar at the age of twenty-one, FitzGerald was appointed a Queen's Counsel at thirty-one and a cabinet minister before his fortieth birthday.* While his intellect was not in question, it was his fearsome work ethic that stood out. He was invariably at his desk before dawn, and would get up as early as three in the morning to prepare a case – or at least that was what he liked to tell his overawed opponents. At forty-one, he was still recognisably the fresh-faced prodigy who had lorded it over the Munster circuit two decades earlier, though the hairline was starting to recede, and – perhaps in an attempt to add some gravitas to his youthful features – he now sported a straggly grey neckbeard.

Mr FitzGerald was not the sort of barrister who indulged in cheap theatrics or rhetorical flourishes. He spoke plainly, choosing each word with care and raking the jury box with a piercing, intelligent gaze.

---

* At least one of his descendants also achieved high office. A hundred and sixty years after FitzGerald's own elevation to the cabinet his great-great-granddaughter Amber Rudd was appointed the UK Home Secretary.

'Gentlemen of the jury, it now becomes my duty to lay before you, as shortly as I can, the details of the evidence which will soon be submitted to you on the part of the prosecution. It is not a case of direct and simple proof, but a case of circumstantial evidence – a long chain of circumstantial evidence which, by irresistible inference, points to the prisoner as the person guilty of this crime.'

In an ordinary murder trial Mr FitzGerald would have limited his opening remarks to a brief outline of the circumstances of George Little's death and a summary of the evidence against James Spollin. But, as he acknowledged, this was no ordinary murder trial. There was no star witness likely to seal Spollin's fate, no killer fact or damning piece of forensic evidence. Instead, the prosecution would attempt to construct a case from the testimony of almost fifty witnesses, from a multitude of facts and observations, many of which would seem trivial if considered in isolation. Mr FitzGerald called it a 'long chain of circumstantial evidence', but it was more like some enormous and intricate jigsaw. The Attorney General's task was to explain to the jury what the pieces of the puzzle were, and how they all fitted together.

Mr FitzGerald told the jury a story that began with the appointment of George Little as railway company cashier in May 1856, and ended with the arrest of James Spollin and the recovery of the missing cash just over a year later. He was particularly careful to demonstrate that Spollin had ample opportunity to commit the crime. He stressed that the prisoner lived and worked at Broadstone, was well known there and could come and go as he pleased. There was the fact that the prisoner had been working in the cashier's office less than a week before the murder, his familiarity with the roof, and his knowledge of the duckboards and ladders that would allow a robber to make a swift escape. He explained in great detail who he intended to call as witnesses, and what they would say.

Mr FitzGerald concluded his address by remarking ingratiatingly that a jury so educated and experienced scarcely needed his advice. But he felt it necessary to say a word about the grave responsibility they now faced.

'Your duty to the prisoner in such a case as this is to examine the evidence with the utmost care, nay, with the most jealous and scrutinising caution; to sift every grain and particle of it, and if you think it does not point unerringly to the prisoner – if you entertain upon that evidence a reasonable doubt, it will be your duty towards the prisoner to give him the benefit of that doubt, and to acquit him of the charge. But if, on the other hand, you do not entertain any rational doubt, then it will be your duty – though your painful duty – to find a verdict of guilty, even though that verdict may consign him to an untimely end.'

And the Attorney General resumed his seat, having spoken for two hours and forty-three minutes.

There was no witness box in the Green Street courtroom. Those called to give evidence did so from a mighty high-backed oak chair placed on top of the barristers' table, surrounded by lawyers and overlooked by the judges to the front and the public to the rear. It was an intimidating experience, even for those who had been involved in a criminal trial before. From the moment a witness climbed the steps leading up to the table they were the centre of attention, like an actor in a solo show.

First to brave this daunting arena was Frederick Franklin, surveyor to the Irish Board of Works. A pleasant young man in his late twenties, Franklin had supervised the construction of the models that now surrounded him, and he was there to confirm that they accurately represented the terminus. His appearance should have been a mere formality, but James Spollin's counsel Mr Curran surprised his opposite number by asking to cross-examine the witness, and then trying to prove that his measurements were flawed. The mild-mannered surveyor proved equal to the interrogation, and Mr Curran left the fray without drawing blood. It was a strangely inconsequential fight to pick, and it may be that the defence barrister simply wanted to show the jury his mettle.

Combative and quick-witted, Mr Curran was the defence team's best asset, and he planned to cross-examine most of the prosecution witnesses himself. But given the abundance of talent available on the other side of the table, the Attorney General could share much of the work with his colleagues. The man who would shoulder most of the burden was Gerald Fitzgibbon QC, a grizzled legal heavyweight. Fitzgibbon was the son of a tenant farmer, an unusual background for a barrister at a time when the profession was still dominated by a well-heeled elite. He had grown up on a smallholding in Limerick but now, in his sixties, occupied a fine Georgian house in Merrion Square. His neighbours there included the ophthalmologist and antiquarian Dr William Wilde, whose three-year-old son Oscar would one day become even better known than his eminent father.

After these lengthy preliminaries the jury was finally given the opportunity to hear some evidence. Mr Fitzgibbon called the first witness with first-hand experience to relate: William Chamberlain, George Little's assistant. Wracked with nerves, William had cut a sorry figure at the police court – but the experience seems to have exorcised those demons, because this time he bore the pressure of the witness table well. Speaking clearly and confidently, the clerk confirmed that he had last seen Mr Little alive at 5.00 on the afternoon of Thursday 13 November. William testified that the builder Mr Tough and the cash porter Mr McCauley had both visited the office near the end of the working day, but that the cashier had been alone when he, William, had left the office.

Mr Fitzgibbon asked whether William had ever seen the prisoner, James Spollin, in the cashier's office.

'Yes, sir. I saw him varnishing the railings of Mr Little's office about five weeks before his death.'

'And was that the only occasion on which he visited the office, or were there other times?'

'I last saw him there about a fortnight or three weeks before the thirteenth of November. He came into the office shortly before five o'clock, before I left.'

'What happened on that occasion?'

'Spollin made some remark about "coming up" and Mr Little stood up and said that he had come too early, that he was not ready for him. Spollin said he would leave his things there and come back later. He did leave a paintbrush and some things rolled up in a cloth.'

Mr Fitzgibbon concluded his examination by asking William to identify the handwriting on the packages of money found at Broadstone after Spollin's arrest. The clerk confirmed that both Mr Little's writing and his own were on the scraps of paper placed in front of him.

The implication was so obvious that it hardly needed stating: the money found buried by the wall of the workhouse, and underneath the latrine, was the same money that had been taken from the cashier's office. But Mr Curran, when he began his cross-examination, was not so sure.

'Mr Chamberlain, staff and servants at Broadstone such as yourself are paid on a Thursday, I believe. Who is it that distributes their wages?'

'Mr Hodgens, the superintendent of the railway police.'

'And at this time, last November, where would Mr Hodgens get the money from?'

'From Mr Little.'

'I see. And what form would that money take?'

'He generally gave Mr Hodgens a docket, and silver, notes and gold out of the common funds, according to the amount of the docket.'

'How much would the amount be, in a normal week?'

'It might be two or three hundred pounds.'

It was a minor point, but a telling one. Mr Curran had demonstrated to the jury that large amounts of money, accompanied by the cashier's handwriting, could be found in places other than Mr Little's office. The defence barrister meant to test every easy assumption to destruction, to cast doubt wherever it might be found.

William Tough was next to climb the steps to the witness table, and the builder did not remain there long, merely confirming that he had visited Mr Little's office at 4.50 on the day of the murder, in order to cash a cheque. Mr Curran rose to cross-examine him, paused for effect, and then asked:

'You didn't kill him, I suppose?'

'I won't tell you that.'

There was laughter, Mr Tough was dismissed and the cash porter William McCauley took his place. He testified that he had visited the cashier's office several times during the day, and that when he left for the last time, shortly after 5.00, Mr Little had been alone. One of the junior defence barristers, William Sidney, asked Mr McCauley whether he had noticed anything unusual during that last visit.

'No, sir. The boxes were waiting for me outside the counter.'

'What was Mr Little doing?'

'I did not notice, sir. I just took the boxes and walked away.'

'Well, do the same now.'

The defence had apparently decided that if there was nothing useful to be gained from cross-examination they might at least provoke a little amusement. There was no such levity when Anne Gunning settled into the heavy chair in front of the two judges. She told the by-now familiar story of her movements through Directors' House on the evening of the murder, including the light she had seen coming from Mr Little's office at about 7.30. The first moment of real interest came when the Attorney General asked whether she knew James Spollin.

'Yes, sir. I have seen him cleaning windows in the boardroom and corridor. He also wallpapered my bedroom and sitting room.'

'Mrs Gunning, on the landing of the back staircase, next to the cashier's office, is a swivel window.' The lawyer pointed it out on one of the models in front of him. 'If a person wished to reach the roof, could they climb out through that window?'

'Yes, there is no difficulty in doing that.'

'And did you ever see the prisoner do that?'

'I have seen Spollin get out that way repeatedly.'

Mr Curran began his cross-examination by remarking suavely that Mrs Gunning seemed to remember her route around the building very exactly, given that it was nine months ago.

'I have told the story to so many different persons that I can never forget it.'

'I suppose now you could tell us how many cups of tea you took that night?'

The quip fell flat, Mrs Gunning merely observing that she 'always took the same compliment' of two cups.

Mr Curran asked how many people could gain access to the cashier's office after business hours.

'Any person that knew the way there could have access until eleven o'clock that night, but a stranger could not find the way.'

'My right honourable and learned friend –' he indicated the Attorney General – 'has suggested that the swivel window on the landing was the means used by the murderer to effect his exit. Are there any other windows by which one might leave the building unobserved?'

'Yes, there is a window in the hall near the secretary's office.'

'And is it possible that somebody climbed through that window on the night of the murder?'

'Well, sir, on the morning after the murder I saw marks on that windowsill that seemed to have been made by the nails of a shoe.'

'And what did you conclude at the time?'

'That some person had got down to the platform that way.'

With the unhurried nonchalance of a cat pushing china trinkets off a mantelpiece, Mr Curran was breaking down the certainties of the prosecution's case. Spollin knew how to reach the cashier's office, but so did plenty of others – and what did it matter that he was familiar with the roof, if the murderer might have escaped via another route?

Bernard Gunning followed his wife on to the table and had so little to offer, beyond the unremarkable information that he had known the accused for several years, that it was difficult to know why the prosecution had opted to call him at all. The decision began to look even more dubious when under cross-examination he revealed that Spollin, far from being the sole employee familiar with the station roof, was often accompanied there by a large team of assistant painters. While this was hardly terminal for the prosecution, it was not exactly helpful.

The carpenter James Brophy, on the other hand, had done some useful research since his appearance at the police court. After describing how he broke into the cashier's office and found the body, he explained how an intruder might escape from the roof by climbing down a ladder to the third-class lavatory on the station platform. Mr Fitzgibbon asked how long this would take, and Brophy was able to tell him exactly.

'It took me two minutes and twenty-five seconds to get to the platform from the swivel window next to Mr Little's office.'

'How far is it, would you say?'

'It is one hundred and sixty-eight yards from Mr Little's door to the foot of the ladder. From the office door to the swivel window is forty feet, which took me twenty seconds.'

'And how much further is it from the platform to Spollin's cottage?'

'Another two hundred and six yards. It took me two and a quarter minutes to walk it.'

Mr Fitzgibbon moved on to ask Brophy about the hamper of

money he had found in the loft over the locomotive works. The barrister did his best to link Spollin with this hiding place.

'Mr Brophy, the prisoner had a workshop in the same building. How far is it from where you found the basket?'

'A very short distance.'

'Did you see him nearby before the bag was found?'

'I cannot say that I did, although he was often there afterwards.'

'Could you be more precise? When exactly?'

'On the day after the basket was found. The police were in the workshop where he normally worked, and I saw him peeping in through the gate, instead of going to his work. I said to him, "Is that you, Spollin?" "Yes," said he, "who are those people in there?" "The detectives," said I. Then he turned around and went away.'

Mr Curran was invited to question the witness. He did not disappoint.

'Mr Brophy, you said that the prisoner's workshop is a short distance away from where the hamper was stored. How many other people work near the stairs leading up to that loft?'

'About fifty or sixty men and boys.'

'I see! And yet of all these fifty or sixty people you single out the prisoner.' The defence barrister had the bit between his teeth. 'Come now, Mr Brophy, have you any ill feeling towards Spollin?'

'I never had a quarrel with him.'

'Did you ever say you would hang him?'

Brophy was flustered, but held his own.

'I never did. He injured my brother, and I had a disagreement with him.'

'I thought so.' Mr Curran's triumphant reaction implied to the jury that this was an admission of some significance.

The surgeon George Porter was next to be examined. He described the wounds he had found on Mr Little's body and agreed that the blunt instrument used to kill him might have been the hammer found in the canal. The Attorney General asked about the incised wounds on the neck and face. What had caused them?

'They must have been inflicted by a very sharp instrument.'

'Would a razor be enough to do it?'

'I would have thought a razor very likely to have inflicted these wounds.'

Mr FitzGerald picked up something from the table in front of him and handed it to the witness.

'Could the injuries you describe have been caused by the razor you are now holding?'

Mr Porter opened the razor and examined its blade minutely before replying.

'It would have done it very well, and I see gaps at the end of the blade.'

'Would you explain what you mean by that, Mr Porter?'

'To make an incision such as I described, the blade must have come into contact with the teeth, and doing so would injure the edge of a sharp instrument.'

The Attorney General turned to the jury, and with the air of a conjuror completing a successful card trick revealed that the razor he had shown to the surgeon was the one with Spollin's name written on its handle.

His triumph was short-lived. Mr Sidney began his cross-examination by handing the witness another razor.

'Mr Porter, the razor you now have in your hand was found in the canal some nine months ago. Might the wounds have been caused by that blade?'

'Yes, quite possibly.'

'And do you agree that this razor also has gaps in it?'

'Yes, it does.'

'My learned friend has just shown you a hammer which was found during a search of the canal, and you agreed that it might have been the murder weapon. But I have another hammer here. Do you recognise it?'

'Yes. I saw it on the day that the body was exhumed.'

'And for what purpose?'

'I fitted it to the wounds on the head to see if it was a match.'

'And was it?'

'Yes, it fitted exactly.'

'And did you check whether any other hammers matched the wound?'

'Yes, I tried one more, which I believe to have been about the same size.'

'So you cannot be certain that it was the first hammer – that is, the hammer found in the canal – that was the murder weapon?'

'No. Indeed, I never said that another hammer would not fit the wounds.'

Archibald Moore and Mr Beausire were then questioned about their memories of the crime scene, but without producing a word of evidence that even threatened to be useful. Equally unenlightening was Dr John Aldridge, a chemist who had tested the red stains found on the door frames on the ground floor of the station. All he was able to say was that they were not blood; how this helped either side was anybody's guess.

It was now a quarter to six in the evening, and after more than five hours of evidence the jurors were starting to wonder how much longer they would be required to remain in the stuffy courtroom. The Attorney General chose this moment to call Lucy Spollin. The ten-year-old passed within touching distance of the dock as she skirted the lawyers' table. Her father, who had listened impassively but attentively to all that had gone on, could no longer control his emotions as he watched his little girl climb the few steps up to the table and clamber into the great chair, her feet swinging free. But before the clerk could reach her with the Bible, Mr Curran stood up to say that he intended to cross-examine this witness, and since it was likely to take a considerable time he asked for it to be postponed to the following morning.

The only people disappointed by this sensible request were the occupants of the public gallery, who had been looking forward to the encounter between Spollin's daughter and the barristers with keen anticipation, and who now faced another anxious wait in an early-morning queue if they were to have any chance of seeing it. The judges agreed with Mr Curran, so Lucy left the court without uttering a word, and Thomas O'Byrne took her place. O'Byrne, the foreman of the painting department at Broadstone, had been Spollin's superior at the station, and confirmed that the accused had been employed in Mr Little's office about a fortnight before the murder, varnishing a table and covering some of the fixtures with morocco leather. Mr FitzGerald asked about Spollin's behaviour on the day that the hamper of money was found above the locomotive works.

'I remember seeing him while the police were in my workshop. I was speaking to a policeman; he came to the door, and opened it to come in. But then he closed it quietly, and I noticed him peeping in through a gap.'

Mr Sidney, in his cross-examination, was unimpressed.

'Mr O'Byrne, the day you saw Spollin "peeping in", as you put it, the police were in your workshop, weren't they?'

'Yes, sir.'

'That was an unusual occurrence, surely. Were the other men not interested in finding out what was going on?'

'Yes, that day there was a great deal of gossip about the murder. Every time the detectives came there was whispering.'

'We have heard much about the basket that was found that day. Would it take any great effort for a person climbing the staircase to reach it?'

'No, anybody passing up that way could put their hand on it.'

'How many people have access to those stairs?'

'A great number.'

'Would you be more precise? There were about four weeks between the murder of Mr Little and the discovery of the basket.

How many people might have passed that way during those four weeks, do you think?'

'I would not swear that a hundred and fifty did not pass during that time.'

The Broadstone storekeeper Henry Osborne was next to take his place on the table. Mr Fitzgibbon asked whether he would recognise the prisoner's handwriting, to which he replied in the affirmative. The barrister handed him Spollin's time-book.

'Mr Osborne, what does this book have to say about the prisoner's movements on the day of November the thirteenth last year?'

Mr Osborne flicked through until he found the right page.

'It appears that he left work at half-past five p.m., which was the usual quitting time.'

'What had he been doing that day?'

'This is not stated in the book, but I happen to know that he had been working on some new carriages in the paint shop.'

Mr Curran took over the questioning for the defence.

'I believe the prisoner also earned some extra money in his free time, by doing painting and wallpapering for individuals on a private basis. Did he ever do any work for you?'

'Yes, he did.'

'And how did you find him?'

'He was always quiet, temperate and inoffensive.'

And after this glowing character reference the first day of the trial petered out to an unremarkable close. Constable Meares related the discovery of the package by the workhouse wall, and the stationmaster of Athlone railway station – as well as his booking clerk – gave wholly superfluous evidence about the provenance of the money in it. It was 7.00 before these unnecessary witnesses had been dealt with, at which point the Lord Chief Justice announced that the court would rise, and asked for four bailiffs to be sworn in to look after the jury. This development caused some consternation, as the jurors realised that they were about to be placed in something like captivity. One of their number, John Johnston, addressed himself to the bench.

'My Lord, are we not to get home?'

The Attorney General took it upon himself to answer.

'That is out of the question, gentlemen.'

'Many of us have important business to discharge. Our detention will be most inconvenient.'

The Lord Chief Justice explained patiently that in a trial of such gravity it was essential that the jurors were kept together, and did not communicate with anybody else. The response to this statement was near-mutiny. The exhausted jurors spoke all at once, complaining bitterly at the effect this deprivation of liberty would have on their business affairs. It was eventually agreed that if necessary they could send messages to their families – carefully vetted to ensure that they contained no reference to the case – via mounted police officers. And with that the court was declared adjourned until the following morning.

Outside the courthouse the weather had taken a turn for the worse. The continuous heavy rain was not enough to deter the crowds who had spent all afternoon discussing the case, their curiosity fed by occasional scraps of information thrown to them by those leaving the building. As the public galleries emptied and their occupants poured out into the street, they found themselves being pressed for intelligence about the latest evidence against the prisoner. For a few minutes Green Street turned into the Curragh on the day of a race meeting, with little knots of people exchanging prognostications and shaking their heads in frustration at each other's ignorance.

Meanwhile at the rear of the building a prison van containing James Spollin emerged from the courthouse yard, surrounded by an escort of mounted police, and proceeded rapidly and almost unnoticed towards Richmond Bridewell.

15

Friday 7 August

The rain continued to fall that evening as the jurors made the best of a bad job, reluctantly tucking into an expensive meal at the nearby European Hotel under the watchful eyes of the court-appointed bailiffs. It was still falling the next morning when they hurried back to the Green Street Courthouse, the twelve burghers of Dublin with their official escort, obediently scuttling along in formation like a crocodile of schoolboys. The weather seemed to have dampened public enthusiasm as well, for at 9.30, when a convoy of horses and vehicles rattled down Halston Street and dropped off James Spollin and two prison officers, there was hardly anybody there to see it.

The courtroom itself was as packed as on the previous day, and with good reason. Most of the lucky ticket-holders knew that the prisoner's children were to be examined today, and since the Crown appeared to be relying on their evidence to secure a conviction it seemed possible that Spollin's fate would be decided in the coming hours – *de facto* if not *de jure*.

Mr Curran seemed to think that he had missed a trick during his cross-examination of Anne Gunning, because he immediately requested her recall for further questioning. The judges conferred briefly before assenting. This time it was one of the junior defence counsel, William Sidney, who was given the responsibility of cross-examining her. The purpose of this tactic instantly became clear when Mr Sidney began by asking more questions about the swivel window near Mr Little's office. Mrs Gunning testified that this window was near her own apartment, that the stairs beneath it had no carpet, and that she would have expected to hear a person walking up the staircase or opening the window – and yet she had heard no noise. She also confirmed the existence of a third window through which an interloper might have made an escape. The profusion of doors and windows, corridors and stairs, so complicated her narrative that there was a lengthy digression as first Chief Justice Monahan, and then the Attorney General, sought clarification. Once the baroque complexities of the Broadstone floor plan had been cleared up to the satisfaction of the bench, Mrs Gunning was allowed to step down. Mr Kemmis slipped out of the courtroom with her, and when he returned he was escorting Lucy Spollin.

Lucy wore a pink spotted frock, with a black velvet cape and a blue and amber silk bonnet – neat but not formal, dressed for a birthday party rather than Sunday Mass. She was a picture of innocence, and it hardly seemed possible that what she said in the next hour might determine whether a man lived or died. As she was led in silence to the witness chair, every eye was upon Lucy – or darting between her and her father to see how her appearance would affect him. He grew agitated at her approach; his face flushed, and he appeared to weep as she climbed the few steps up to the table. He did not utter a sound, but wiped his single eye with a handkerchief as he shifted his seat to one side in the dock so as to get a better view of his daughter.

The Attorney General began gently, putting Lucy at her ease by asking her where she lived, and the names and ages of her brothers. She betrayed no hint of nervousness, giving her answers in a firm, clear voice – apparently unperturbed by the presence of her father, and by the hundreds of spectators who hung on her every word. Mr FitzGerald asked about the daily routine in the Spollin household at the time of the murder. She replied that the family had lunch together at 12 p.m., and at 5.30 every evening her father and elder brother would leave work and come home for tea.

'Miss Spollin, do you remember the day that Mr Little was killed?'

'Yes.'

'Did your father dine at home that evening?'

'Yes.'

'What time did your brother James come home from work that day?'

'At half-past five.'

'Did your father come home with him?'

'No.'

'Was your father there for tea?'

'No, not till after James and my mother had eaten.'

'What time did your father return home?'

'About seven or eight.'

'And what about you? Did you have tea with James and your mother?'

'No, my brother Joseph and I took our tea after them.'

'And was your father at home by then?'

'No, not till after.'

'So when did you first see your father at home that evening?'

'I did not see him indoors till he came in to take his tea by himself.'

'Before he came in for his tea, did you see your father out of doors?'

'Yes.'

'Where did you see him?'

'He was on the roof opposite our cottage, on the forge where the smiths used to work.'

'Where were you at the time?'

'Looking out of the window of our cottage.'

'Was anybody else with you?'

'Yes, all my brothers. James came to look out of the window with me. Joseph also came, and both of them saw my father.'

'It was dark, surely. How were you able to see him?'

'There was moonlight.'

'And what was your father doing on the chimney?'

'He had a ladder and was putting something down the chimney.'

There were gasps from the public gallery, which the Chief Justice silenced with a glare. The Attorney General continued.

'What was he putting down the chimney?'

'It was something round in a lump.'

'And what was your mother doing all this time?'

'She was standing at the hall door.'

'And when did your father come in for his tea?'

'About an hour and a half after I saw him on the roof.'

'So what time was he on the roof?'

'I do not know the clock myself. It was about six or seven that he was up there, after I took my own tea.'

The Attorney General moved on as swiftly as possible. He wished to avoid bringing attention to his key witness's damaging admission that she could not tell the time.

'Did you yourself go outside after you had your tea?'

'No.'

'And what did you do afterwards?'

'I went to bed. That was after my father had taken his tea.'

At this point a juror interrupted to ask for more information about the ladder. The intervention was welcomed courteously by the Attorney General, who relayed the question to his witness.

'When you saw your father on the roof of the old smithy, where was the ladder?'

'On the roof.'

'So the bottom of the ladder was not on the ground?'

'No, it was from the roof to the chimney.'

'How did it get up there?'

'He brought it up after him.'

Judge Monahan broke in to ask how she knew that that was what her father had done.

'I saw him climbing up, and when he got on the roof he pulled up the ladder after him.'

Both jurors and judges having now satisfied themselves on this point, Mr FitzGerald decided that it was time to introduce a crucial exhibit. At his direction, one of the ushers handed Lucy the piece of calico in which some of the money had been buried.

'Miss Spollin, do you recognise this cloth?'

'Yes.'

'What is it?'

'When I first saw it, it was a sun bonnet. I was given it as a present by my cousin Julia Lyons.'

'When did she give it to you?'

'A long time ago. I think it was a year before last Christmas.'

'What happened to it after she gave it to you?'

'I never wore it. It was used as a duster.'

'You are quite sure that this is the same piece of cloth given to you as a bonnet?'

'I am quite sure. I often saw it about the cottage.'

'Have you seen it in the cottage since Mr Little was killed?'

'No.'

'When do you last remember seeing this piece of cloth?'

'About three months before Mr Little was killed.'

'Where was it then?'

'It was in the cottage, being used as a duster.'

'Do you remember when the canal was drained, shortly after the murder?'

'Yes.'

'At that time the police were near your home, searching the canal and the land around it. What did your father say to you about that?'

'He said that if I was shown a piece of chamois or red rag, I was to say I had not seen it before.'

'Now, let us turn to the time of your father's arrest a few weeks ago. Do you recall that your mother was ill around then?'

'Yes, about a week before my father was taken.'

'Do you recollect your father being present when your mother was sick, and your mother asking him to send for someone?'

Mr Sidney leapt up to protest that the Attorney General was asking leading questions. Mr FitzGerald replied that it was a perfectly proper question to ask, since the answer would correspond with a statement made by the prisoner. Mr Curran retorted that this was not relevant, and might prejudice the case. After a bit of wrangling between the barristers, Chief Justice Monahan settled the matter.

'Ask the question,' he said.

'On the grounds that it will have a bearing upon the case,' said Chief Justice Lefroy, completing his brother judge's sentence for him.

'I am obliged to your Lordships,' said the Attorney General, turning back to face Lucy. 'Will you tell me what she said?'

'She said she was very ill, and wanted the priest and the doctor.'

'What did your father say to that?'

'That he would not let a priest or doctor into the house, and that if anybody left the house for them he would have their life.'

It is gratifying for any barrister to finish examining a witness secure in the knowledge that their evidence has made some impression, and when the Attorney General sat down it was to a background of shocked gasps and muttered conversations in the public gallery.

The suggestion that James Spollin had made threats to kill against his own flesh and blood was certainly one that looked bad for him, but as Mr Sidney stood up to begin his cross-examination he knew that there were already signs that Lucy might prove a greater asset to the defence than to the Crown. He had been entrusted with this delicate task because Mr Curran appreciated that his own approach to challenging a witness – combative, acerbic, witty – might be counterproductive if deployed against a young girl. William Sidney was a different type of advocate: urbane and courteous, he presented himself as the witness's ally rather than their antagonist. He had just turned thirty, not yet a Queen's Counsel but clearly destined to be one, endowed with brains and an easy charm.

Following the example given by the Attorney General, Mr Sidney began by asking Lucy a series of innocuous questions about the schools she and her brother attended, before striking out into more contentious territory. The girl spoke softly, so Mr Sidney repeated her answers to ensure that the jury did not miss a word.

'Miss Spollin, when did you first hear that Mr Little had been killed?'

'He was murdered on a Thursday, and I heard that he was murdered on the Friday, at about half-past five.'

'Who was it that told you?'

'My brother Joseph. He heard it among the workmen in the sheds.'

'And what about your brother James? When did he hear it?'

'The same time that Joseph knew it.'

'You have described seeing your father on the roof of the forge. Are you quite sure that that was on the evening before you heard Joseph say that Mr Little had been murdered?'

'Yes, I am.'

'Might it not have been some other evening?'

Lucy had so far answered every question calmly, but now she replied with some heat, her vehemence drawing gasps from the public gallery.

'No, I am quite sure, as sure of that as anything else I have said.'

Mr Sidney changed tack abruptly. 'Miss Spollin, there is a clock on the wall behind you. Can you tell me what time it says?'

The clock in question hung opposite the judges, immediately above the dock. Looking at it would entail meeting her father's gaze. Perhaps this was the barrister's intention; if so his ruse was unsuccessful, because without moving in her chair Lucy said emphatically that she did not 'understand the clock' at all.

'Do you know in which month Mr Little was murdered?'

'No.'

'Well, then, do you know whether it was at the beginning or end of the year?'

'No.'

'You've told me what your father was doing that Thursday. Do you recall what he was doing on the Monday before that?'

'No.'

'Well, then, let me ask you something simpler. Do you remember what time he came home from work that Monday?'

'No.'

'Or the Monday after that?'

'No.'

'Could you tell me what time your father came home any night that week?'

'I think he came home at the usual hour, but I can't remember.'

'I see,' said Mr Sidney. 'You see we have a beautiful model here of your cottage. There is a large building overlooking it, is there not? Do you know what that building is?'

'Yes, sir. It is the asylum.'

'How close is the asylum to your home?'

'Very close. A boy standing on the roof of our cottage could hit it with a stone.'

There was a ripple of amusement at this curiously specific choice of illustration.

'If a person were standing at a window in the asylum would they be able to see your father standing by the chimney?'

'Yes, they would see him as clearly as I did.'

'You say that you were standing at the parlour window when you saw your father. Does that window have curtains, or a blind?'

'Yes, there is a curtain, but it only covers the bottom half of the window.'

'Was that curtain drawn across the window on the night that Mr Little was murdered?'

There was a long and meaningful pause before Lucy answered in the affirmative.

'And was there a light in the room?'

'Yes, there was a lamp lit and a candle burning.'

The piece of calico was produced again, and Mr Sidney handed it to her.

'Will you swear upon your solemn oath, as you expect to be believed, that you have ever used that piece of cloth?'

'I will.'

'How do you know?'

'By the pattern.'

'Did you ever wash it?'

'I don't know. I can't be certain.'

Mr Sidney paused, and changed direction once more.

'Was there any conversation at home about the fact that a three-hundred-and-fifty-pound reward had been offered for information about the murder of Mr Little?'

'Yes.'

'How often did you have these conversations?'

'I could not say. I did not speak of the matter myself, but I heard my father, mother and brother discuss it.'

'Before you went to the police station to swear your information a few weeks ago, did you speak to anyone about what you would say?'

'No.'

'Come, now. Was there really nobody? How about your mother?'

Lucy was adamant.

'No. I don't think my mother even knew I was going to the police station.'

'Where did you go after giving your evidence in front of the magistrate?'

'To a lodging in Sackville Place where my mother was being looked after by the police.'

'How long did you stay there with your mother?'

'Two or three days.'

'During that time, did you speak to anybody about what you had said in your evidence?'

'Nobody.'

'Your mother was with you for the whole of the two or three days that you were in that house. Are we to believe that you said nothing about it to her during that time?'

The little girl seemed genuinely offended at the suggestion.

'I never opened my lips to her, nor she to me.'

'After you went home to the cottage, you shared a bedroom as usual with your brothers?'

'Yes.'

'And you ate at the same table with your mother and brothers?'

'Yes.'

'And did you speak to any of them about what you had said in the police station?'

'No, I never spoke a sentence to them about it.'

Mr Curran asked for the jury to be allowed to hear the evidence Lucy had given at the police court a few weeks earlier. This rather tiresome duty fell to Mr Smart, the deputy clerk, who read the two statements. By and large they tallied with what the jury already knew – but there were also a couple of important discrepancies, and the canny defence barrister knew that these might prove awkward to explain. But since Lucy was the Crown's witness, Mr Curran could not challenge her about them until the Attorney General had done a bit of damage limitation first. Mr FitzGerald stood up.

'Miss Spollin, I am about to remind you of the answers you gave today with reference to the cloth. You told me that the last time you saw it before the day of Mr Little's death was about three months before that day.'

'Yes, sir.'

'But at the police office, in front of the magistrate, you said this: "I remember the day of Mr Little's murder, and I saw that duster (the lilac cloth) about the house that day or the day before, but I have not seen it since, until today, nor do I know what has become of it." Have you any explanation to give to the court and jury connected with those statements?'

His oblique phrasing defeated Lucy, who looked blankly at him and said that she didn't understand the question.

'Very well, I can't make it plainer. Now, you said here today that when you looked out you saw your father on a ladder getting on to the roof, and that he pulled up the ladder on to the roof with him. But in the second information you gave you said, "I saw my father at the chimney; he did not take the ladder up on the roof with him." Have you any explanation to offer?'

This time Lucy grasped his meaning.

'Well, sir, when I was at the police station I said I *thought* my father brought up the ladder with him, but I was not sure. But the man put it down wrong and said that I *was* sure about it.'

'Do you now have a clearer recollection of what you did see?'
'Yes.'

'And what was it?'

'I saw him with the ladder on the ground, and climbing up it to the roof; and when he reached the top he took the ladder up after him and leant it against the chimney. The chimney was up as high as his neck, and he was putting something down it.'

Chief Justice Lefroy returned to the vexed subject of the piece of lilac calico, which according to Lucy's original statement she had seen on the day of the murder.

'You said today when asked about the duster that you had not seen it for three months before Mr Little's death. Do you perceive the difference between your two answers?'

'Yes.'

'Can you give any reason for the difference between them?'

'I can. When they ask me now I remember that it was three months before.'

'Do you now say positively that you had not seen it for three months before?'

'Yes.'

And with this not entirely convincing answer Lucy's examination was brought to a close. To the neutral observer it was difficult to judge what the effect of her evidence might be. On the one hand she had made some extremely damaging allegations about her father's behaviour; on the other, the defence had exposed her inability to tell the time, or even to name the months of the year. And the inconsistencies within her testimony might play badly with a jury that would, in all likelihood, be asked to rely upon it for a guilty verdict.

If the Attorney General had concerns about the way things were going, they were about to get a lot worse. Lucy's replacement on the witness chair was her older brother Joseph, a few months short of his fourteenth birthday. Mr Fitzgibbon began by asking him to recall when he first heard about Mr Little's death.

'I heard of it on a Friday evening, between five and six o'clock.'

'Where were you at the time?'

'At the turnpike, near the Broadstone.'

'And where were you in the earlier part of the day?'

'At school.'

'When did you return home from school?'

'Some time between three and four.'

'And the previous evening, the Thursday, do you recall seeing your father?'

'Yes. The first time I saw him it was between half-past five and six.'

'Where was he then?'

'Crossing the railway lines.'

'When you saw him crossing the lines, where was he going?'

'Towards the terminus.'

'Did you notice anything in particular about his appearance?'

'Yes, I noticed that he had something swinging in his hand.'

'Could you see what it was?'

'No. It looked like something long.'

The defence barristers exchanged glances of surprise. Joseph had not made any such claim at the police court hearing. Now he was more or less claiming to have seen his father carrying the hammer.

'When was the last time you saw him before that occasion?'

'It was at dinnertime, between twelve and one.'

'And after you saw him crossing the lines, when did you next see your father?'

'At about eight o'clock, when he was on the roof of the forge.'

Joseph described the scene: how he and his three siblings had been in the parlour together after their tea; how they had all looked out of the window, wondering what was keeping their father out so late, and noticed him clambering up on to the roof of the building opposite.

Mr Fitzgibbon paused and moved on.

'Your father owned two razors which he used to shave with at the time of Mr Little's death. Do you recognise them?'

A clerk handed Joseph four razors, two of which he immediately identified as his father's. They were then passed over to the bench, where both judges examined them minutely. One of them was the razor found in the canal during the most recent search, with 'Spollin' carved into its handle. The other had been among the prisoner's effects on the day of his arrest.

'What about this piece of calico, Master Spollin? Have you seen this before?'

'Yes, my sister used to wear it. It was a sun bonnet. Later she used it as a duster.'

'When did you last see it before Mr Little was killed?'

'It was a couple of days earlier, in the old workshop behind the cottage.' Joseph pointed out the semi-derelict building on the model in front of him.

'Did you see the bonnet, or duster, or whatever it was, after the day of Mr Little's murder?'

'No; the next time I saw it was when Mr Kemmis showed it to me.'

For the benefit of the jury, Mr Fitzgibbon asked Joseph to clarify: he had not seen the calico again until after its discovery wrapped around the package of money. The boy also backed up two of Lucy's more incendiary claims: that their father had threatened to kill them if they fetched a doctor; and that he had directed them to lie to the police.

Mr Fitzgibbon asked Joseph if his father owned a padlock.

'Yes, he used them for locking the tops of his oil cans. He had two that I know of.'

'Is this one of them?'

The clerk handed Joseph the padlock that had been found embedded in the bucket of red lead.

'Yes.'

'When did you last see that padlock?'

'He had them both up to the time of Mr Little's death, but soon afterwards I only remember seeing one of them.'

'Did he own a hammer?'

'Yes, more than one.'

Two hammers – one large, one small – were handed to Joseph. The large hammer, which had been seized at Spollin's cottage at the time of his arrest, had a small patch of putty on its head.

'Are these your father's hammers, Master Spollin?'

'Yes.'

'Did your father own these hammers at the time of Mr Little's death?'

'Not the small one. He got that after Mr Little was killed. But he had the large hammer.'

'And what did he use that large hammer for?'

'He kept it in the old workshop for nailing up planks. I saw him hammering in spikes to train the runner beans.'

'So it was in, or near, the cottage at the time of the murder?'

'Yes.'

'What about after the murder?'

'I did not see it again until Mr Kemmis showed it to me.'

Mr Fitzgibbon had completed his examination, but one of the jurors wanted Joseph to explain where his father had been when Joseph saw him crossing the railway lines. He indicated a spot on the model. Judge Monahan asked a question.

'When you saw him crossing the goods yard was it the general time when other employees were leaving work?'

'No, sir. It was some time after. James had already returned from work.'

Mr Curran began his cross-examination where the Chief Justice had left off.

'You have already said that you did not see him for very long. Can you really be sure that it was your father you saw?'

'He was long enough in my view to make me perfectly sure it was him.'

'Come, now. I have seen the goods yard. It is a busy place; there are piles of timber lying about, and cattle wagons coming and going. It was already dark. Yet you recognised a face from the other side of the railway lines?'

Joseph was adamant. 'There was no timber near the cottage, and no wagons there that evening.'

'Were you going to school at the time of Mr Little's death?'

'Yes, at the Black Church, off Dorset Street.'

St Mary's Chapel of Ease – whose nickname alluded to the dark limestone from which it was built – was also the site of a Catholic school recently founded by the Irish Christian Brothers.

'At what time of day did you go to school?'

'I used to go between nine and ten o'clock in the morning, and return home between three and four in the afternoon.'

'Did you return home for lunch?'

'No, I would take bread with me.'

'How long were you at school at the Black Church?'

'I went there for nearly a year.'

'And were you there every day?'

'Yes, except a few days when my shoes needed repairing.'

'So on the day that Mr Little was murdered you would have been at school?'

'I don't think so.'

Mr Curran was brought up short.

'You weren't at school that Thursday?'

'No.'

The barrister was suddenly aware that the Fates had thrown a free gift into his lap.

'By virtue of your oath, and your father on his trial for his life, did you previously swear that you were at school that day?'

'I did not.'

Having secured this emphatic declaration, Mr Curran moved on to the piece of calico.

'Earlier you were shown a piece of cloth which you identified as a sun bonnet given to your sister. Did you ever see her wear it?'

'Yes, but not often.'

'When did you last see her wear it?'

'It must be nearly three years ago.'

'Did you ever use it as a duster?'

'No, never.'

'So how could you know that this tattered fragment of cloth was the same as the sun bonnet you last saw her wearing three years ago?'

Joseph was rattled. 'I know it by the pattern.'

'When your father was arrested, did you talk to your mother about what had happened, or to your sister?'

'No.'

'You sleep in the same room as your sister, do you not?'

'Yes.'

'And you did not talk to her about why he had been arrested?'

'No.'

'Did you dine with your mother, brothers and sister that evening?'

'Yes.'

'And eat breakfast with them the following morning?'

'Yes.'

'And yet you did not have a conversation with them about what had happened, or why the police might have taken your father away and locked him up?'

'I never did.'

Mr Curran handed him the padlock.

'You told my learned friend Mr Fitzgibbon that this padlock was identical to one owned by your father. How did you recognise it?'

'It has a crown on it, and the letters "VR".'

'There are no other marks on it by which you can identify it?'

'No.'

Mr Curran's approach with Joseph had been subtle. Rather than challenge his story directly, he had tried to demonstrate that many of the boy's most damaging claims were open to multiple interpretations – and, without stating it openly, had hinted at a possible conspiracy involving Mary Spollin and two of her children. But the barrister now produced a shocking *coup de théâtre*.

'Master Spollin, did you swear an information at the police office in Capel Street a few weeks ago?'

'Yes.'

'And after you had given your information was it read back to you?'

'Yes. Once in the clerk's office and then in the police court.'

'And did you hear it read clearly and distinctly?'

'Yes.'

Mr Curran was leaving no room for doubt. 'And did you swear that it was all true?'

'Yes.'

The defence barrister asked the deputy clerk to read the statement sworn by Joseph at the police court. It was long, and for many occupants of the public gallery the wholesale repetition of evidence they had just heard from the witness's own lips was an unwelcome diversion. But it soon became clear why Mr Curran had inflicted it on them. In his first statement, Joseph claimed to have been at school every day during the week of the murder, but the courtroom had just heard him swear the exact opposite. Nor was it the only discrepancy. A sudden frisson passed through the room.

When the clerk had finished his recitation, Mr Curran continued.

'Now, Master Spollin, can you explain how it was that in that statement you made no mention of having seen your father that evening before you saw him on the roof of the old forge – and that you said you never saw him between lunch and when he was on the roof?'

Joseph was floored. He wrestled with the question for some time, apparently trying to think of an adequate reply, before giving up, defeated. There are times when silence is a barrister's most lethal weapon. Mr Curran let the moment linger before repeating his question. Joseph remained mute.

'Today you testified that you were not at school on the day of the murder. But at the police court you swore that you went to school all the week of the murder. Can you give any explanation of that, Joseph Spollin, on your father's trial?'

There was no answer. Mr Curran adopted a more conciliatory tone.

'Since your father's arrest, have you been living at the Broadstone cottage?'

'Yes, sir.'

'And your mother?'

'Yes, sir.'

'How have you been occupying yourself? Playing games, I imagine?'

'Yes, sir. Building a little bridge and doing a variety of things.'

'Does your mother scold very much at times?'

'Sometimes.'

'She is very passionate sometimes?'

'Yes, sir.'

'Scolds a great deal, speaks loudly, and brawls?'

It was a crude trap, and one that Joseph easily avoided.

'No, sir, she does not brawl.'

And after completing a devastating cross-examination, Mr Curran resumed his seat once more. Mr Fitzgibbon was given a chance to salvage something from the wreckage by re-examining Joseph, but his explanation that there were details he had forgotten to include in his previous evidence was too little, too late. The damage had been done.

16

Saturday 8 August

One of the mysteries of the Spollin trial is what happened to Superintendent Augustus Guy. The detective notionally in charge of this murder inquiry for most of its seven months was not even asked to give evidence, and his name was mentioned only once. Barely three weeks earlier Mr Guy had watched from the front row of a police court as the man he had arrested faced a charge of murder. The superintendent had been the public face of the inquiry, and now he was nowhere to be seen. Where was he?

There are good reasons for suspecting that he was in disgrace. Certainly he had been relieved of his responsibilities, and not willingly. In a memorandum written some months after the trial, the Crown Solicitor Thomas Kemmis refers in passing to the fact that Mr Guy had been removed from the investigation. Mr Kemmis evidently distrusted the detective's instincts from the outset, casting doubt on his initial theories as to the identity of the murderer. Signs of more general dissatisfaction with Superintendent Guy's performance first surfaced in January, when the Crown Solicitor and the Chief Secretary shared their private reservations about the quality of his work. But it seems likely that the final straw was the revelation during the police court hearings that the superintendent had detained Spollin's son James illegally for three weeks. If Mr Guy were called as a witness he would be forced to admit that he had broken the law, and the entire trial might collapse. These circumstances would also explain why the eldest Spollin child – undeniably an important witness – was not asked to give evidence.

In the absence of the superintendent it was Inspector Ryan who climbed on to the table to face the barristers. He did not trouble the court for long. He gave an account of the alibi James Spollin had offered when first questioned, and confirmed that the razor and hammer exhibited to the court were those found in the canal.

More intriguing was the evidence given by Lewis West, a cutler, who testified that the name 'Spollin' scratched on to the handle of the razor was his doing, explaining that when blades were brought to him for sharpening he routinely marked them with the owner's name.

Mr Curran challenged the cutler's view that the razor had lain underwater for a considerable time before its recovery.

'Have you reached that conclusion because of the rust on the blade?'

'Yes; but a bright steel instrument might also remain a long time in water without rusting.'

'Do you say this of your own knowledge?'

'Yes. In order to form an opinion on the matter, on the twenty-third of last month I threw a razor with some spots of rust on it into water, and on taking it out of the water this morning I found the bright parts of the razor were not at all discoloured.'

Mr Curran did not bother to spell out what must have been obvious to the jury: the cutler's experiment showed that it was impossible to tell whether the razor had been in the canal for ten minutes or ten years.

Next to settle into the witness chair was James Magill, an overseer at the railway company. At the Attorney General's invitation he recalled a conversation he had had with the accused six months earlier.

'Towards the end of February I was with a draughtsman named Boylan, measuring a table. Spollin came up and asked what we were doing. I said that we were going to knock down the old sheds and put up new ones. He said that it would be an inconvenience to me, to which I replied that it would inconvenience him more, as the rubble would be thrown into his garden. He said that if they took down the sheds they would surely find the money. "What money?" said I. "The money that was taken from Mr Little," he said. Another time I came up while Spollin was talking to a man named McClean, a tin-plate worker. McClean asked Spollin whether he thought the murderer had been one of the men recently laid off. He replied no, that the murderer was still here, and laughing at us all.'

Mr Sidney, for the defence, was sceptical. Under pressure from the barrister, Magill admitted that most of the railway workers had shared Spollin's view that the killer was still on the premises.

Two police officers described the various searches of the Broadstone terminus, and then an expert witness was called to offer his opinion on a piece of evidence for which the prosecution had high hopes. William Mullen was a locksmith, and as soon as he had sat down he was handed the padlock found in Spollin's cottage, with its key. Following the instructions of Mr Fitzgibbon, he fitted the key into the lock and opened it, confirming to the court that they were a match. Mr Fitzgibbon then gave him the padlock found in the bucket of money, and the locksmith observed that it was choked with red lead.

'You have your tools with you, I believe,' said Mr Fitzgibbon. 'Do you think you could pick away that obstruction?'

Muttering that he could certainly have a go, Mr Mullen set to work. The lead flaked off quite easily, and shortly afterwards he tried the key in the lock. It opened.

The successful outcome of this experiment provoked gratifying noises of surprise from the public gallery. But that was not the end of the matter. Judge Monahan asked the locksmith whether this meant that the key belonged to the padlock found in the bucket.

'It may, but this key would open every lock of the same pattern.'

Mr Curran stood up and pressed home his advantage.

'Would I be right in thinking, Mr Mullen, that there are a great many padlocks identical to this one?'

'Yes. These are made in Birmingham, and when they make a new padlock they manufacture thousands to the same design.'

'So I might purchase a lock just like this one, which would be opened by this key, more or less anywhere?'

'Not anywhere, but I imagine they could be bought in many places in Dublin.'

It was a disaster for the prosecution, and their attempt to prove that the padlock was Spollin's fell apart entirely when the next witness was called. Thomas Bambrick told the court that until 1853 he had been employed by the railway company. He knew the prisoner, he said, and remembered that Spollin had some lockable oil cans. He could not be sure, said Mr Bambrick, but he had a faint recollection of seeing padlocks.

Lord Chief Justice Lefroy was exasperated.

'Surely there ought to be someone more competent to give evidence on this point than a person employed so far back as four years ago?'

The unfortunate prosecution counsel, Mr Beytagh, ploughed on regardless. He pointed out the wooden bucket on the exhibit table and asked the witness whether he had ever seen the prisoner using it. Thomas Bambrick scrutinised it carefully before replying.

'I remember him getting red and green paint from the storekeeper, but he used to carry them in a square box. I don't recollect this tub at all.'

The spectators could have few complaints about the entertainment they had seen so far. There had been the high drama of Lucy and Joseph's evidence, then the light relief afforded by the comical mishaps of the prosecution. It was now late afternoon but another fifteen witnesses were still to give evidence, testing the endurance of judges and jurors to the limit. It was not as if they had much to add. Several recalled the discovery of the body, the minutiae of which had already been discussed and which were not in dispute. Five described the search of the canal in stultifying detail; and the elderly Broadstone watchman was even summoned to the witness chair to inform the court that he could recollect nothing useful about the night Mr Little died. It was as if the prosecution had decided to throw every particle of available information at the jury, in the hope of giving the impression that the case against Spollin was substantial rather than just voluminous.

When the court finally rose at a quarter to seven that Saturday evening, the jurors learned that it would be a while before they saw their wives and children again, or slept in their own beds. They could not return home, or communicate with anybody except each other, until the case was concluded. On Sunday morning they were permitted to go to their various churches, each escorted by a bailiff, and after lunch the sheriff arranged carriages to take them on a drive through the genteel wilderness of the Phoenix Park. Then it was back to their enforced confinement at the European Hotel. Still, the cage was a gilded one, and the government would be picking up the bill for anything they ate or drank. Juries were sometimes known to abuse this privilege. During another murder trial in Victorian Dublin, nine jurors (the other three were teetotal) drank copious quantities of beer, wine, champagne, sherry, gin and whiskey, and then ran riot through the hotel, causing such chaos that their behaviour became the subject of a parliamentary inquiry.

The members of the Spollin trial jury were more abstemious, and not a whisper of scandal followed them back to the Green Street courtroom on the morning of Monday 10 August. After two long days the Crown had supposedly finished laying out its case, but as soon as the judges were back on the bench, the Right Honourable Abraham Brewster QC stood up to say that there were one or two things that the prosecution had omitted to mention. A police constable was summoned to talk about the poker and bloodstained towel found in Mr Little's office – even though the former item was agreed by all sides to have nothing to do with the crime. Patrick Hanbury was then recalled to clear up a few details from his earlier testimony. Mr Sidney was offered the chance to cross-examine the stationmaster for a second time, and he chose a surprising and inflammatory line of attack.

'Mr Hanbury, what was the general opinion about the matter amongst the men at the Broadstone?'

He had no time to answer before the Attorney General leapt up to protest that whatever the men at the Broadstone thought, it was hearsay and therefore inadmissible. The judges agreed, so Mr Sidney tried another approach.

'Were any other railway employees besides the prisoner ever arrested by the police?'

'Yes. Catherine Campbell was more than a month in their custody, and about three months altogether in their charge.'

'And were there suspicions against other persons at the railway?'

'Yes.'

'Strong suspicions?'

'Yes.'

'And serious facts against them?'

This time it was Mr Brewster who intervened.

'Do not answer that question. How can he tell whether there were serious facts?'

Mr Sidney ignored the interruption. 'Were these facts not so strong that they were about to arrest another person?'

Mr Brewster could take no more. 'Do not answer, Mr Hanbury. I must object to this line. I have already allowed you to go to a great length, Mr Sidney.'

'I am very much obliged to you, Mr Brewster,' said Mr Sidney, with exaggerated courtesy. It was inevitable that his line of questioning would be ruled out of order, but it did not matter: he had succeeded in insinuating that the police had arrested the wrong man. An underhand trick, perhaps, but an effective one. The jury could not forget what they had heard.

Mr Brewster had one more witness to call: Sergeant Meyers, who had been present at the time of Spollin's arrest. The policeman testified that the prisoner's clothes had been taken from him and sent to Dr Geoghegan, the forensic chemist, for analysis. The scientist should have been in court to reveal what he had discovered, but since he could not be found Mr Brewster declared that the case for the prosecution was at last complete.

Of all the distinguished lawyers in court that morning, only John Adye Curran had experienced this elaborate legal charade from the defendant's perspective. A quarter of a century earlier – by a curious coincidence, twenty-five years to the day – Curran had stood in the same Green Street courtroom accused of taking part in an illegal meeting. As a law student he was involved in the campaign against the tithe, an ancient tax that funded the Church of Ireland. Like many Catholics, he deeply resented being made to pay for the worship of the wealthy Protestant minority while the Catholic churches frequented by peasants and labourers received nothing. The young Curran became an ardent supporter of abolition, and in the summer of 1832 he addressed an anti-tithe rally in the mountains south of Dublin. He was arrested and sentenced to two months' imprisonment, in the week that he was due to be called to the Bar. Instead of beginning in practice he found himself a convicted criminal, handcuffed and sitting in a prison van as it rattled its way to Kilmainham Gaol.

The episode nearly cost him his legal career, but it also proved the making of a great advocate. John Adye Curran had suffered injustice, and knew how it stung. He knew what it was like to cower in the dock, his stomach in knots of terror, while a judge handed down sentence. So when he rose to address the jury he could easily imagine that it was his own life he was pleading for, rather than that of James Spollin.

'Gentlemen, it was a melancholy sight, one I hope we never again shall behold, to see children coming forward on an occasion like this to give evidence where their own father's life was at stake . . .'

In the dock James Spollin slumped forward and buried his face in his handkerchief, his shoulders heaving as he sobbed.

'. . . and coming forward, gentlemen, with a coolness and with a determination which must have struck every one of us; even with a levity of manner and an indifference, as if they were – and I am satisfied they were – the innocent victims of someone behind the scenes.'

Mr Curran was careful not to name her, but nobody in the room could be in any doubt that it was the children's mother he was accusing.

'Gentlemen of the jury, what *is* the case? One of mere suspicion. Take away anything you have heard about those who were not here in person, and take away the evidence of Lucy and Joseph Spollin – because I defy any rational being to come to the conclusion that either of them has told the truth – and what becomes of the case? Mere, mere nothing.'

And the defence barrister spent the next four hours explaining why. Mr Curran was merciless. He picked apart the evidence given by the two children, pointing out every inconsistency as he went. He reminded the jury that the prosecution's case relied on dates and times supplied by Lucy, who 'does not know the month of the year or understand the clock'. As for Joseph, he had given two different versions of his whereabouts on the day of the murder, and changed his story repeatedly. His latest claim was that he had seen his father walking towards the terminus swinging 'something long' in his hand. Mr Curran refuted it brutally.

'The boy said he was standing at the door of the cottage when he saw his father crossing the line. The distance between those places is nearly one hundred and fifty yards. I was there yesterday evening, and a person could not recognise his own friend in the broad daylight at that distance, much less on a dark November night.'

The children had been coached in their evidence and told what to say, the barrister alleged. There was 'somebody behind the curtain' controlling them, trying to ensure that James Spollin – who could be seen sobbing in the dock once more – was hanged for murder.

After rubbishing the prosecution's two most important witnesses, Mr Curran did his best to dismantle the rest of their case. He was angry, incredulous, mocking. He poured scorn on their attempts to incriminate Spollin. They claimed that the prisoner had escaped through a window on to the roof, but not a drop of blood had been found on the window frame. They said that Spollin worked near the place where the hamper of silver was found, but a hundred and fifty other people passed that spot every day.

There was nothing to connect the prisoner with the money, Mr Curran said, once the children's unreliable evidence about the calico bonnet was discounted. Nobody had seen Spollin with the bucket, and there was no record of his obtaining red lead from the stores or anywhere else. There was no evidence that he had ever owned the hammer, or either of the razors – and who would be stupid enough to commit a murder with a weapon engraved with his own name? The barrister suggested darkly that somebody had thrown the second razor into the canal with the express intention of implicating his client.

At the climax of his speech, Mr Curran summarised the case against Spollin in words that dripped with sarcasm.

'You are asked to convict him because money belonging to Mr Little was found near the place where he had worked; because an ordinary padlock was found in red lead under the money. You are asked to find him guilty of this murder because the hammer found in the canal and which fits the wound exactly is not proved to have been his, and because the first razor is not shown to have been his, and another with his name scratched upon it has turned up at a subsequent search in a place where it might have been thrown by any member of his family. You are asked to come to the conclusion that he is the murderer because of a ridiculous story which the children tell of having seen him at the chimney, and about a sun bonnet of a lilac colour which Julia Lyons, who is said to have made it, is not called to identify, and because of some idle talk which took place on the premises. You are asked to convict him because the press in this country and in England have raised an outcry, and public opinion has demanded this man as a victim.

'You are in an awfully responsible position. You are now sitting in judgment, the arbiters of the fate of this unhappy man, but before you come to a conclusion that he is guilty, you must weigh the evidence carefully, and ask yourselves, does the evidence sustain this charge? If it is at all consistent with his innocence you must acquit him. I now leave this case in your hands, gentlemen, confident that you will do your duty to your country, your God, and the prisoner at the bar.'

As Mr Curran sat down, a handful of people in the gallery began to applaud lustily. There was no denying that the defence counsel's performance had been most impressive; but in court such displays of approbation were frowned upon, and those responsible were quickly silenced.

Close to fifty men, women and children had climbed the steps to the witness table and sworn to tell the truth, the whole truth, and nothing but the truth, but James Spollin was not one of them. The defendant at a murder trial in nineteenth-century Ireland was not permitted to give evidence, a measure intended to protect them from wily prosecutors and the dangers of self-incrimination. But if the rules gave a superficial appearance of even-handedness, in other respects the deck was stacked against the prisoner. The defence lawyers were typically allowed little or no access to their client outside the courtroom, often forcing them to piece together a case from the evidence disclosed by the Crown. The most obvious handicap they faced, however, was that they were allowed only one opportunity to address the jury, while the prosecution were given both an opening and a closing speech.

It was Abraham Brewster QC who made the final arguments on behalf of the Crown. He walked the jury once more through the crime and its discovery, doing his best to show that Spollin was uniquely qualified to plan and carry out the murder, and that the location of the money suggested his involvement. But he devoted most of his energies to rubbishing Mr Curran's suggestion of a conspiracy between Mary Spollin and her children Lucy and Joseph. Mr Brewster pointed out that there was no evidence that James Spollin had been a bad husband, or his marriage an unhappy one. Neither of the children had given any hint that their father was unkind to them. So what motive could they possibly have for conspiring to have him sent to the gallows? He ridiculed the idea that they might have risked it for a reward of £350.

As he drew to a close, Mr Brewster's tone became more serious and his delivery more measured. He dwelt upon the awful nature of the decision the jurors would now have to make, and the responsibility that lay in their hands. When he sat down there were renewed manifestations of emotion in the public gallery, and once again these were quickly silenced.

Chief Justice Monahan, who had been keeping a keen eye on the clock, announced that his summing-up was likely to run to 'a very considerable length', and that since it was now 6.30 he had decided to adjourn the court until the following morning – ensuring, to the delight of the assembled journalists, that this most absorbing of murder trials would go into a fourth day.

It was not just the streets outside the courtroom that were crowded on the morning of Tuesday 11 August. Most of the city knew that the jury would be retiring to consider their verdict at some point that day, and rumour had it that they would find James Spollin guilty. That would mean an execution; and, realising the hordes that would inevitably descend on Kilmainham Gaol for this sensational event, many Dubliners went straight there to secure the best views of the gibbet.

The judges arrived on the bench promptly at 10 a.m. Though the less senior of the two, Chief Justice Monahan had taken on the responsibility of summing up. He spoke for four and a half hours, but not a word was wasted. His orderly mind had sifted through reams of evidence, discarded anything he deemed inessential, and then identified which points both sides agreed upon and which were disputed. He laid this all out before the jury as a simple narrative, beginning with the night of George Little's murder. In Judge Monahan's view there was no way of proving what time the crime had taken place, whether it had been committed by one person or several, or even what route the perpetrator(s) had taken in entering or leaving the building. He was satisfied that the hammer, and one of the razors, had been used to kill Mr Little, but told the jury that there was no convincing evidence that either had ever been owned or used by James Spollin.

As he moved systematically through more recent events – the arrest of Spollin and the discovery of the money – it became increasingly clear that neither judge had found the prosecution's efforts to link the prisoner with the physical evidence terribly compelling. Judge Monahan's tone changed markedly when he turned to the testimony of Lucy and Joseph Spollin.

'Were it not for the evidence of these two children,' he said, 'it would be a mere case of suspicion, and perhaps such that neither the Lord Chief Justice nor myself would feel justified in submitting it to a jury.'

Here was the crux of the matter. In his opening speech the Attorney General had spoken of a 'long chain of circumstantial evidence' which would prove the guilt of the prisoner. Judge Monahan was now indicating that there were only two links in that chain that really mattered: Lucy and Joseph. And if the jury disbelieved their testimony, the whole chain crumbled to dust.

'No doubt there are serious discrepancies in the evidence of these children; but they agree in the main fact, that they saw their father upon the chimney of the forge, on the night of the murder, putting something down it. This is the material part of the evidence, and you have to decide whether or not you believe it. The little girl positively states that two days later she asked her mother what her father was doing when she saw him at the chimney, and that her mother did not give any answer. With regard to the discrepancies which do exist, you are told by the Crown that they are not material, and therefore should not destroy the credit of a witness with you; on the other hand, the counsel for the defence alleges that they are mistakes which a truth-telling witness could not make. The defence suggests that the children, in giving evidence, both acted under the control of their mother. Of course, if you believe this, you will not give credence to any statement they made.

'And now, gentlemen, what you are asked by the Crown to believe upon the whole of the evidence is this: that upon the evening of the thirteenth of November, at half-past five o'clock, when his work was finished, the prisoner at the bar, instead of returning home to innocent children to share their humble meal, went to commit a premeditated murder. There is no doubt that murder was committed upon that night, and you are to decide whether James Spollin is or is not the murderer.

'There are still the various other considerations that may arise, but above all there is this: that if you have a reasonable doubt in the evidence, it is your bounden duty to acquit the prisoner, just as much as if you were certain of his innocence. But, on the other hand, if having considered the whole of the evidence, you come to the conclusion that these facts have been proved by the children of this man, that it is impossible that any conspiracy existed to take away his life, that when he said he was with his family he was, in fact, on the roof of the forge – then it will be for you to say whether that be not consistent with his guilt, but inconsistent with his innocence.'

Judge Monahan's voice began to shake with emotion as he reached the final paragraph of his summing-up. A few jurors wiped away tears.

'Gentlemen, if you come to the latter conclusion you are bound in the discharge of a painful duty which you and all of us owe to the public, irrespective of consequences: to bring in a ver-dict of guilty. But let no feeling of the heinousness of the crime induce you, for one moment, to act on the feeling that justice requires a victim. Justice requires no victim; justice requires and prefers that ninety-nine guilty men should escape, than that a hair of the head of one innocent man should be sacrificed to mistake. And may the Almighty guide you to a true and just verdict.'

The Chief Justice seemed overwhelmed at the end of his extra-ordinary address, whose final sentences would resonate for many years afterwards. At the request of the jurors, several exhibits including the hammer and the calico bonnet were handed up for them to examine for one last time, and at twenty to three the jury retired to deliberate. James Spollin was taken back down to the cells, while the judges remained on the bench. Nobody was will-ing to leave the courtroom in case the jury returned unexpectedly, but it was not long before boredom supervened. People started to talk in whispers, and within a few minutes little groups had formed all over the room, having heated but *sotto voce* discus-sions about the likely verdict.

It was 4.10 – much sooner than anybody had expected – when the hum of conversation was cut off as if by the closing of a tap. The jurors had returned to their box. The spectators hurriedly regained their seats, while the prisoner reappeared in the dock and Mr Alley, the clerk of the court, called out the names of the jurors to check that they were all present.

When he was satisfied he asked, 'Gentlemen of the jury, do you agree to your verdict?'

'Yes,' said the foreman, handing him a piece of paper.

James Spollin had risen from his seat in the dock, and leant uneasily against the railing in front of him. Mr Alley unfolded the slip and examined its contents carefully. The courtroom remained in breathless silence as he lifted his eyes and announced in a sonorous voice:

'You say James Spollin is not guilty.'

17

For a few seconds after the verdict was announced, the quiet dignity of the Green Street courtroom gave way to raw emotion. There were gasps of surprise and horror, and an outbreak of applause was quickly stifled by police officers who had been stationed in the public gallery. In the dock, James Spollin struck the iron railings with his fist, and exclaimed, 'My children!' He clapped a hand to his face and collapsed into the arms of the two men guarding him, who helped him into a chair and loosened his necktie. An official fetched a jug of water and swabbed his face and neck, as the newly acquitted man hovered on the edge of consciousness.

After a few minutes Spollin recovered, and was allowed to address the court. He spoke falteringly, his thoughts disordered by the passions raging inside him.

'My lords and gentlemen, I find myself not entirely deceived. I was convinced that I stood before twelve of my countrymen – men of experience, with happy firesides and confidence in their family circles. I thought that they would impartially take my case into consideration, and they have done so. It is not for me to commence to praise myself, but I have been brought here wrongfully . . .'

Spollin raised his hand and crashed it down on the railing in front of him.

'Wrongfully by . . . but I will not condemn the woman. I loved the woman, but it is a dreadful thing to be in the hands of a female tyrant. I should thank the two honourable gentlemen . . .'

He indicated the two judges, who listened impassively to his rambling monologue.

'. . . pillars of law on the bench. I may be too sensitive when I say the servants of the Crown have blackened my character too much in their addresses to the jury. I have, however, thanks be to God, escaped.'

Spollin raised his hands and looked up to the heavens.

'Thanks and praise be to God! Amen.'

After this rousing homily Spollin sat down. But almost immediately another thought struck him, so he got up again.

'My character, I am afraid, must remain triflingly impaired. My children, the only ones I love, I have to provide for.'

He fought back tears as he continued.

'And if I have the means I would like to retire to some silent colony for the rest of my life . . .'

Judge Monahan, who had heard quite enough, spoke over him. 'Is there any other charge against the prisoner?'

An official answered in the negative, but Spollin ploughed on regardless.

'I would like to convey my sincere thanks to the press for remaining silent during my incarceration. And to your honourable friend, Mr Curran, my counsel, for the untiring energy he displayed. May he and Mr Sidney live many a day without a similar case as mine to defend!'

Spollin slumped into his chair, exhausted. The latter part of his speech had been almost drowned out by cheers from outside the courtroom, where news of the verdict had just been announced. Mr Sidney rose to his feet.

'There is a large crowd outside, my lord, and perhaps it would be as well not to discharge the prisoner just yet.'

'Well, then,' said Judge Monahan. 'He is formally discharged, but he can remain with the prison governor until tomorrow morning.'

Spollin was escorted out of the dock by the prison officers, while the Chief Justice dismissed the jury, thanking them for their time and attention. On the street outside a huge crowd waited expectantly, applauding every official as they emerged, and greeting the defence barristers with particular enthusiasm. The not-guilty verdict was, it appeared, a popular one. But the one person they really wanted to see was to be denied his moment of public triumph. There were still plenty of people in Dublin who believed that James Spollin was guilty, and one of them might be hiding in the throng, waiting to administer summary justice. For his own protection the man of the hour was bundled out of a back door and into a van, destined to spend one last night in Richmond Bridewell.

Thomas Kemmis, the Crown Solicitor, made his way through the multitudes on Green Street and walked briskly in the direction of Broadstone. Though well aware of the weaknesses Mr Curran had so skilfully exposed in the prosecution case, he had not been expecting the verdict. Most well-informed observers had predicted a hung jury followed by a retrial, while Mr Kemmis knew from contacts inside the prison that James Spollin had been expecting to be found guilty. There were urgent matters to consider – in particular, what would happen to Mary Spollin and her children, now that her estranged husband was about to regain his liberty. Mr Kemmis had already discussed this contingency with the Chief Secretary, and they had agreed on a plan. The government would offer Mary a new identity, and to resettle her and the children overseas in one of the British colonies.

When Mr Kemmis arrived at the Spollins' cottage a uniformed constable in his navy tunic and top hat was standing guard at the door. He looked somehow out of place amid the roses and hollyhocks of the little garden. Mary and the three youngest children had been under police protection for several weeks; James, the eldest, was now living elsewhere, having fallen out with his mother because he believed his father was innocent. Mr Kemmis had been a frequent visitor throughout the summer, and during the trial he had made a point of dropping in every evening to keep Mary informed of the latest developments. She already knew about her husband's acquittal: at the Crown Solicitor's insistence a police messenger had been dispatched to Broadstone as soon as the verdict was announced, so that she would not hear the news from some gossipy railway employee.

As soon as Mr Kemmis had sat down in the neat parlour he expressed his sorrow that the Crown had not been able to secure the verdict they had hoped for, and assured her that the government believed implicitly in her husband's guilt. He would ensure that the Dublin Castle administration did everything in its power to help her, he said, and told her about the offer to relocate the four of them to another country. One immediate problem was the fact that Spollin had a legal right to custody of the children. Mr Kemmis told Mary that he had asked Dr Dempsey, the curate of their local church, to act as intermediary. The priest was on his way to the prison to tell Spollin that if he did not relinquish his rights Mary would make an application to the Lord Chancellor, who would undoubtedly award her custody.

Mary's greatest concern was what her husband would do when he emerged from prison the following morning. Mr Kemmis told her that he had sent a constable to Richmond Bridewell, carrying Spollin's clothes and the eight sovereigns which the police had confiscated during the search of the cottage. He hoped that the money, and a few words of unambiguous advice, would be enough to persuade Spollin to leave the city, but if this measure was not successful he would leave a police guard at the cottage for as long as necessary.

At 8.00 the following morning a nondescript covered cart trundled out of the gates of Richmond Bridewell and turned up New Street, towards the centre of Dublin. Bystanders quickly divined the identity of the passenger concealed within, and set off in pursuit. The streets were busy and progress slow, and as the vehicle passed St Patrick's Cathedral and then struggled through the maze of streets to the west of Dublin Castle it attracted a tail of hangers-on. By the time it reached Broadstone this entourage had swelled into a large and decidedly hostile mob, whose members banged the sides of the cart and derisively called out Spollin's name.

When James Spollin alighted from his conveyance he was relieved to find a large contingent of policemen on hand to protect him from harm. But this was no welcoming committee. A detective sergeant named Craven stepped forward with a couple of officials from the railway company and told him that he would be denied access to any part of the premises, with the exception of the lock-keeper's cottage where his son James had been staying. Spollin protested: he wanted to speak to his wife, he said, and he had the right to visit his own house and family. Sergeant Craven told him that it was out of the question – but he was willing to pass on a message to her.

Spollin thought for a moment.

'Would you tell her . . . that I do not blame her for what she has done. I entertain no ill feelings for her on that account. All I want is that we should resume the same amicable relations that we enjoyed before I was arrested. And I have not eaten this morning. Perhaps she would be good enough to send me out some breakfast?'

A constable sauntered off to the cottage to deliver this presumptuous communication. A few minutes later he returned, empty-handed and looking faintly embarrassed. There was little need for him to describe the substance of Mary's response, or the manner in which it was delivered. Rebuffed, Spollin went in search of his son James, for a reunion both had been eagerly looking forward to. He would never speak to his wife, or lay eyes on their three youngest children, again.

A few hours later, father and son ventured out of the lock-keeper's cottage and headed for town. They were disconcerted to find that there was still quite a crowd loitering outside Broadstone, and these unasked-for disciples trailed after them down Dominick Street, past Simpson's Hospital and all the way to their destination in Stafford Street. There the pair disappeared into number 28, a cramped house squeezed between two tenement buildings which contained the modest offices of Charles Fitzgerald, his solicitor at the trial.

Mr Fitzgerald greeted his guests coldly. The visit was unexpected and not entirely welcome. Spollin explained his business. Despite his acquittal he had lost everything: job, home and family. His worldly possessions consisted of ten gold sovereigns – the eight returned to him by police, plus two in outstanding pay from the railway company – and the clothes he was wearing, and he had a young son to support. He felt that if only the Dublin public knew of his plight they would want to help him. Spollin had decided to solicit donations by means of a subscription list, and would like the firm's senior partner, Mr Cane, to put his name to this charitable enterprise.

Mr Fitzgerald reacted much as Mary Spollin had earlier when asked to provide her husband with breakfast. He declined the request tersely, and suggested that it might be better for Spollin to remove himself from Dublin in general, and his office in particular. The solicitor tried to escort the pair off the premises, but when he flung open the front door to eject them he was astonished to find the narrow street blocked in both directions by an immense throng. Perceiving that their intentions were not entirely friendly, he locked and barred the door and shepherded Spollin and his son through a back passage that brought them out into Great Britain Street. As he watched them making their escape into the tangle of alleys behind the hospital, Mr Fitzgerald hoped that Spollin would take his advice and leave town. But the solicitor had a feeling that Dublin had not seen the last of him yet.

*

On the morning of Tuesday 18 August, a week after the conclusion of the trial, an advertisement appeared on placards all over the city:

PRINCE PATRICK'S THEATRE, FISHAMBLE STREET
FOR ONE WEEK ONLY
JAMES SPOLLIN,

being about to leave this Country, and not having the means to do so, will deliver a Personal Narrative of the proceedings taken against him for the murder of the late Mr Little – commencing THIS DAY, August 18th, from 1 till 4. Evening, from 6 till 10. Admission, One Shilling.

Prince Patrick's Theatre was rather less salubrious than it sounded. Fishamble Street, a poverty-stricken thoroughfare on the south side of the Liffey, lay between the Castle and the city coal yard and was home to artisans including basket makers and tool manufacturers. Tucked away in an unobtrusive corner, behind an arch and a line of iron railings, was a dilapidated building built in the 1740s. First opened as a concert hall, it had since been through numerous, but only sporadically successful, incarnations as a venue for lotteries, entertainments and public meetings. In 1850 two entrepreneurs had given it a lick of paint and reopened it as a variety theatre – named, it seems, in honour of Queen Victoria's seventh child.* Now the artists who trod the boards of Prince Patrick's were mostly a colourful assortment of acrobats, comedians and performing dogs. It was a far cry from its glory days in 1742, when on the same stage George Frederick Handel had supervised the world premiere of his *Messiah*.

This was the venue that James Spollin had hired to deliver his 'personal narrative', an event that he hoped would provide him

---

* Prince Arthur William Patrick Albert was born on 1 May 1850, and may therefore have been conceived during Victoria's two-week tour of Ireland the previous August.

with both public vindication and sufficient capital to emigrate. Half a dozen policemen waited, bored, outside the theatre as the hour of the first performance approached. They were there in case of trouble, but apart from a few unruly local children there was little to concern them.

After entering the building one climbed a staircase to the lobby, where tickets could be bought at a little window with 'Pay here' painted over it. Inside the booth was young James Spollin, who was assisting his father as box office attendant, usher, and stage manager. After paying their shilling, audience members then went up a second, filthy, flight of stairs and entered a gloomy auditorium with a low stage at one end. There was no curtain, and a decaying backdrop depicted a gaudily painted interior, the ghost of some long-forgotten production. Behind this sheet of canvas the star of the show could be heard pacing up and down. At the front of the stage were a rickety table and chair. The hour of 1.00 came and went, without any sign that the show was about to begin. The organisers were, no doubt, hoping for some late additions to the audience, who numbered seventeen: eight newspaper reporters, five detectives and just four ordinary citizens.

It was almost 1.30 when young James entered the room, stood at the foot of the stage and in a loud whisper informed his father that there were 'some gentlemen here', whereupon Spollin made his entrance. He was wearing a dark coat over a blue jacket, with a black silk neckerchief. In his hand he carried a sheaf of notes, to which he referred occasionally during the ensuing monologue. To the surprise of his audience, he said nothing about the Broadstone murder or his part in the drama, instead making a brazen appeal for financial donations.

'I have come to lay my case before those who are now present. You are all aware of my situation, without money or reputation. I need not enter into details connected with my present circumstances; my object is for the simple purpose of obtaining the means of leaving the country. In Dublin it would be difficult enough to obtain employment. I am burdened with a portion of my family – a young man who has been renounced by his mother. I have not entered into this without very good advice, knowing that the public would cheerfully respond and give me what I need. I am not confining you to the price of admission; if any gentleman feels inclined to contribute he is welcome to do so. A long passage will necessarily entail a heavy expense that I am otherwise totally incapable of meeting.'

Spollin picked up a copy of the *Freeman's Journal* from the table and launched into a lengthy complaint about the way the newspaper had treated him. He was stopped in his tracks by an interruption from an elderly man who had just entered the room. The newcomer was William Fitzpatrick, an eighty-two-year-old grocer who owned a shop in nearby Dame Street. To the tiny audience, however, he was much more than that. A tireless campaigner for Catholic emancipation, Fitzpatrick had been a close friend of the Liberator himself, the popular hero Daniel O'Connell. He had served as a member of the Dublin Corporation, and was outspoken in his support of Irish independence. William Fitzpatrick was afraid of nobody; and when he spoke, Dubliners listened.

'As I see the gentlemen of the press are here, perhaps they would ask the public whether they wish to allow this man to exhibit himself in this way. If he is allowed to make a speech here today to obtain money, he will do the same in every town in Ireland.'

'That I deny, sir,' said Spollin hotly.

'At all events,' Mr Fitzpatrick continued, 'the citizens of Dublin will not countenance such a thing. The scarcity of this audience shows that the public are so disgusted that they will not listen to this man. I came here today determined to do my best to show a good example to my fellow-citizens. It is a monstrous thing for that man to come forward to make speeches, and to expect to have an audience of the citizens of Dublin.'

Mr Fitzpatrick turned and addressed Spollin directly.

'You got off through the merciful charge of the judge, but there was not a man of the jury that was convinced of your innocence.'

Spollin was given temporary relief from this attack by the entrance of his son, who asked Mr Fitzpatrick whether he had paid for his ticket.

'I did, sir,' said the grocer. 'I will not be stopped.'

Spollin appealed to the police to eject his heckler, but the detectives were enjoying the spectacle far too much to intervene.

'Who,' continued Mr Fitzpatrick, undaunted, 'was it that told your wife where the money was?'

'That is nothing to you, sir,' said Spollin junior.

'Oh, but it is, sir, and if I have to stay here until six o'clock I won't let you go any further till you answer that question.'

Spollin responded with a question of his own.

'Supposing I was the most guilty man in existence, would you run me into a hole to starve? Now, answer that humane question.'

'Upon my word, I would run you into wherever you would be away from the public, that you might not do further mischief.'

'That is not a very Christian opinion,' observed Spollin.

'The Lord Mayor ought to stop these proceedings. At any rate, there is no one to listen to you now, so I may as well leave.'

Having driven home his point with some elan, Mr Fitzpatrick made his exit.

Spollin drew the chair to the side of the stage and sat down. After a pause, he continued.

'I will put my case to the gentlemen who remain. What am I to do?'

He waited for an answer, but none came.

'Were it not for my family it would be easy for me to retire and go into one of the poorhouses.'

He fell silent, and wiped his eye with his handkerchief. At length he resumed.

'I thought it would have been the aim of every humane person to assist me in leaving the country, and not make the sort of display that Mr Fitzpatrick did just then. There is nobody here that would deny that the best thing would be for me to emigrate. By taking this step I can't bring myself more public notoriety than what my trial has done, but if I remain here you all know what the consequences will be. Supposing that I was the guilty man, it is a most dreadful thing that the sacred bond of matrimony should be destroyed by my wife. I have nothing more to say to you.'

He rose to his feet.

'I hope, gentlemen, you will admit that I am deserving of some support. You will admit that Mr Fitzpatrick—'

Another member of the audience interrupted.

'You did not answer Mr Fitzpatrick's question. Who told your wife where the money was? Explain that now.'

'It would be difficult to explain what the police could not find out,' said Spollin. 'That is totally out of my power.'

His interlocutor was not satisfied. 'You did not say you were innocent?'

'I held forth my innocence, but as I said before, even if I were the guilty man—'

'Who put the money there, do you know?'

'I know nothing at all about it, sir,' insisted Spollin.

A third heckler joined the fray. 'I paid a shilling to see how far your audacity would carry you. Now I would willingly give a second shilling to buy a rope to hang you.'

And with that he departed. Spollin waited for the door to close before continuing.

'Of course some will disagree. But I am sure that the public would rather help me leave than have me knocking about the country.'

Another pointed out that the result of the afternoon's performance gave some indication of public feeling on the matter. Spollin had been given his eight sovereigns; why had he not simply used that to emigrate, when a passage to America could be had for £3?

'Would you have me walk the streets of New York without a shilling, to be worse off than I am now? Now, gentlemen, I leave my case in your hands, and I hope you will not make it worse. I put it to your own conscience to do anything you possibly can to help me. I will not detain you any longer.'

After barely half an hour of diversion – none of it the 'personal narrative' that had been advertised – the audience departed. None responded to Spollin's invitation to 'volunteer and contribute' as they left.

The turnout that evening was only slightly better than it had been for the matinee, with the audience numbering no more than twenty. Spollin's monologue covered the same self-pitying ground as earlier in the day, and was received with similar disdain. He was evasive when questioned about the murder, and only answered with candour about his own background, revealing that most of his family had emigrated to America. One man stood up to tell him that the people of Dublin were too moral and religious to have any sympathy with him. He faced a simple choice: he must either establish his innocence by clearing up the doubts that surrounded the case, or confess his guilt. He could not be tried again, so a confession would not harm him – but it might at least bring him forgiveness from God and man.

After a while the audience became restless, and one attendee stood up to ask when Spollin would be delivering the 'narrative' promised on the posters. Spollin replied that he had no such speech to give, and that he had not written the advertisement. His aim was merely to gain public sympathy and raise funds. Things grew rowdy, and one particularly insulting troublemaker had to be ejected by the police. But it was even worse outside the building, where hundreds had gathered to protest against Spollin's appearance. The theatre management ordered the doors to be locked and barred, and when the crowd found that they could not get inside they began throwing stones at the theatre and abusing innocent passers-by. Sensing that the situation might quickly develop into a riot, the police decided to bring the event to a premature close. And so for the second time that day, the unlikely theatrical artiste departed the stage with taunts ringing in his ears, and scuttled off ignominiously through a back door, out of sight of the mob.

The first-night reviews of James Spollin's theatrical debut were perhaps not what he had been hoping for. The *Dublin Evening Post* condemned the 'unparalleled audacity and indecency' of his conduct, adding that it was impossible to describe 'the reprehension and disgust with which it is viewed by an indignant and outraged public'. The *Daily Express* declared his appearance on stage a 'shocking outrage on decency', while the *Dublin Evening Mail* opined loftily that 'we cannot imagine that any similar occurrence ever took place in a community professing to be civilised'.

In fact it seemed that Spollin had merely succeeded in driving away his supporters. Many ordinary Dubliners had been willing to give him the benefit of the doubt, seeing him as a working-class Catholic used as a scapegoat by an incompetent police force. They cheered his acquittal, but his subsequent behaviour was baffling. Everyone knew a family who had emigrated, counting the pennies until they scraped together enough for the passage to America. But here was a person with £10 in his pocket, more than he needed, exploiting his infamy – and the death of an innocent man – for financial gain. At best it was improper; at worst, the act of a guilty man.

Whatever else could be said of James Spollin, he was not stupid, and he did not make the mistake of persevering with his theatrical venture. At 1.00 the following afternoon Prince Patrick's remained closed, the pavement empty of people except a noisy gaggle of children, and a few people hanging around to see if Spollin would show his face. These idlers passed the time by discussing the murder of George Little and their increasing confidence that James Spollin was indeed the killer. After half an hour or so a police officer walked to the door and had a brief conversation with somebody inside, before announcing that Spollin would not be appearing there again. He was wise to stay away, for in the evening another large and hostile crowd gathered outside the theatre, apparently intent on doing him some mischief.

Unknown to his antagonists, Spollin and his son were only a few streets away, holed up in a seedy boarding house in Exchange Street. For the next few days they kept a low profile while they waited for the furore to die down. On the rare occasions that they ventured outside they were followed at a discreet distance by plain-clothes policemen, who had kept a constant watch on the pair since Spollin's release from prison. It was not clear what they should do next: the 'personal narrative' had brought in barely a pound, and their funds were dwindling by the day. It was finally dawning on James Spollin that they had no future in Dublin, where public opinion was so fiercely against him. Instead he intended to take his story to Cork or Limerick, trusting in the charitable instincts of those outside the capital.

But he was never given a chance to put this plan into action. Late on Saturday night he received a visit from Inspector Ryan, who informed him that he was under arrest, and would be charged with robbing £350 from the Midland Great Western Railway Company. Spollin looked astonished, then defeated.

'Well, it cannot be helped. But I know nothing about it,' he said.

'I suppose this will be another three months' job,' said his son.

'We must only bear it with patience,' replied the father.

Cleared of murder by a jury of his peers, James Spollin could not be tried again on the same charge. But the authorities at Dublin Castle were convinced of his guilt, and desperate for justice to be seen to be done. If they succeeded in getting him convicted of robbery, they could at least reassure the public that the perpetrator of this most heinous crime had been punished for his deeds.

When news of Spollin's recapture broke, there were rumours that the detectives had uncovered some crucial new piece of evidence. But at the police court hearing two days later the Crown presented nothing new, merely relying on the witness statements given in front of the magistrates two months earlier. The proceedings were brief, and concluded with Spollin being sent back to Richmond Bridewell to await trial in a couple of months.

On 5 September Spollin wrote a 'memorial' (petition) to the Lord Lieutenant of Ireland, requesting financial assistance to fund his defence. The Chief Secretary objected to the idea of giving Spollin any more public money, scribbling a brusque note in the margin of the letter: 'No reply should be given to this memorial.' But Spollin would not be left to fend for himself. A few days later John Adye Curran received a letter from the Chief Baron, the senior judge of the Court of Exchequer, informing him that he would be required to defend James Spollin at the next Dublin Commission; he would receive no fee. Mr Curran was furious. The government had paid him a pittance for the murder trial – one of the most difficult and high-profile cases Ireland had ever seen – and now he was being asked to do it all again, and for nothing. He made his displeasure known, but had no option but to accept: one did not say no to the Chief Baron.

The autumn Commission opened at the Green Street Courthouse on Monday 26 October. The case of James Spollin, who was charged with 'larceny in a dwelling-house of property to the amount of £5 or higher', was one of several due to be heard by the two judges that week. But before any of these trials could begin, a grand jury would scrutinise the facts to assess whether there was a case to be answered. If they determined that the evidence against the prisoner was compelling, they would return a 'true bill', and the defendant would stand trial. If, on the other hand, they felt that the case was flimsy, they would declare 'no true bill' – also known as 'ignoring' it – and all charges would be dropped. Once the jurors had been sworn in, one of the two judges, Baron Richards, addressed them briefly about each case. When it came to James Spollin, he cautioned them that they were to disregard anything they had heard or read about the murder trial.

'Gentlemen, I am bound to tell you that you are to act as if you had not heard of James Spollin before. You will examine the witnesses sent before you carefully and cautiously, and if you come to the conclusion that the evidence is sufficient to sustain this charge of larceny against James Spollin, you will be bound to find a bill against him. If, on the other hand, you are not prepared to come to the conclusion that the evidence is sufficient to establish his guilt, you will be bound to ignore the bill and discharge him.'

The jurors retired to their room to deliberate. They had been given copies of the informations to browse, and were also expected to interview a few of the prosecution witnesses in private, free from the scrutiny of barristers or judge. It was a surprise when the members of the grand jury filed back into their box after only two hours, and an even greater shock when the foreman Mr Kinahan announced their unanimous decision. They had found 'no true bill' against James Spollin. After four months in prison, two prosecutions and one lengthy trial, his ordeal was over. Declared innocent of any crime, he was a free man.

'And thus,' observed the *Dublin Evening News*, 'ends all judicial inquiry into the circumstances of the famous Broadstone murder.'

PART FIVE

The Phrenologist

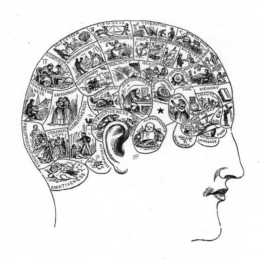

18

Tuesday 17 November

On a chilly evening just over a year after the Broadstone murder, three men dressed in greatcoats and top hats made their way through the crowds of St John's Market in Liverpool. It was 8 p.m., but the five avenues of the great building were still alive with activity, brightly lit by more than two hundred gas lamps. At this time of night the more genteel of the market's patrons were no longer in evidence; most of the customers were labourers or their wives, taking advantage of the cheaper produce on offer towards the end of the day, as stallholders attempted to wring every penny from the last of their stock.

After leaving the market the three men crossed Whitechapel and plunged into the gloom of Preston Street, a narrow and unlit thoroughfare lined by mean-looking tenements. They were watchful and anxious, for while still only a few hundred yards from some of the busiest streets in the city, they were now entering its most notorious slum. The first thing that hit them was the smell, an overpowering stench of raw sewage emanating from the open drains that ran through the courtyards at the centre of each group of houses. The buildings were squalid and overpopulated, and some were in a dangerous state of disrepair. A few years earlier one of these tenements had collapsed without warning, although the only person injured was an unfortunate policeman who had been trying to raise the alarm.

Many of the houses were occupied by burglars, prostitutes, and receivers of stolen goods. Number 55 was home to the infamous Hunt family, three generations of delinquents and ne'er-do-wells;

309

the fearsome matriarch of this criminal dynasty was Old Granny Hunt, known locally as the 'Queen of Demons'. A short distance further on was Fallows' Marine Stores, one of the few legitimate businesses on the street, whose owner had chosen the location because it was only a short walk from the docks. But few of the sailors who frequented Preston Street were interested in buying rope or salt beef. Most came in search of sex or alcohol, both of which were readily available at any time of day or night. The cheapest booze – and the bloodiest fights – could be found in the 'jerry-shops', illegal drinking dens set up in outbuildings and coal cellars. There was also one licensed pub, albeit a rough one: the Auld Lang Syne.

It was to this establishment that Frederick Bridges and his two companions were heading. This was not a social occasion; Bridges had asked his friends to accompany him as a precaution. After ducking through a low door and descending a flight of stairs they found themselves in a subterranean liquor vault, where they were accosted by the proprietor. Mr Bridges told him the purpose of their visit, and the landlord waved them on into the next room, a filthy low-ceilinged chamber with benches around the walls and great chunks of wood, like butchers' blocks, doing service as tables. The landlord, a man called Thomas, followed and sat down on a bench opposite Mr Bridges. Behind him was a window which in daylight hours gave a worm's-eye view of the grimy houses opposite. Now all outside was dark, but on the panes somebody had painted in white the incongruous phrase 'Happy Land'.

This was an unfamiliar environment for three respectable Liverpudlians, but they were relieved to find that their host was an affable and talkative fellow, and gave no hint of being suspicious of his unlikely customers. There was only one subject that Mr Bridges wished to talk about, and he looked for an opportunity to steer the conversation in that direction. This proved unnecessary, however, for Thomas soon launched, unprompted, into an impassioned monologue on the topic in question: the life and travails of James Spollin.

Thomas had strong views about the various injustices suffered by Spollin, and he did his best to persuade his guests that the man reviled by most of Ireland had been deeply wronged.

'All reasonable, right-minded persons must view Mr Spollin's case as I do: from the fact of his having been legally acquitted of the charge against him. He is, therefore, according to the laws of this country, not guilty.'

Having staked his claim to the moral high ground, the landlord rather undermined his efforts by broaching the subject of money.

'All that I have said and done for Mr Spollin has been done from pure charity on my part. But the fact of the case is, gentlemen, that Mr Spollin is a very poor man, and he is anxious to get out of this country, but he lacks the means to do so. I am sure that you would not expect that Mr Spollin could allow himself to be seen without some . . . consideration, shall we say. If any of you gentlemen wishes to see Mr Spollin for yourselves, you may do so by presenting a small sum – sixpence, or a shilling, or any amount you feel inclined to contribute to so charitable a cause.'

Mr Bridges did not hesitate. This was, after all, the reason for their visit. He suggested a whip-round, and his friends fished in their pockets for coins. The landlord seemed satisfied with this display of good faith, and disappeared behind the scenes. A few minutes later he came back into the room, followed by a newcomer who Mr Bridges recognised at once – although he had only ever seen his face, imperfectly rendered, in an illustrated newspaper. There was no mistaking him. It was James Spollin.

The Irishman was an intimidating presence, a powerfully built man with the solid appearance of a boxer. He wore a brown double-breasted overcoat, and underneath it a black waistcoat and black trousers. Over the collar of a white shirt he wore a smart black neckerchief. As he entered the room he had removed his cloth cap, exposing a flat bald head ringed by light red hair. His moustache had the same auburn hue, but the untidy beard that covered the greater part of his face was darker in colour.

The landlord introduced this object of fascination to his three guests. The visitors could not help noticing the smooth and concave expanse of skin in the place where his right eye should have been. It contrasted painfully with the remaining left eye, which was large, bright and blue.

When Spollin spoke, his manner was entirely at odds with this unnerving exterior. He was self-possessed and courteous, and observed suavely that he was glad to see that so many gentlemen had sympathy for his predicament. When the money was presented to him he accepted it gratefully, and sat down to join in the conversation. He seemed perfectly happy to talk about his trial and the events leading up to it. Spollin spoke in glowing terms of his own barristers, and praised their generosity in defending him virtually without fee. He was vicious in his criticism of the Crown prosecutors, who he said had turned his children against him, poisoning their minds until they were willing to send their own father to the gallows. The only one who had remained loyal, he said, was his eldest son James.

This was all very interesting, but Mr Bridges had hoped for rather more than a fireside chat with a suspected murderer. At his request, one of his friends took Thomas aside and explained that Mr Bridges wanted an interview with Spollin in private. The landlord beckoned to Bridges to follow him. He was taken to a small bare room, and shortly afterwards the Irishman joined them. Since this was now a business meeting, the landlord thought it appropriate to make some formal introductions.

'James, this is Mr Bridges. He is a phrenologist.'

Spollin shook the proffered hand, but did not say anything. Mr Bridges switched on the charm.

'Mr Spollin, I am very grateful that you agreed to meet me. My friends and I came especially to see you. But I have a favour to ask. Since you were charged with the murder of Mr Little you have become quite a well-known character. I would very much like your permission to examine your head, to determine whether you have the type of brain capable of doing such a deed.'

Spollin looked thrown by this unconventional demand, and gave the matter considerable thought before answering.

'No, sir. I will not agree to your request. But I have no objection to your examining my head on the day that I depart for America or Australia.'

It was not the answer Mr Bridges had been hoping for. But he sensed that he might yet succeed in winning Spollin over.

Examining people's heads. It was a strange way to earn a living, but Frederick Bridges was passionately devoted to his calling.

By any standards the forty-seven-year-old was an eccentric. According to his own account he was one of seventeen children born to a Manchester architect and inventor who devised several machines which were adopted by the Lancashire cotton mills. His father's ingenuity was not matched by his business acumen, however, and for most of Frederick's childhood the family lived in poverty. Frederick received almost no formal education and started work as a printer's apprentice while still a child. Little more is known about his early life, but at some point in the 1830s, when he was in his mid-teens, he became fascinated by the discipline that would become his life's work: phrenology.

Frederick Bridges himself described phrenology as the science of 'the faculties of the mind, and the organs by means of which they are manifested'. The discipline emerged in the 1790s in the work of Franz Joseph Gall, a German physician who believed that he had discovered a relationship between an individual's talents and the shape of their skull. Gall believed that the functions of the mind could be divided into twenty-seven distinct faculties, each associated with its own 'organ' or area of brain tissue. There was an organ specific to musical talent, another for cunning, and even one for religious sentiment. The relative size of each organ was an indication of the individual's personality and aptitudes, and also determined the shape of their brain. Gall suggested that by examining the skull it was possible to infer the configuration of the brain tissue beneath, and so to reach meaningful conclusions about a person's moral and intellectual characteristics.

Gall called his doctrine 'Organologie'; it was a few decades later that the term 'phrenology' – from the Greek meaning 'study of the mind' – came into general use. In Britain its heyday began in the 1820s, when the first phrenological societies and journals were founded. Its adherents believed that they had succeeded in putting psychology on a sound scientific footing: for the first time, the mysterious workings of the mind could be related to specific features of brain anatomy.

By the 1850s phrenology had lost much of its scientific credibility. Physiologists disputed the idea that discrete mental faculties could be located with any precision inside the brain, and animal experiments appeared to justify their scepticism. The phrenological 'readings' offered by practitioners to their clients were often vague and inconsequential, and had little practical value. It was easy to mock a supposedly 'scientific' discipline that seemed to offer no more insight than a visit to a fairground fortune-teller.

But Frederick Bridges was absolutely convinced of the scientific rigour of his work, and of its potential benefits for all humankind. He was evangelical about his cause, giving public lectures and writing for the local newspapers. Parents and teachers were encouraged to take children for a private consultation, at which Mr Bridges would examine the subject's skull before offering his opinion on the child's particular aptitudes, and the profession or trade to which he thought them best suited. He also offered tuition in practical phrenology ('Day classes for ladies; evening classes for gentlemen') at the organisation he had founded, the grandly named Phrenological Institution. This august establishment was in fact a modest town house occupied by Mr Bridges and his wife Hannah.

As well as making his expertise available to the masses, Frederick Bridges had a particular interest in the criminal mind. He had devoted several years of research to one absorbing problem: was there something distinctive about a murderer's brain? If so, the implications for law and order were momentous. Detectives could identify a killer simply by asking a phrenologist to examine the skull of their prime suspect: there would be no need for expensive inquiries or the laborious gathering of evidence. And why stop there? Mr Bridges predicted an age in which people were routinely screened for their phrenological characteristics, and those recognised as potential murderers pre-emptively imprisoned for the protection of society. In the future, he reasoned, dangerous individuals would be taken out of circulation before they had broken any law.

In order to investigate this problem thoroughly, Mr Bridges needed to compare the skulls of a number of murderers to see whether they had any features in common. To gather this essential data he hit upon the simple, if macabre, solution of attending their executions. Prison governors were usually happy to admit a distinguished scientist to witness the last moments of the condemned man, and afterwards Mr Bridges was permitted to examine the body, and to take a plaster cast of the head.

In June 1856, for instance, the phrenologist travelled to Stafford for the execution of William Palmer, the notorious Rugeley Poisoner. Bridges was allowed to enter the prison at 6 a.m. on the day of the execution, and noted the murderer's 'perfect calm' as he left his cell for the last time. He then joined a large crowd of spectators to watch the hangman tie the noose around Palmer's neck, and witness the sickening jolt that put an end to his life. When the lifeless body had been left swinging gently in the wind and rain for the allotted time, it was cut down from the scaffold and removed to the prison morgue, where Mr Bridges was waiting with a select group including the city's High Sheriff, the prison governor and chaplain, and a number of local medics.

As the phrenologist prepared his equipment, he gave his audience an impromptu lecture based on his initial observations of Palmer's head. From a cursory examination, he said, he had noted the 'extreme predominance of secretiveness, his utter want of conscientiousness, and his defect in the higher reflective powers'. Mr Bridges believed that Palmer was not the sort of person predisposed to violent murder, but had the qualities of a 'secret and subtle' poisoner. His disquisition over, he then shaved the dead man's head and proceeded to make a cast in plaster of Paris.

Over the course of several years Mr Bridges had amassed a huge collection of these plaster heads. Newspaper advertisements urged the public to visit the Phrenological Institution to view this unique rogues' gallery, which included busts of some of the foulest criminals ever brought to justice. Beneath each model was a label in Mr Bridges's neat handwriting, identifying the salient phrenological features and explaining their relevance to the crimes each man had committed.

After comparing the heads of these murderers with those of his law-abiding clients, Mr Bridges noticed something he believed significant. By drawing an imaginary horizontal line starting at the subject's earhole, he could determine the angle between their ear and their eyebrow. This measurement he termed the 'basilar-phrenometric angle', and to make it easier to ascertain he devised an instrument he called the phreno-physiometer. It resembled a navigator's quadrant, with a brass semicircle, graduated in degrees, mounted on a rectangular frame of mahogany. Moveable brass pointers were fixed at the centre of the semicircle; by placing the instrument next to the subject's head and rotating the pointers, he could read off the angle formed by their ear and eyebrow.

In normal, well-adjusted individuals he found that the size of the basilar-phrenometric angle was close to 25 degrees. An angle much smaller than this he associated with a lack of energy and willpower, and general feebleness of character. But Bridges also found to his delight that his murderers all had one thing in common: a basilar-phrenometric angle of between 35 and 45 degrees. William Palmer's head gave an angle of 40 degrees; so did that of John Thurtell, perpetrator of the 1823 Elstree Murder. William Dove, executed in 1856 for poisoning his wife; Robert Marley, hanged at Newgate for beating a jeweller's assistant to death; John Gleeson Wilson, reviled killer of a woman and two small children; all displayed the dread angle of 40 degrees.

Frederick Bridges had succeeded in proving to his own satisfaction – if not to everybody else's – that he could distinguish a murderer from an innocent member of the public by measurement alone. He was convinced that the unyielding laws of nature would soon replace the fallibilities of judge and jury, while Lady Justice would give up her scales for a Bridges phreno-physiometer. But so far he had only been able to test his theory retrospectively, on the bodies of those known to be guilty of the crime. Now he yearned to use his discovery in earnest, to detect a murderer who was still at large.

And what better candidate could there be than James Spollin? The Irishman had been acquitted of murder, but the police and a large proportion of the public remained convinced of his guilt. If he could only examine Spollin's skull, Mr Bridges could settle the question once and for all. He would be serving the interests of justice, and also making a historic contribution to the progress of science. The only question now was whether Spollin would submit to examination. If he was innocent, of course he had nothing to fear: his cranial geometry would declare him not guilty, and that would be the end of the matter. If, on the other hand, he knew himself to be a murderer, he surely would not want to run the risk of exposure.

After their brief interview in 'Happy Land' Mr Bridges felt that there were some grounds for optimism. Spollin had declared his intention of moving abroad and starting a new life with his son in America or Australia. Emigrating was an expensive business, and it was clear that the pair were desperately short of cash. If their situation in Liverpool became intolerable, money might succeed where negotiation had so far failed. Mr Bridges left his address with Thomas the landlord, with a note informing Spollin that he would always be welcome to visit if he needed a friend. The phrenologist hoped that this would do the trick; but for the time being he could only wait.

19

Tuesday 24 November

The week after Mr Bridges's adventure among the slums, an unexpected visitor rang the doorbell of the Phrenological Institution – or number 30 Mount Pleasant, as the postman persisted in calling it. It was Mr Thomas, the proprietor of the drinking den at which Spollin was staying. The phrenologist was surprised to see him, but invited him inside. Thomas explained that Spollin wanted to commission a model of the Broadstone terminus and its surroundings, a replica of the one that had been used in court as a visual aid for the jury. His intention was to exhibit the model, and to use it in public lectures at which he would prove why he could not possibly have killed Mr Little. Thomas asked Mr Bridges if he could recommend a craftsman who might undertake such an assignment.

The phrenologist was nonplussed.

'I do not know a model-maker who would be willing to work for such a man as Spollin. No doubt he could make a replica much better than anyone else, given his perfect knowledge of the place.'

Ever since his arrival in Liverpool, Spollin had been obsessed with the idea that public appearances would provide the funds for his escape. The debacle in Dublin seemed not to have deterred him in the least, and he remained stubbornly convinced that English audiences would give him a more sympathetic hearing than their Irish counterparts. On the evening before his first meeting with Mr Bridges, Spollin had paid a visit to Liverpool's central police station in Gore Street, accompanied by Thomas. The pair presented themselves at the front desk, and asked to see the officer in charge. They were admitted to the office of Superintendent Clough, where Thomas introduced his companion as 'Mr Spollin, from Dublin'. Without waiting for a reply, Spollin issued his demands.

'I want the assistance and cooperation of the police in opening a place where I intend to show a model of the premises where the murder took place, and also of my house and situation, so that I can more clearly explain the incidents relating to it. I hope you will give me your assistance, for I want to raise the means to get out of the country.'

The superintendent already knew all about Spollin – indeed, his plain-clothes detectives had been discreetly tailing the Irishman ever since his arrival in Liverpool. He was incensed.

'Mr Spollin, I am astonished by your request. The police will deal with you as we would with any other of Her Majesty's subjects, without reference to past events. But we will not extend to you any protection beyond that usually offered to any other persons. It would be out of the question to give you special protection after what has happened.'

Spollin looked irritated by this outburst, but kept his composure. He thanked the superintendent coolly and left the building, closely followed by the obedient Thomas.

That incident had been a setback, but was not enough to persuade Spollin to reconsider. He continued to live quietly in Thomas's Preston Street tavern while working out what to do next. Although he did not advertise his presence there, the occasional brave Liverpudlian, keen to satisfy their curiosity, made the trip to the Auld Lang Syne in the hope of seeing him. A shilling was usually sufficient to gain an audience, as long as the stranger looked respectable and professed sympathy for Spollin's situation.

One of these visitors was an undercover reporter from the *Liverpool Mercury*, who succeeded in engaging him in conversation. Spollin was probably unaware that he was talking to a journalist, since the press had been unremittingly hostile towards him since his acquittal, and the feeling was now mutual. If the reporter had been hoping for some dramatic admission, he was out of luck. As soon as the subject of the murder was broached Spollin became guarded and careful in his answers, saying nothing that he had not said before.

He was more forthcoming when the reporter asked about his current plight. His eldest son was still in Dublin, he explained, but would soon be joining him in England, and then the two would emigrate together. To America, he hoped, or possibly Australia; they had not yet decided which. His other children were still with 'the woman' – as he called his wife, contemptuously – 'and they are being supported by Government, no doubt of it'.

As for his reception in Liverpool, Spollin said that the locals had welcomed him. He claimed not to have experienced any hostility, although while walking through Toxteth he had been recognised, and such a large crowd gathered that he thought it best to return home. He became most animated when talking about his plans for the model of Broadstone, which in his imagination had evolved into an attraction to rival Madame Tussaud's. Spollin was apparently the only person not to have noticed a flaw in his moneymaking scheme: the initial outlay was likely to cost him almost as much as the fare to New York.

But he pressed on, and somehow managed to collect enough donations to commission his models. On Monday 7 December an advertisement appeared on the front page of several local newspapers:

SPOLLIN IN LIVERPOOL

Mr James Spollin, who was falsely accused by his wife, and honourably acquitted, will exhibit, this day (Monday), at the Brunswick Rooms, Hunter Street, Byrom Street,

MODELS OF THE BROADSTONE RAILWAY TERMINUS,
Dublin, including his own cottage.

For the purpose of obtaining funds to enable him to emigrate.

N.B. – Mr Spollin returns his sincere thanks to those gentle-men who came forward so kindly to assist him in procuring those models.

Open each day from 11 a.m. to 3 p.m., and from 4 p.m. to 7 p.m. Admission 1s each.

On the morning of this much-anticipated event a modest queue gathered outside the assembly rooms where Spollin was waiting, his models neatly laid out before him. But before he could admit the first paying customer, a police inspector and several consta-bles barged into the room. They bore a message from their superintendent, informing Mr Spollin that in accordance with local law, those wishing to exhibit to the public must first seek authorisation from the Lord Mayor. Since no such permission had been obtained, the police were obliged to shut down his exhibition with immediate effect.

Sorting out this bureaucratic nicety would only have meant a couple of days' delay, but Spollin could see straight away that the decision had little to do with enforcing the city's by-laws. He felt persecuted by the police, whose stifling presence was apparent every time he ventured out of the front door of the Auld Lang Syne. The faces of the plain-clothes officers who followed him on every minor errand had become so familiar that they no longer bothered with any attempt at secrecy. The previous week Spollin had even engaged one of them in conversation, asking him jocu-larly, 'Well now, what do you think about my case? Do you think I was guilty?'

The detective considered the question seriously.

'Since you have asked me, I will answer honestly. If ever one man murdered another, you murdered Mr Little.'

Spollin winced. This was rather more candour than he had been expecting.

'And that is *your* opinion!'

But it was not just one policeman's opinion: the entire force was against him, and he knew it. There was no point in persevering with his public exhibition, he decided, since the superintendent would soon find another excuse to shut it down. So he packed up his models without complaint, and headed back to the less salubrious surroundings of Preston Street. A couple of days later a second advertisement informed readers that Mr James Spollin's models were now on display at the Auld Lang Syne, where the man himself would be present to 'receive the voluntary contributions of the charitable and humane'.

To call this enterprise a failure would be an injustice, since it would imply that Spollin had simply been unsuccessful in his aim of raising the funds he needed to emigrate. The reality was far worse. The few visitors who came to inspect his models left the Auld Lang Syne absolutely convinced that nobody but Spollin could possibly have robbed and killed Mr Little. Disaster turned into catastrophe when customers started to boycott the pub in protest, and in less than a month the business collapsed. The landlord and his family went to live in lodgings. It seems, however, that the Thomases did not blame Spollin for their troubles, as he and his son – recently arrived from Dublin – were invited to stay with them.

On the evening of 28 December, Spollin and Thomas paid a second visit to the Phrenological Institution. Frederick Bridges showed them into his study and asked what they were after. They wanted some advice, they explained: they were considering putting on another exhibition of the model of Broadstone, and would like to know whether Mr Bridges thought this a good idea.

The phrenologist was astounded. It was obvious that Spollin had no inkling of the contempt in which he was held. Mr Bridges strongly advised his guests against taking this course of action: he felt that it would arouse public disgust, and only harm Spollin's cause. Thomas looked disappointed but put a brave face on it, muttering that perhaps they could try in St Helens instead. Spollin sat in silence, dejected. He had squandered all his money on the models, and now there seemed no way out of his predicament.

Mr Bridges sensed an opportunity. But he was also wary of Thomas, who for all his fine words about charity had clearly latched on to Spollin with an eye to improving his own financial situation. It was essential that he find a way of getting the Irishman on his own. As casually as he could, the phrenologist made Spollin an invitation.

'If you are not already engaged, you can call tomorrow night.'

The effect was exactly as he had intended. Thomas assumed, wrongly, that Mr Bridges was offering to advise them in their future business endeavours. Satisfied with the outcome of the interview, he got up.

'I must leave. I have to go to Wales in the morning to see my sister. I hope to borrow some money from her.'

The following evening Spollin arrived at the house on Mount Pleasant with his son James. They were sullen and seemed suspicious; Mr Bridges decided that their behaviour was characteristic of 'studied low cunning'. He did his best to put them at their ease, but had little success until his wife Hannah came to greet their guests. Her warmth and compassion were quite genuine, and the Spollins soon relaxed in her presence. She expressed great sympathy for young James, saying what a pity it was that a youth of his age should be placed in such circumstances.

This was a sure way to win the confidence of Spollin senior, who was fiercely protective of his eldest son. Unexpectedly he turned to Mr Bridges, and asked whether he would be willing to examine the boy's skull. The phrenologist was happy to oblige. He picked up his phreno-physiometer from the desk and applied it to the boy's head. After adjusting the brass pointers he told Spollin that the angle registered 25 degrees.

'That is the average. It indicates that the organ for destructiveness is no greater than the usual.'

'That is as I expected: James shows great aversion to acts of destruction.'

Mr Bridges saw his chance.

'Now, Mr Spollin, allow me to measure your angle.'

He attempted to place his measuring instrument next to the father's head, but Spollin was having none of it. He pushed it away good-humouredly and grinned.

'Oh no, Mr Bridges, don't go too far. You shall have your opportunity in a little while. You, and nobody else.'

Mr Bridges decided to try a different tack. He placed the phreno-physiometer back on the table and then said, as if noticing it for the first time, 'Why, Mr Spollin, your organ of veneration is much larger than that of your son!'

Mr Bridges explained that the organ of veneration was the part of the brain responsible for piety and religious sentiment, and was situated at the top of the brain. He laid his hands on Spollin's bald pate as if to demonstrate. While the Irishman was distracted by a rambling monologue about the distinctions between the organs of self-esteem and benevolence and their relative positions, the phrenologist made a surreptitious examination of his skull.

Some hours later, after the departure of his guests, Mr Bridges sat down to make a note of his observations. The first thing he had noticed was that the base of Spollin's skull was unusually large. This indicated to him that the organs of acquisitiveness, secretiveness, cautiousness, preservativeness and destructiveness were all highly developed. The head was conical, with the organs of veneration, benevolence and conscientiousness all very small. These qualities would predispose Spollin to plan and execute schemes of great sophistication – and to do so without a twinge of conscience, whatever the consequences for others. The basilar-phrenometrical angle was about 40 degrees: the perfect angle for a murderer.

Spollin was evidently intelligent, quick to grasp new concepts and careful in his analysis of any new problem. In Mr Bridges's view this made him a uniquely dangerous individual, possessor of a brain 'of the true assassin class'. The phrenologist felt that he had a responsibility to do something. After sitting in thoughtful silence for a while he reached for a sheet of paper, and composed a letter.

TO THE RIGHT HONOURABLE SIR GEORGE GREY, HOME SECRETARY

Sir – I beg to inform you that James Spollin, who was tried lately at Dublin for the murder of Mr Little, has called upon me several times, and offered to allow me to take a cast of his head, for phrenological purposes, if I will find him the means to enable him and his son to leave this country. He has been trying to get the means by the exhibition of himself in public, but did not succeed: as a last resource he came to me for help.

The configuration of his head is of a most dangerous type. It is, therefore, not prudent to allow such a man to be at large in this country. No one appears to have any sympathy for him, but the strongest feelings against him. He and his son cannot starve; they will be driven to commit some outrage upon society.

If I had been able to pay their expenses I should have gladly done so, to prevent him from doing more mischief in this country.

His mental powers are of a higher order than I generally meet with in such men, particularly the reflective faculties, which render him more dangerous, as he is better able to lay his plans to defeat detection.

I have deemed it my duty, on public grounds, to inform you of the strong characteristics and danger of this man, with a hope that something may be done to remove him and his son from this country. The expense would be from £25 to £30.

I have the honour to be, sir, your most obedient very humble servant,

FREDERICK BRIDGES

Phrenological Institution, Mount-pleasant, Liverpool

Mr Bridges folded this peculiar missive, sealed the envelope and placed it on the hall table, ready for posting. He never received a reply.

When Spollin next visited the Phrenological Institution a couple of days later, he came alone. This time he seemed far more comfortable in his surroundings, and gladly accepted an invitation to dine with Mr Bridges and his wife. Under the gentle interrogation of Hannah Bridges, and aided by generous quantities of wine, the Dubliner soon became quite forthcoming.

'How was it that you came to Liverpool, Mr Spollin?'

'It was Thomas who invited me. He wrote a letter addressed to the prison in Dublin, and it was forwarded to my lodgings. I agreed to come, on condition that I would receive half the profits from any public appearances I might make.'

'And when did you travel here?'

'I arrived here a fortnight before the papers wrote about my visit to Superintendent Clough at the police office.'

Spollin acknowledged his debt to Thomas, who had paid his fare from Dublin and given him accommodation, but he also felt cheated. He believed that his ostensible benefactor was intercepting his letters, and continually misrepresented the opportunities he was laying before him. Mr Bridges interrupted to say that he had tried several times to leave messages for Spollin at the Auld Lang Syne, but that Thomas had never passed them on.

By the end of the evening the phrenologist and the murder suspect were on good terms. And Mr Bridges had made a promise: he would do his best to help Spollin find the means to enable him and his son to leave the country.

When Spollin took his leave he was effusive in his thanks.

'I am very grateful for the way you have treated me. I have not met with such kindness since I came to Liverpool.'

Affable, polite and engaging, the Irishman had been the

perfect guest. Most would have been reassured by his demeanour, but not Mr Bridges. In his notes he recorded that 'this evening's study of Spollin fully confirmed my conviction of the dangerous type of his brain'. He dismissed the bonhomie as an act, a 'cloak of deception' that enabled him to conceal the true wickedness of his nature. 'Criminals of the class to which Spollin belongs,' he wrote, 'are allowed to move in circumstances without being suspected. I can now well understand how people were mistaken in Spollin's character, and that he would be the last man on the works at the Broadstone terminus that would be suspected.'

The following Saturday, New Year's Day 1858, Spollin appeared again. He had not been expected, but Mr Bridges welcomed him into his study, wished him a happy new year and fetched him a chair, which he placed in a position convenient for making covert observations of his guest's skull. Hannah joined the gathering, and for a while Spollin was cheerful and carefree. But when the conversation turned to his plans for the future, the mood changed abruptly. The turning point came when Mr Bridges admitted that he had no idea how to raise the money Spollin needed to leave the country. The Irishman's easy good humour suddenly evaporated and he sat silently contemplating the floor; it was as if his last shred of hope had departed, leaving him outcast, utterly miserable, alone.

Mrs Bridges took pity on him. She broke the awkward silence.

'Come, Mr Spollin. I will see what I can do for you. Women can often do more in these cases than men. If I can raise the sum you need to take your son abroad, will you allow my husband to take a cast of your head?'

Spollin sighed heavily, and fell silent for a while before answering.

'Yes, madam. I will give Mr Bridges all power to do as he likes, and will sign any document to that effect.'

'And will you leave the country?'

'I will, madam, and will be only too glad to have the chance to do so.'

'Then I will do all I can for you.'

Spollin seemed relieved at this possible resolution to his difficulties. Mr Bridges asked where he intended to go. He seemed not to care, as long as it was a long way from England – and he would disguise his appearance so that nobody could possibly recognise him.

Mr Bridges remembered something.

'Mr Spollin, did you see the sketch of yourself in the *Illustrated Times*, about the time of the trial?'

Spollin said that he knew nothing about it. A few months earlier the newspaper had devoted an entire page to the story of his arrest, with a large picture of Spollin making his first appearance in the police court, drawings of various locations around Broadstone, and even a map of the station. Hannah went to fetch a copy from her husband's study. She returned with the paper opened at the relevant page, folded in half so that only the picture of Spollin was visible. He contemplated it silently for some moments before asking whether they thought it was a good likeness. It was, they agreed, a very competent portrait.

Spollin turned the paper over and glanced at the other side. The bottom half of the page contained a drawing of his family's cottage at Broadstone, and under that a sketch of the office where George Little had been murdered. Spollin was transfixed. His face coloured, and his hands began to tremble violently. He threw the paper away, rose from his chair and buried his face in his hands.

Mr and Mrs Bridges looked on uncomfortably. Was Spollin's sudden distress a tacit admission of guilt? That is how they both interpreted it; later, Hannah would say that it was as if Spollin had seen George Little's ghost. When the Irishman finally recovered his composure, he explained himself.

'It was the sight of the cottage that affected me, once my happy home, which I spent many pleasant hours in decorating.'

Over the next couple of days Mrs Bridges did as she had promised, calling on philanthropically minded Liverpudlians in the hope of raising the funds that Spollin needed. She told them that a donation would be a charitable act towards a man who had been found not guilty by twelve of his peers, and yet walked the streets in fear for his life; a loving father who could not provide for his son. As well as appealing to their sense of Christian charity, she also emphasised the significance of her husband's work, and the consequences for scientific knowledge if he could only make a cast of Spollin's head. But her entreaties fell on deaf ears, and she returned to Mount Pleasant empty-handed.

This was all as Frederick Bridges had predicted. He had seen Spollin abused on the street and spat at by strangers, and now appreciated that even the most public-spirited of Liverpool's residents was unlikely to give money to the city's most reviled individual. But there was no way that Bridges could pass up this opportunity. He could already see the cast of Spollin's head taking its place among those of Dove, Palmer, Gleeson Wilson and the other murderers in his private gallery – but it was also a talisman, the physical proof of the theory to which he had devoted so many years. He had reached a decision. If necessary he would buy the Spollins' ticket himself. He was not a rich man, by any means, but he had some savings and could borrow a little more if need be.

Mr Bridges went into his study and took out a fresh sheet of paper. If he was going to be Spollin's saviour he wanted their agreement formalised in a contract, so that he would be protected in the event of any dispute. After giving the matter some thought he picked up a pen and began to write.

Bridges had asked Spollin to return the following Monday to discuss matters further, and at a little after 7 p.m. the Irishman arrived with his son. Hannah told him as gently as she could about her efforts on his behalf, and how they had ended in failure. Spollin slumped in his chair, disheartened. But his mood was about to improve dramatically. Mr Bridges spoke.

'Mr Spollin, as no one will do anything for you, I shall have to do it myself.'

Spollin was overjoyed. But his stammered thanks were soon followed by demands. He wanted to dictate the terms of the agreement in order to ensure that he was not taken advantage of. He would need Mr Bridges to buy him a new winter coat, and to help him redeem a number of possessions which he had been forced to pawn.

Mr Bridges listened patiently to this list of requirements before telling his guest what he thought of his impudence.

'Then I will not allow a cast of my head to be taken.'

'Very well, then my business with you is at an end. The sooner you leave this place the better. You have been consorting with scoundrels, and you judge me from the fullness of your own heart.'

Spollin leapt up, reclaimed his hat and made for the door. On the threshold he turned to deliver a parting shot.

'When I came here I took you for a gentleman.'

Hannah realised that there had been a misunderstanding.

'Mr Spollin, you seem to think that my husband has called you a scoundrel. He meant the people you have been with since you came to Liverpool. Now sit down, if you intend to do business with him. You do not appear to understand your position.'

Spollin's son, who had so far remained silent, backed her up.

'Father, he did not call you a scoundrel, but those who deceived us.'

The Irishman grew calmer, and returned to his seat. Mr Bridges pressed home his advantage.

'Now, Spollin, I know the kind of man I have to deal with. You must either submit to my conditions or quit this house. Every inch of your path is tracked by detectives.'

Spollin muttered a few words about the police and his feelings towards them. Mr Bridges told him that before they went any further with their business together he would require both father and son to sign an agreement. He picked up the document, which he had left out on a table, and read it to them:

In the year of our Lord one thousand eight hundred and fifty eight January the eighth I, James Spollin, do hereby agree to allow Frederick Bridges practical phrenologist 30 Mount Pleasant Liverpool in the county of Lancashire, to take a cast from my head and face, and a photographic portrait of myself in consideration that the said Frederick Bridges will find me and my eldest son the means to enable us to leave this country: and that I will on no pretence or consideration whatsoever allow any person but the said Frederick Bridges to take a cast from my head and face, or a photographic portrait of myself or otherwise make any drawing or painting of me whatsoever and that I give the said Frederick Bridges all power over the said cast and photograph to do with them and say whatsoever his judgement may seem proper and right.

Spollin considered this text in silence for a while before responding.

'I cannot allow my photograph to be taken, because if one is taken, any number could be made from it.'

Mr Bridges was relentless.

'If that is your decision the business is now at an end. I will have nothing more to do with it.'

Spollin had no alternative but to back down.

'Well, I do not care much for it, but the last part of your agreement gives you great power.'

'That it does, I grant, but nothing less will satisfy me.'

He produced a pen and thrust it expectantly at Spollin. The Irishman managed a smile and said, with forced good humour, 'Well then, if I must do the thing, I might as well do it effectually.'

He seized the pen and signed with a flourish.

'Spollin is now dead,' he said, and passed the pen to his son, who added his signature. Frederick and Hannah Bridges then witnessed the document, and the agreement became official.

Now the business was completed, the tension in the room eased palpably. Spollin and James gave a brief account of what had happened to them since they were forced to move out of the Auld Lang Syne. As Thomas, their former host, had lost his livelihood they soon found themselves in poverty: he was able to give them a place to sleep, but little else. They had pawned everything they owned except the clothes they wore. Spollin rummaged in his pockets and produced the tickets, which Mr Bridges examined and found to amount to 18s 4d.

Mr Bridges had based his assessment of Spollin's personality on a brief survey of the Irishman's skull. There had not yet been the opportunity to perform a full examination, but he believed that he had seen enough to assess the configuration of his brain. He knew his new acquaintance to be untrustworthy, scheming, secretive – and a murderer. This was not the subjective judgement of Frederick Bridges, but the disinterested verdict of Nature. His faith in the accuracy of phrenology was unshakeable.

But phrenology was a pseudoscience, an ill-conceived theory cobbled together from inconsistent observations and irrational assumptions. We now know that specific areas of the brain do in fact perform specialised functions, such as problem-solving, initiating movement, or processing stimuli. But these areas bear little relation to the 'organs' hypothesised by the phrenologists, and meticulously mapped on the porcelain heads that are still a familiar relic of their beliefs. The phrenology heads produced and sold by Mr Bridges indicated no fewer than forty organs, each numbered to aid the beginner. All, from number 1 on the list (Amativeness) to number 40 (Casuality), were imaginary, without any basis in scientific fact. Spollin had no organ of destructiveness to measure, and his basilar-phrenometric angle revealed nothing about his personality – least of all whether he was a murderer. Mr Bridges's detailed appraisal of his character traits was worthless, at least from a scientific point of view.

That is not to say that it was entirely incorrect. An astrologer or palm-reader will often speak the truth, even if their insights have nothing to do with the movements of the heavens or the lines on their client's palm. Mr Bridges soon felt vindicated in his description of Spollin as greedy and untrustworthy, because he only succeeded in obtaining his plaster cast and photograph after the Irishman made repeated attempts to modify the terms of their agreement, or to pull out of it entirely. Spollin's efforts were futile, for as he well knew – and Mr Bridges did not fail to remind him – it was only by cooperating fully that he could hope to leave England for good.

Spollin endured without complaint the tedious process of making a cast of his head, but the taking of the photograph prompted their last and bitterest confrontation. Mr Bridges took him to the studio of Mr Wilmot, a photographer friend who was familiar with the phrenologist's peculiar requirements. Spollin at first refused to show the right side of his face, with its missing eye, to the camera, but his objections were eventually overruled. He then asked Mr Wilmot to take a second picture for his own use, a request the photographer was happy to fulfil.

Two days later, on Thursday 14 January, Mr Wilmot went to the Phrenological Institution to deliver the finished photographs in person. They were daguerreotypes, images made directly on to delicate copper plates and then developed using mercury vapour. Since even gentle rubbing might damage them, Mr Wilmot had given the pictures a coat of varnish to protect them.

Mr Bridges thanked him, and gazed at the photographs in admiration. Spollin sat in three-quarter profile gazing out to the left, smartly dressed in overcoat and bow tie. It might have been the portrait of a bank manager or family doctor. The images were virtually identical, one intended for the phrenologist and the other for Spollin himself. Mr Bridges calmly picked up one of the plates and broke it in two, bending the thin copper until it snapped. The photographer was aghast.

Mr Bridges thought he had better explain. The previous day, he said, he had been walking along Lime Street when he was recognised by a stranger, who stopped him to ask when he had last seen Spollin. 'Why do you want to know?' Mr Bridges had retorted. It transpired that the man knew all about the photographs, and he let slip that he had struck a deal with the Irishman to buy his portrait from him. The phrenologist was exasperated, although not entirely surprised, to learn that the unscrupulous Spollin had not been able to resist the opportunity to make a bit of extra money. Well, he would not stand for it. He would rather destroy the picture than see his generosity abused in this way.

Spollin arrived at the house on Mount Pleasant just as Mr Wilmot was leaving. Mr Bridges took him into his study and explained the situation. Spollin was incredulous and then outraged. He wanted his photograph.

'I will have one. I will not leave this country without one.'

Hannah Bridges, who had often been an unexpected ally to James Spollin, now backed up her husband.

'There is nothing in the agreement to say that you are to have one.'

'I do not care for the agreement. No agreement shall bind me. I shall have a portrait.'

Frederick Bridges had heard enough.

'Yes, to sell it, you vile scoundrel. Now I tell you, if you break one condition of the agreement, I will have you transported for obtaining money under false pretences. You found it easy to rob and murder Mr Little, but you will find that now you have a different man to deal with. I know you, I know what you are capable of doing. I know what you have done. A man with a head of your type ought not to be allowed at large.'

Whether it was the strangeness of the insult, or the sheer fury with which it was delivered, this was the blow that put an end to Spollin's resistance. He sank into a chair, his energy spent. Frederick Bridges, a man he had known for less than two months, had promised him the one thing he desperately wanted. Helping him to emigrate would cost the phrenologist at least £20 – as much as Spollin had earned at Broadstone in four months – and what had he asked in return? To take a photograph and make a model of Spollin's head. By any reckoning this was a good deal for the Irishman, and yet he had been unable to resist the urge to ask for more. His greed, which poisoned so many of his dealings in Liverpool, had finally been neutralised by practical necessity.

He had also run out of time. Mr Bridges was as eager to get rid of Spollin as the Irishman was impatient to leave, and the phrenologist had already secured two berths on a ship that would set sail within a few days. The tickets were sitting on his desk, but there was one more formality to be completed before he would hand them over. Mr Bridges wanted a clean end to an association that had been characterised by mutual suspicion and distrust. He had fulfilled his side of the bargain; there must be no ambiguity about it, no room for manoeuvre.

He placed a piece of paper in front of Spollin, and handed him a pen. A short document, a single sentence. A receipt. One more signature, and their business was done.

January 14th 1858
30 Mount Pleasant
Liverpool
    This is the receipt in full of all demands on Frederick Bridges according to agreement.
    James Spollin

*

A freezing January morning at Liverpool docks. A wind that whipped off the Mersey and chilled to the bone, yanked at tarpaulins till they threatened to fly loose, and whistled through the rigging, making the halyards snap incessantly against their masts. Stevedores, their workwear strangely insubstantial for such a bitter day, hurried between warehouse and quayside with the last of the cargo. Many of the ships that sat gently rolling at their moorings were steamers, modern wonders capable of crossing the Atlantic in less than ten days. But the vessel now being prepared for departure was a clipper, a three-masted, square-rigged sailing ship that even under favourable winds would take twice as long to make the same journey. She was an emigrant ship, and most who boarded her were prepared to endure a little discomfort for the chance of starting a new life overseas.

The passengers had already embarked, and were settling into the cramped quarters that would be their home for the coming weeks. A few families had scraped together the money for a private cabin, but the majority – several hundred men, women and children – were in steerage, a dark, low-ceilinged space immediately underneath the main deck. Two tiers of broad wooden bunks lined both sides of this chamber, with a narrow aisle running in between. Eight guineas would secure a bunk to share with two or three others – though not the bedding, which passengers had to supply themselves. Also included in the ticket price were rations of bread, flour, meat, potatoes and other foodstuffs, which were carefully weighed out to the nearest ounce and doled out once a week. The passengers would prepare their own meals, using their own utensils; there was a ship's cook, of course, but he could not be expected to cater for a deck full of emigrants as well as two dozen hungry sailors.

Those who used these emigrant ships were a diverse bunch: German, Dutch, Irish, English. Few had friends or family in Liverpool to wave them off, but a small crowd of spectators had nevertheless gathered on the quayside to watch the ship depart.

Among them, unremarkable and unremarked, was a middle-aged couple, both heavily muffled against the cold. They exchanged a few words as they stood watching the ship intently, their eyes never deviating from the decks and gangplank. Frederick and Hannah Bridges had decided to brave the elements not out of any sentimental desire to wish James Spollin a fond farewell; in fact, they wanted to make sure that he really left.

A few hours earlier, Hannah had supervised the final preparations for the great departure. She had managed to engage an amateur make-up artist of some local renown, a woman who specialised in fancy-dress balls. They had begun by getting Spollin to shave off his whiskers, the outsize ginger moustache and beard that made him so instantly recognisable. Then the expert went to work, altering his appearance so successfully that when young James was admitted to the room he did not recognise his own father. An effective disguise was essential, for there would inevitably be Irish labourers aboard their ship, and even five months after his acquittal it was not improbable that somebody would recognise Spollin from his likeness in the newspapers.

But, so far at least, all had gone without a hitch. Father and son had queued to present their tickets to the purser, and then given false names for him to write in the ship's manifest. Now they would have to remember to stick to these new identities, at least until they reached their destination. They had introduced themselves to a few of their new shipmates, none of whom seemed to be aware that they were meeting one of the most reviled men in Britain. It was a dangerous game, but a blessedly brief one. In a month or two the Spollins would be free of all persecution, free of their toxic reputation, free to do as they chose. And nobody – not the police, not the government stooges of Dublin Castle, not the vipers of Fleet Street – would have the slightest idea where they had gone.

Nobody, that is, apart from the nondescript couple who remained on the quayside long after the great vessel had slipped its moorings and begun its stately progress along the Mersey shipping channel towards the Irish Sea. And they had promised never to tell a soul.

EPILOGUE

20

Saturday 13 March 1858

Her proud owners called the *Emerald Isle* the 'fastest packet in the trade'. Launched in 1853, she was one of the larger passenger ships plying the transatlantic route, her three enormous square-rigged masts supporting what looked like several acres of canvas. Her figurehead was a leaping Irish wolfhound, while her stern was ornamented by a carved golden harp, supported on one side by another wolfhound, and on the other by an American eagle. Below decks she boasted a fine mahogany-panelled saloon cabin, with thick carpets and green velvet settees.

But few of those on board would even lay eyes on such luxury. The *Emerald Isle* was designed to carry people in great numbers rather than great style. While no more than a dozen of the wealthiest passengers were likely to enjoy the plush furnishings of the saloon, as many as nine hundred could be crammed into the squalor of steerage. The food and accommodation were dire, and provided ideal conditions for contagious diseases to flourish. There was a reason that doctors travelled free of charge, and it was not simple benevolence. Any medical man unwise enough to take up the offer was likely to spend much of the journey in the ship's hospital, tending to the sick and dying.

The passage to America was rarely easy at this time of year, and the *Emerald Isle* spent almost eight weeks at sea, battered by violent snowstorms and heavy winter gales. She finally dropped anchor off the tip of Manhattan on Saturday 13 March, and after the usual customs formalities the passengers were taken ashore on a small flotilla of barges and tugs. They disembarked at a pier next to a cluster of buildings known as Castle Garden, New York's recently opened reception centre for immigrants. The new arrivals were filthy and unkempt, not having had a bath or a change of clothes in almost two months. To add to their indignities they were then driven into the nearest building between two lines of officials, like sheep being rounded up into a pen.

In the midst of this ragged crowd were a man in his forties and his teenage son. There was no sign of a wife or any other children, and they did not appear to be part of a group. The pair surrendered their scanty luggage for inspection, and then waited in line to be examined by the medical officer. When they had been declared free of disease they joined the slow procession into a great rotunda, where they were met by a series of unsmiling officials who scrutinised the immigrants closely and bombarded them with questions: Where were you born? What is your trade? What is your first language? Where are you going? What is your name? The pair answered that they were Irish labourers who intended to remain in the United States; the older man gave his name as Charles Lowther, and his son as Thomas.

This interrogation was not the end of the ordeal, because nobody was allowed to leave until every last immigrant had been questioned and their details logged. Though it was cold and many were sick, they were shepherded into an open-air holding area, where at intervals an official would read out a long list of names, for reasons which were never made entirely clear. After what seemed an eternity of waiting, the Lowthers were free to reclaim their baggage and leave Castle Garden. They picked their way through the touts peddling dubious railroad tickets and questionable boarding-house accommodation; past the bona fide money-changers and the crooked ones; the clerks offering letter-writing services to the illiterate; the porters, food vendors, beggars, drunks, cabmen, police officers and myriad other species that made up this exotic new ecosystem; and finally emerged blinking on to Broadway, the gateway to a new continent, new opportunities, a new life.

An Irish father and son calling themselves Charles and Thomas Lowther really did arrive in New York on the *Emerald Isle*. Were they the Spollins travelling under an assumed name? It is impossible to be sure, but there are good grounds for suspecting that the Lowthers existed only as a convenient fiction.

The Spollins were certainly in Liverpool until Thursday 14 January, when they visited Frederick Bridges for the last time and signed a receipt for their passage abroad. The following Tuesday the *Liverpool Mercury*, whose reporters had kept close tabs on their movements, announced that James Spollin had 'taken his departure for a distant part of the globe . . . within the last few days'. Both the newspaper and Mr Bridges agree that the pair left the city by sea, and records show that fifty-one vessels set sail from the port of Liverpool during that four-day period, all but a few on Sunday 17 January. They were heading for ports all over the world: Adelaide, Bahia, Barbados, Calcutta, Ghent, Gibraltar, Havana, Lima . . . the list goes on, all the way down to Veracruz.

While the Spollins might theoretically have been on board any of them, the majority were cargo vessels and carried no passengers. Moreover, the manifests for most of the remainder have survived, making it possible to see who was travelling, their nationalities and ages. The emigrants who appear in these lists were typically young single men, or travelling as a family, and it is unusual to find a man in his forties accompanied by a teenager.* None of the ships that left Liverpool that weekend for Boston, Philadelphia, New Orleans or Melbourne carried two passengers who might plausibly have been the Spollins. In fact, of all the vessels bound for North America or Australia – the two most popular emigrant destinations – it is only the *Emerald Isle*'s

---

* Even if Spollin and his son travelled under different surnames, they would still be an obvious anomaly in the passenger manifest of an emigrant ship.

passenger list that includes two Irishmen who were not merely the right ages, but evidently father and son.

The choice of New York would make sense. The city was overwhelmingly the most popular destination for Irish emigrants, more than half a million of whom had settled there in the immediate aftermath of the Great Famine. Spollin's own family were part of this mass exodus, and during his infamous theatrical appearances he seems to have given a hint of his intended travel plans when he asked his audience whether they would have him 'walk the streets of New York without a shilling'.

Journalists assumed that that was where he had gone, too. On Friday 5 March the Dublin *Daily Express* had this terrific piece of gossip:

> Spollin, the alleged murderer of Mr Little in Dublin, has arrived in New York, and notwithstanding his endeavour to change his appearance so as not to be recognised, the first tavern he entered the landlady presented him with his portrait, to the back of which a drawing of the scene of the murder was affixed. The fellow was completely unnerved, and burst into tears.

It's a neat story, but almost certainly fabricated; apart from anything else, the timings would require the Spollins to have caught a steamer to New York in a week when none left Liverpool. Similarly implausible is the claim, made by a few Irish newspapers in September 1858, that James Spollin had just been hanged in New York for murder. Executions were rare and newsworthy events in 1850s New York, and tend to be well documented – and yet there is no other report that this one took place.

After these two – probably apocryphal – sightings the trail goes cold. Wherever the two Spollins travelled in January 1858, and whatever befell them thereafter, they got what they wanted: they disappeared.

*

Was James Spollin the Broadstone murderer?

The police and Dublin Castle officials certainly thought so. In a detailed report written for his superiors on the day after Spollin was cleared of murder, the Crown Solicitor Thomas Kemmis suggested that the verdict was not as disastrous as it might appear. He pointed out that the trial had at least succeeded in removing 'unjust suspicion from innocent persons', and 'fix[ed] the guilt incontestably' on Spollin – at least, as far as the public were concerned. Two months later, after the failed attempt to prosecute him for robbery, nobody even suggested that the investigation should be reopened. There was nothing to investigate: as far as government, prosecutors and detectives were concerned, they knew who had committed the Broadstone murder, and he had got away with it.

Even among those who believed that James Spollin was guilty, few suggested that the jury had reached the wrong decision. In a thoughtful editorial published immediately after Spollin's murder trial, *The Times* argued that 'it would be impossible to say that the evidence was conclusive, and the verdict a wrong one'. Reading the transcript of the trial today, it is difficult to see how a competent and impartial jury could have reached any other verdict. The prosecution had no physical evidence connecting Spollin with the crime scene. They could not link him to the supposed murder weapons, or prove that he had been anywhere near Mr Little's office on the night of the cashier's death. The most damaging evidence offered against Spollin was the allegation, made by two of his own children, that he had lied about his whereabouts on the evening of the murder – but the inconsistencies in their testimony, ruthlessly exposed in cross-examination, rendered their contribution almost worthless.

Once the evidence of Lucy and Joseph Spollin was disregarded, the case against their father looked not so much flimsy as non-existent. The Crown argued that he knew the station buildings well, and that the stolen money had been found near his cottage. But these facts made him no more likely to have committed the crime than dozens of other railway employees. There was a gaping void at the heart of this prosecution, and everybody knew it. The one person whose evidence might have proved James Spollin's guilt was not allowed to testify.

If the law had permitted Mary Spollin to give evidence against her husband, she could have told the court that she had seen her husband in bloodstained clothes, that he had admitted to the crime, and that she had helped him hide the stolen money. Perhaps the most compelling evidence – which the jury was not permitted to consider during the trial – was the fact that she had been able to lead the police straight to the missing cash. If it did not prove that her husband was the murderer, it suggested that her claim to have helped conceal it was true. But of course Mary's story would not have gone unchallenged; there is no way of knowing how robustly she would have stood up to a skilful cross-examiner like the defence counsel Mr Curran.

While most contemporary commentators agreed that the case against James Spollin was simply not strong enough, none suggested that he might be innocent. It is possible that there were people in Dublin or Liverpool who passionately believed it, but if so they have left no trace. The overwhelming impression conveyed by the historical record is that James Spollin's behaviour following his acquittal was enough to convince the most ardent sceptic that he was a guilty man.

If that was indeed the case, who was to blame for Spollin's escape from the hangman's noose? In his report Thomas Kemmis, who had supervised both the investigation and the eventual prosecution, refrained from criticising either detectives or lawyers. The public and media were not so generous. One Dublin paper railed against the 'bungling and stupidity' of the police, while another compiled a long list of the detectives' mistakes. It began with their botched examination of George Little's office, which had resulted in the erroneous assumption that the cashier had taken his own life. Then there was their repeated failure to find several large packages of money, hidden under their very noses; and, worst of all, Superintendent Guy's disastrously premature arrest of James Spollin. If the detectives had instead kept a close watch on Spollin's movements, it would surely have been only a matter of time before they caught him in the act of visiting his hidden stash – and then they would have had incontrovertible evidence linking him with the stolen money.

Other detractors focused on the court case. The prosecution was criticised for its obsession with irrelevant minutiae, while the Attorney General was castigated for a 'lame, impotent, and inconclusive' closing speech. A devastating analysis published in the *Midland Counties Advertiser* went still further, asserting that the management of the entire case was 'a disgrace to the officers of the Crown, both legal and detective, and from the highest functionary down to the humblest policeman concerned'.

There was an unpleasantly jingoistic edge to much of the debate, and some elements in English journalism delighted in attacking the perceived shortcomings of Dublin's officials. Opponents retorted that it was not Irish lawyers, but English laws, which were to blame. As a direct result of the Spollin case there were demands for legal reform, with the most obvious target being the principle that wives were not competent to give evidence against their own husbands. But the campaign fizzled out after a few months, and it was not until the Criminal Evidence Act of 1898 that the antiquated rule was finally abolished.

Another suggestion was that the courts should add the Scottish verdict of Not Proven to the existing options of Guilty and Not Guilty, allowing juries to signal when they believed a defendant might be guilty but the case against them weak. The English MP William Ewart – an effective campaigner whose many successes included the establishment of publicly funded libraries* – announced that he would be introducing a bill to Parliament, by which he hoped to make the Not Proven verdict available to juries in England and Ireland. Perhaps his views changed, or maybe he had more pressing legislative proposals to consider, because he never tabled the promised motion or even mentioned the subject in the House of Commons.

Like her husband, Mary Spollin had also made clear her desire to melt away into anonymity. She and her three younger children – Lucy, Joseph and George – continued to live under police protection in the Broadstone cottage until October 1857, when her husband was cleared of wrongdoing for the second and final time. But they could stay there no longer, as they had been living rent free on railway company property, and the directors now wished them to leave. At the suggestion of William Kemmis, Mary and her children were taken from their home at the dead of night and relocated to a safe house in a provincial town a short distance from Dublin. This was carried out in conditions of such secrecy that only two people – Mr Kemmis and a single senior member of the police force – knew where they could be found. They remained there for the next six months under an assumed name, supported by a weekly allowance of £1 10s paid to them by the government.

On 2 March 1858 the Crown Solicitor sent Inspector Ryan to speak to Mary about her future. Ryan raised the possibility of emigration, and Mary replied that 'nothing would induce her to go to America'. She was terrified of encountering her husband and eldest son, who she was sure had settled there. She also ruled out Australia, but was happy with the idea of moving to England or even staying where she was. She believed that she was unknown and unsuspected in her new surroundings, and the children were

* He was also the inventor of the blue plaques which commemorate the distinguished former residents of London buildings.

happy there. It is not clear whether they remained in Ireland or settled in the English countryside: the officials responsible sensibly avoided committing the final decision to paper.

Mary and her children retained their original Christian names, but took the surname Doyle. They were awarded a government annuity of £36 per year for life, but William Kemmis was keen to do more for her. The police were still looking after £246 of railway company money which had been recovered thanks to Mary's tip-off. Mr Kemmis wrote to the company secretary Henry Beausire to ask whether the Midland Great Western Railway might consider donating this sum as a goodwill payment to Mary and her children. Mr Beausire replied promptly to say that the directors had approved his plan. Mary received £200, with the proviso that she could touch only the interest. The capital was for her three children, who would each receive £50 on reaching their twenty-first birthday – or sooner, if they needed funds for education or an apprenticeship.

That is the last we know of the Spollins, except for a letter retained in the Irish national archives. In May 1895 the youngest Spollin child – now calling himself George Doyle, and aged in his early forties – wrote from London to Patrick Coll, the Chief Crown Solicitor for Ireland. His message, written from a cheap and crowded boarding house in Lincoln's Inn Fields, is poignant:

Dear Sir

I write to know about a matter which may be of some benefit to me. I am the youngest child of the late Mrs Doyle (Spollin) who was the informant in the case tried (Spollin for the murder of Mr Little of the Broadstone Railway Terminus) in Dublin in July and August 1857. Some company or the government, I don't know which, gave a sum of money for the maintenance of the family, and each child was to receive £50 at the age of 21 years. When I was 21 I was out in the Far East and was late in sending in my application. I wrote I think towards the end of 1872 and received, I think early in 1873, through the Bishop of Southwark's hands, £44, 4 or 6 shillings and a few pence. Mr Lane Joynt was the solicitor.

As I was then fairly well off I did not trouble about the balance. I also remember reading on the receipt I signed something which gave me to understand that I might be entitled, at a future period, to something more. I wish to know if there be any money to which I might be entitled now. Mother died in October 1876. As I am now in very straitened circumstances a little money would be very welcome. The winter was severe and has caused much misery over here.

Hoping you will make enquiries about the matter and begging to be excused for encroaching on your valuable time,

I beg to remain your obedient servant,

George Doyle

The following week he received a brief reply informing him curtly that the Chief Crown Solicitor had checked the departmental records and determined that Mr Doyle was due no further money from the Crown.

It must have been a bitter blow. George had not been exaggerating when he referred to his 'straitened circumstances'. He was making his living selling newspapers on the streets of London, and census records show that six years later he was still living at the same insalubrious address in Lincoln's Inn. It was probably a dosshouse, as there were at least twenty other residents – all men in their fifties or sixties, and all scraping a living by cleaning windows, carrying sandwich boards or painting theatre scenery. But it was not long before George was struggling to pay the rent even for this miserable accommodation. Within a couple of years he was homeless, and his name started to appear with depressing regularity in the register of the

Lambeth Workhouse. By the time of the 1911 census he was listed as a permanent resident of the institution; and five years later the youngest member of the notorious Spollin family died there in abject poverty, aged sixty-six.

Another name that cropped up repeatedly in the flurry of letters and memos between police, lawyers and government administrators following the collapse of the Spollin case was that of Catherine Campbell. The Gunnings' young servant had been taken into police protection in November 1856, and shortly afterwards she divulged information that implied the guilt of her employer Bernard Gunning. Although Catherine and her evidence were subsequently deemed unreliable, the detectives refused to let her go, and she remained in confinement for another ten months. It was only after Spollin's departure for Liverpool that she was finally granted her liberty.

On 19 November 1857 she made an unannounced visit to the Dublin Castle office of Joseph Finnamore, the superintendent in charge of the detective division. Catherine told him that she wanted to be compensated for her loss of time and the damage to her reputation. The superintendent forwarded her demand to the Crown Solicitor, who in turn passed it on to the Attorney General. Mr Kemmis's brief memorandum on the subject is faintly sinister, concluding that 'you might now deem it advisable to dispose of Catherine Campbell'.

The Attorney General, Mr FitzGerald, responded in a similar vein: 'Catherine Campbell has no claim whatever, but I think that she should be finally got rid of by the payment of such moderate sums as to the Crown Solicitor should appear proper.' Mr Kemmis proposed to give Catherine £10 in two instalments: the first would buy her a passage to America, and she would receive £5 on arrival to fund her first few months as an immigrant. This is the last reference to Catherine in the official papers, which might indicate that she accepted the offer.

The behaviour of the Dublin Castle administration towards Catherine Campbell seems inexplicable. For a few weeks she was treated as the Crown's star witness; then she became a pariah, deprived of her freedom in extremely dubious circumstances. Even though the officials believed that she had tried to pervert the course of justice, they granted her a generous weekly allowance for the next ten months. When she finally regained her liberty they paid her a substantial sum – which all involved agreed she did not deserve – to leave the country. Why was the mighty British state so exercised by an illiterate teenager, an orphan from a peasant family? It is possible that officials simply accepted that their conduct had permanently deprived Catherine of her livelihood, as without reputation or references her hopes of employment were nil. But the manner in which her case was dealt with suggests that she posed some sort of threat: perhaps the residents of the Castle feared the damage her story would do to the administration's credibility, and decided that Catherine should be on another continent when she told it.

Catherine Campbell was not the only person whose reputation was dragged through the mud. Her former employer Bernard Gunning had been accused of murder; much of Dublin had believed him to be the killer, and his wife Anne his accomplice. But on 11 November 1857 the *Dublin Evening Mail* revealed that the Gunnings had at last been given some recompense. Under the headline 'Railway Compensation', the newspaper announced that the directors of the Midland Great Western Railway had awarded them £100, and put Mr Gunning in charge of the hotel at Athenry railway station, at a nominal rent.

The report drew an immediate denial from Mr Beausire, who wrote to point out that the hotel was not owned by the railway company, and therefore not in its gift. The newspaper's 'apology' was a masterpiece of withering sarcasm:

Mr Beausire's letter makes it perfectly clear to us that these gentlemen were quite incapable of appreciating the sufferings endured in their service by their clerk Mr Gunning, in the way we were unwarily led to suppose, and we sincerely regret having countenanced any such misapprehension.

In fact Bernard Gunning had resigned his position at Broadstone and used his compensation money to secure the tenancy of the railway hotel, a small but rather high-class establishment set in its own gardens. The fact that such a business could now prosper in a town whose name had become a byword for poverty was a sign of renewed economic optimism, a decade after the Great Famine. While Mr Gunning's relationship with his former employers had irreparably broken down, he was still held in great affection by his old colleagues. The following March the proud landlord of the Athenry Railway Hotel was the guest of honour at a dinner in Dublin at which they presented him with an elegant silver tea service, engraved to mark the occasion of his retirement. But this pleasant new chapter of his life was cut short when he contracted tuberculosis, to which he succumbed in 1865. His widow Anne continued to run the hotel on her own until she died six years later from kidney disease, aged sixty – or 'at a very advanced age' as the local newspaper described it.

Only a few people emerged from the aftermath of the Broadstone tragedy with their reputations enhanced. James Spollin's lawyer John Adye Curran was one of them: his scintillating performance in court confirmed his status as one of Ireland's most gifted defence barristers. The senior presiding judge, Thomas Lefroy, barely uttered a word during the trial, and did little to dispel the widely held opinion that he was senile; but there was no doubting the competence of his colleague on the bench, James Henry Monahan. Chief Justice Monahan handled a difficult case with calm authority, keeping a roomful of self-important lawyers in check as effortlessly as if they had been Sunday-school pupils.

That said, few Dubliners would have approved of the praise he lavished on the police. The judge made a point of expressing his approbation of their work 'in the highest terms', provoking such delight in official circles that Mr Kemmis forwarded a transcript to the Attorney General, commenting that it might be appropriate to give some sort of bonus to the officers concerned. This proposal was approved by the Chief Secretary, and five detectives were given substantial cash rewards: Daniel Ryan received £25, and four others £15 each. Ryan was also promoted from acting to full inspector. The awards were never made public, which was probably just as well: the government would have been hard pressed to justify them, with so many people hungry and homeless on the streets.

There was one glaring omission from the list. The work of Augustus Guy, who had been in charge of the investigation until its closing stages, was not deemed worthy of recognition. It was an obvious snub for a man who had once been the most senior detective in Ireland, and Superintendent Guy ended his career in relative obscurity. He was transferred to the seaside suburb of Kingstown (now Dún Laoghaire), a genteel resort a few miles south of Dublin. It would normally be a nice gentle posting for a policeman nearing retirement, but his time there was not without incident. During the terrible winter storm of February 1861, when more than a dozen ships were wrecked in Kingstown harbour, Mr Guy and five of his men risked their lives to rescue the crew of a vessel which had been thrown on to the rocks, earning well-deserved praise for their bravery. Two years later, after twenty-six years in the Dublin Metropolitan Police, Augustus Guy retired and returned to England, settling in the Buckinghamshire village of Whitchurch.

Daniel Ryan was on the opposite trajectory. By 1859 he had risen to superintendent of 'G' division, in charge of the detective force. The remainder of his career would involve more politics than policing, as the campaign for Irish independence – quiescent for much of the previous decade – was once again gathering steam. Ryan ran a network of informers and gathered intelligence on separatist groups, who loathed him heartily as a result. The height of his unpopularity came in 1866, when in a single night he rounded up ninety-one suspected nationalist activists and detained them without charge. Suspending civil liberties in this dramatic fashion did nothing to deter those struggling for Irish independence, as another attempted rebellion the following year – the Fenian Rising – showed. Daniel Ryan remained in charge of the British police state in Ireland, what Friedrich Engels once called its 'iron fist', until his retirement in 1874.

In March 1858 Frederick Bridges travelled to Dublin to give a series of six lectures entitled 'Phrenology and its application to daily life'. The advertisements, which emphasised the moral and educational benefits of his work, made this sound like a philanthropic venture, but Mr Bridges was not there out of any benevolent instinct. He hoped to cash in on his association with a suspected murderer. In his luggage were copies of a hurriedly thrown-together pamphlet, *The Phreno-Physiological Characteristics of the Head of James Spollin*, and several of his plaster casts of killers' craniums. Expecting lively interest in his anecdotes about the notorious Spollin, he had booked the Music Hall, a splendid building in Lower Abbey Street, for six consecutive nights.

When the phrenologist arrived in the Irish capital he was basking in the glow of one of his greatest triumphs. A few weeks earlier Mr Bridges had received an unexpected invitation to the London home of Lord Palmerston. The recently ex-Prime Minister – his entire cabinet had just resigned – was keen to learn about phreno-physiometry and discuss how it might be employed in the criminal justice system. The phrenologist was given the honour of a lengthy private audience, and after explaining the outlines of his system he was even permitted to examine the great man's head.*

With signs that his ideas were permeating even to the heart of government, Mr Bridges must have felt that his stock was on the rise. But the endorsement of Palmerston counted for little in Dublin, and the phrenologist found that his choice of venue had been unduly optimistic. In a hall that could accommodate four thousand paying customers he lectured to audiences described – by the only newspaper that bothered to send a reporter – as 'exceedingly small'. The public had tired of hearing about James Spollin and the crime that had shamed their city; and besides, there were more important matters to think about. Every week brought news of more casualties in India, hundreds of young Irishmen killed while serving in the British army. Families all over the country were mourning their dead, and helping to support those left behind. Picking over the squalid details of a homicide seemed an indecent pursuit while so many were grieving. In Ireland, at least, the murder mania was over.

One of the more unsavoury aspects of the brief public obsession with the Broadstone murder was the way in which it made a celebrity of the suspected killer, while the victim was almost forgotten. George Little's immediate family kept a low profile throughout the police investigation and did not attend the trial, at which they were represented by one of George's cousins. Afterwards his mother Frances and sister Kate continued to live quietly at their home in Waterloo Road, their only income coming from the charitable fund set up through the generosity of their fellow Dubliners. The Littles never received a penny from the British

---

* When Palmerston returned to government as Prime Minister the following year, he made a special award to Frederick Bridges of £50 from Treasury funds in recognition of his work. But there is no indication that the phrenologist's ideas ever influenced public policy.

state, and were apparently neglected in other ways as well. The Crown Solicitor visited Waterloo Road to interview Kate a couple of times after her brother's death, but there is no record of any official contact with the family after December 1856. In the mass of correspondence that followed the trial there is no mention of the Littles, or any suggestion that they might deserve an apology or explanation. A bureaucracy that handsomely rewarded its own police officers for failure could not even bring itself to express sympathy for those they had failed.

Frances Little died in January 1861, four years after the senseless murder of her firstborn. She was buried in the same grave as George, and her name was added to his headstone. The inscription has been worn almost smooth by 160 years of Dublin weather, but it is just possible to make out the first part of the epitaph, and the sentences of scripture Frances chose to commemorate her son.

Sacred
to the memory of
GEORGE SAMUEL LITTLE
who fell asleep in Jesus
November 13th 1856
aged 42 years

Blessed are the dead which die in the Lord. Revelations XIV: 13
Behold, I come as a thief; blessed is he that watcheth.
Revelations XVI: 15
The Lord is my helper; I will not fear what man shall do
unto me. Hebrews XIII: 16

A NOTE ON SOURCES AND
FURTHER READING

The principal source for this book was a collection of documents from the Registered Papers of the Chief Secretary's Office held by the National Archives of Ireland. A file (catalogued as CSO/ RP/1858/12594) compiled by the government officials of Dublin Castle at the time of the murder inquiry – and added to for some years afterwards – contains the transcripts of more than forty police interviews, correspondence between police, legal officers and government officials, minutes of meetings, surveillance reports, and much else besides.

Many contemporary newspapers took a close interest in the case and also published transcripts of every court hearing. One particularly valuable source is the *Freeman's Journal*, a Dublin daily newspaper whose reports on the murder inquiry were generally the most extensive and reliable.

A complete transcript of James Spollin's murder trial was published in book form shortly after his acquittal. Though rare, it is held by some libraries and can also be found online: *Trial of James Spollen, for the Murder of Mr. George Samuel Little, at the Broadstone Terminus of the Midland Great Western Railway, Ireland, August 7th, 8th, 10th & 11th, 1857* (Dublin: E. J. Milliken, 1857).

The phrenologist Frederick Bridges wrote an eccentric but colourful pamphlet about his encounters with James Spollin, which can be found in the British Library: Frederick Bridges, *Phreno-Physiometrical Characteristics of James Spollin, who was tried for the murder of Mr George S. Little, at the Broadstone terminus of the Midland Great Western Railway, Ireland, on the 13th of Nov, 1856, with an account of the author's interviews with Spollin* (London: William Horsell, 1858).

I learned a great deal about the idiosyncrasies of the nineteenth-century Irish justice system from W. E. Vaughan's comprehensive and scholarly *Murder Trials in Ireland 1836–1914* (Dublin: Four Courts Press, 2009).

And two useful works on the history of the Dublin Metropolitan Police are Jim Herlihy, *The Dublin Metropolitan Police: a short history and genealogical guide* (Dublin: Four Courts Press, 2001); and Anastasia Dukova, *A History of the Dublin Metropolitan Police and its Colonial Legacy* (London: Palgrave Macmillan, 2016).

LIST OF ILLUSTRATIONS

p. v 'The Murder of Mr Little' woodcut. Source: *Illustrated Police News*, Saturday 9 September 1882, page 4 (© British Library Board. All Rights Reserved / Bridgeman Images)

PLATE SECTION

Dublin's Broadstone Terminus as it appeared in 1860, showing the pontoon bridge over the Royal Canal. (© Royal Collection Trust)

A contemporary engraving of George Little's office, the scene of his murder. Source: *Illustrated Times*, Saturday 11 July 1857, p.21 (© British Library Board. All Rights Reserved / Bridgeman Images)

Bernard Gunning, the assistant storekeeper, in later life (Family collection, reproduced by kind permission of Pat Parsons and Anne Taylor)

The railway company cottage occupied by the painter James Spollin and his family in the grounds of the station. Source: *Illustrated Times*, Saturday 11 July 1857, p.21 (© British Library Board. All Rights Reserved / Bridgeman Images)

James Spollin, in his first public appearance since his arrest, hears the charges against him at the police court. Source: *Illustrated Times*, Saturday 11 July 1857, p.21 (© British Library Board. All Rights Reserved / Bridgeman Images)

Memorial (petition) written by James Spollin from his prison cell to the Lord Lieutenant of Ireland (© Irish National Archives)

Frederick Bridges, the Liverpool phrenologist who helped James Spollin and his son to emigrate. Source: Frederick Bridges, *Phreno-Physiometrical Characteristics of James Spollin* (© British Library Board. All Rights Reserved / Bridgeman Images)

Portrait of James Spollin taken a few weeks before his departure from Liverpool. Source: Frederick Bridges, *Phreno-Physiometrical Characteristics of James Spollin* (© British Library Board. All Rights Reserved / Bridgeman Images)

Plaster cast of James Spollin's head. Source: Frederick Bridges, *Phreno-Physiometrical Characteristics of James Spollin* (© British Library Board. All Rights Reserved / Bridgeman Images)

ACKNOWLEDGEMENTS

Most of this book was written in lockdown, an experience which made me all the more grateful for the existence of our great libraries and the archivists who look after their contents. In particular I would like to thank the staff of the National Archives of Ireland, who were friendly and unfailingly helpful; and I also greatly appreciated the assistance of staff at the National Library of Ireland and the British Library.

Thank you to my editor Jade Chandler, whose suggestions have been invaluable, and to all at Harvill Secker who have made the editorial process so painless. Also, as ever, to my agent Patrick Walsh for his enthusiasm and advice. And finally to my wife Jenny, for everything.